The Dismal State of the Great Lakes

The Dismal State of the Great Lakes

An ecologist's analysis of why it happened, and how to fix the mess we have made.

JAMES P. LUDWIG, Ph.D

To order additional copies of this book, contact:
Xlibris LLC
1-888-795-4274
www.Xlibris.com
Orders@Xlibris.com
131023

TABLE OF CONTENTS.

GLOSSARY OF TECHNICAL TERMS AND ACRONYMS

AOC = One of 43 Great Lakes' *Areas of Concern* over the degree of pollution.

Bioaccumulation = The accumulation of substances from the aquatic environment

Bioconcentration = The concentration of substances within a food chain

BOD = Biological Oxygen Demand

BWT = The Boundary Waters Treaty of 1909

CGLRM = The Council of Great Lakes Research Managers

CSA = A Community Supported Agricultural venture (usually certified organic)

DDT_r = The sum of all congeners of DDT and its breakdown products

DES = Diethylstilbestrol, a potent synthetic diaromatic estrogen

ERS = Ecological Research Services, Inc. a small ecological consulting firm

FERC = The Federal Energy Regulatory Commission in the United States

GIGO = Garbage In of data and assumptions = Garbage Out of modeled results

GLFC = The Great Lakes Fishery Commission

GLPF = The Great Lakes Protection Fund

GLRCEC = The Great Lakes Regional Corporate Environmental Council

GLWQA = Great Lakes Water Quality Agreement of 1972 (amended 1977, 1987, 2012)

IJC = The International Joint Commission

MDNR = The Michigan Department of Natural Resources

NAFTA = The North American Free Trade Agreement

NGO = A Non-Governmental Organization (often an environmentalist organization)

PAH = Polyaromatic Hydrocarbons

PBB = Polybrominated Biphenyls

PCB = Polychlorinated Biphenyls

PCDE = Polychlorinated Diphenyl Ether

PBDE = Polybrominated Diphenyl Ether

Ppm = part per million or 1×10^{-6}, or mg/kg concentration

Ppb = part per billion or 1×10^{-9}, or ug/kg concentration

Ppt = part per trillion or 1×10^{-12}, or ng/kg concentration

PHH = Polyhalogenated Hydrocarbon Pollutants

POPs = Persistent Organochlorine Pollutants

RAP = A Remedial Action Plan to restore a contaminated Area of Concern

SAB = The Science Advisory Board of the IJC

Synthetic Toxicant = A human-produced poisonous substance

JAMES P. LUDWIG, Ph.D

TBT = Tri-butyl Tin

TCDD = 2,3,7,8 tetrachlorodibenzo-*para*-dioxin

TCDD-EQ = Sum of toxic effects to equivalent to toxicant of TCDD in ng/kg

TCDF = 2,3,7,8 tetrachlorodibenzo-*p*-furan

TMDL = Total Maximum Discharge Limit

Toxin = A biologically-generated natural poisonous substance

Toxicant = A synthetic man-made poisonous substance

TTR = Transthyretin, a protein that transports thyroid hormone and vitamin A in blood

UMBS = The University of Michigan Biological Station

WQB = The Water Quality Board of the IJC

WTO = The World Trade Organization

FOREWORD AND DEDICATION

IN LATE AUGUST, 1996 I found myself on the Lake Michigan shoreline in Chicago, drinking coffee at seven AM, watching tiny waves lap in from an almost calm lake. I had an eight AM appointment at the Great Lakes regional USEPA office to discuss a client's progress on a water quality remediation project. After a long drive through the night from Ontario, I arrived early when traffic was light. So, I went to the lake to see the sunrise, gather my thoughts and simply enjoy a quiet hour before a meeting that promised to be stressful.

I noticed a young black man, perhaps nineteen, sauntering along the lakeshore. Dressed in baggy jeans worn low, he sauntered along the sidewalk above the beach, affecting a cool, black, urban male image. On impulse I waved, then beckoned him down to the lake edge. After a momentary hesitation, he strode down to the water. I offered my hand. He responded with the classic black power clasp, and I met Andre. He was a bit furtive, looking along the walkway he had stepped down from to come to the water's edge. I suspect he did not want to be seen talking with an older white man. What might his friends think about that? But, with just the two of us from very different worlds on a deserted beach in early morning, it was OK. He was safe. He was cool. I asked why he came to the lake and offered some of my coffee. His eyebrows went up. Certainly, an older professional white man dressed in coat and tie for a business meeting did not offer a black street kid dressed like a rapper his coffee. After a moment's hesitation he reached for the cup and took a good gulp, handing it back just a bit defiantly. When I took a drink immediately, he relaxed. Curiosity had captured him.

We talked about the lake and what he thought about it. I was especially interested to know if the threats of toxic contamination had penetrated his urban-oriented mind. I have never forgotten his comments and wrote them down when he left. *'Man, this place is quiet and gentle, not like my place where its always loud and somebody gets hurt all the time. There ain't nothing wrong with this place. When I'm down here I feel real good.'* We talked for a bit longer, finishing the coffee; then he moved on. But, neither Andre's ignorance of the health of southern Lake Michigan, or its intrinsic value as a place to recover from the persistent stresses of his life has ever left me. Even though crippled by pollution and neglect, Lake Michigan still had immense powers to heal.

As a scientist, I see the evidence of the hidden toxins, synthetic chemicals, other pollutants, invasions of exotic species, distorted food webs and the pathetic responses of governments that were far beyond his ken. I have studied these Great Lakes for five decades, have some sense of what has been lost, why it has happened and a few practical ideas of how we can fix these problems. The immense damage already inflicted on these lakes cannot be remediated for many generations and certainly never repaired fully. We cannot recover what has been extinguished or permanently despoiled. I have no idea whether Andre even remembers that somnolent August morning on the beach for I never saw him again. He said he was marrying his pregnant girlfriend later that week. That Andre may be raising a family near Lake Michigan has been one goad to write this book. For, it is we old white men that are pretty well those responsible for the poor condition of these world-class treasures. This book is my attempt to chronicle the pathways we all followed to Great Lakes pollution and poor ecological health, followed by what we must do to restore these Great Lakes, or at the very least manage them for the health of people and wildlife. I have written this for our great grandchildren, the eagles, mink, otters, terns, and even those pesky cormorants that so bedevil our frustrated sport fishermen.

The second more powerful goad came from friends, colleagues and co-workers on Great Lakes issues. I discuss the milestones of my personal journey through the Great Lakes, but many colleagues should be acknowledged by name. My family imbued me very early with curiosity about these waters, especially my father, the late Dr. Fred Ludwig from Port Huron. As a child my backyard was the shore of the St. Clair River, and my vacations were spent banding birds on Great Lake islands with the family. As a nascent professional ecologist, I spent most of eleven years learning the crafts of scientific research and field ecology at the University of Michigan. There I had exposure to an outstanding faculty and facilities while learning research techniques. A life-long interest in

Great Lakes research and management was developed and nurtured there, especially during six summers of work at the University of Michigan Biological Station (UMBS).

I was privileged to work with many others during my Great Lakes research. Great inspiration came from three giants of American ornithology—Robert Storer, Owen Sewell Pettingill, Jr. and Joseph Hickey, as well as Alfred Stockard, the longest-serving director of UMBS. The eminent ecologists Nelson Hairston and Fred Smith provided insights into population ecology and were my advisors in Graduate school. Sweat equity for many field research projects were provided by a host of colleagues. Early collaborators were my Dad, first wife Kay Howard who supported my stubborn Great Lakes focus for 28 years, Carl Tomoff, Denny and Cathy Bromley. Once established as an owner of Ecological Research Services, Inc. I had a succession of marvelous employees and associates who helped on many Great Lakes research projects including Lynne Herman, Lynn Carli, Sally Jo Churchill, my son Mark and daughter Maikwe, Mike Penskar, Steve Apfelbaum, Steve Voice, Hiroko Kurita-Matsuba, Heidi Auman, nephews Matthew and James Ludwig, Loraine (Rainy) Campbell, and Cheryl Summer. For many years, my older brother Ted has kept banding Great Lakes water birds: he is a continuous source of inspiration and logistical support.

Many professional colleagues from agencies and academia helped me formulate and test hypotheses or participated in my research, including Glen Fox, D. Vaughn (Chip) Weseloh, Mike Gilbertson, and Hans Blokpoel from Canada; Catherine Howard, Sylvia Taylor, Tim Kubiak, Keith Grasman, Wayland Swain, Don Tillitt, Bill Bowerman, Miguel Mora and John Giesy from America; Shinsuke Tanabe and Nobu Yamashita from Japan; and Paul Jones from New Zealand. My most recent collaborators have included Mel Visser and my second wife, Alison Kilpatrick, who helped me collect over 300 blood samples from dying cormorant chicks infected with Newcastle Disease Virus just after we were engaged in 1992. Incredibly, notwithstanding the guano and desperately sick birds we bled, she married me anyway. Both wives were exceedingly tolerant and supportive of my life-long obsession with these Sweetwater Seas. All of these people contributed to my published papers substantially and were inspirations in one way or another during my five decades of Great Lakes work.

Jane Elder, Mike Gilbertson, Steven Schneider, Loraine Campbell, Linda Wires, Dave Dempsey and Mel Visser all read early versions of this manuscript, offered insightful suggestions and were helpful critics. Dave and Theo Colborn each offered endorsements of the final text. But, they have no responsibility for the opinions expressed in this book. Any errors are my own.

I give thanks to all of them for their work to support the Great Lakes, their friendship and support these many years. It has been both a wondrous and incredibly frustrating voyage. This book is dedicated to them all in sincere thanks for their unstinting efforts to preserve and restore these waters to health and self-sustaining ecologies. That we have failed does not diminish the intrinsic value of their continuous efforts to improve our management of the magnificent 'sweetwater seas' we call the Great Lakes.

. . . At Fort Vermilion, Alberta, July 25, 2013.

I.

Chronology and events of an ecologist's career.

W E ARE ALL products of the human genetic pool, the circumstances of birth and the environments of our youth. From experience, I suggest that genetics account for most personality traits, but experiences and opportunities are what drive one toward a specific career. I was fortunate on both counts. I come from long-lived stock with relatively few genetic problems. My parents lived into their 90's and had good health until the last five years of their lives. Similarly, all grandparents lived beyond the life expectancy of their times, averaging about a decade longer lives than expected. One great grandmother was 97 when killed in a car accident. In short, nature was kind in the genetic lottery. However, on the debit side I inherited my maternal grandfather's volcanic temper, his tendency for rigid thinking and Dad's decided lack of patience for nonsense.

On the nurture side, I was similarly privileged. When my parents married they settled in Port Huron on the St. Clair River at the outlet of Lake Huron where Dr. Fred practiced family medicine and general surgery for the next 62 years. In 1939 they built a lovely home on the then undeveloped St. Clair River, opposite what would become the infamous 'chemical valley' of Canada during and after WWII. I grew up in a privileged home, taking for granted the magnificent St. Clair River that flowed past at three knots, experiencing the river much like Huck Finn on the Mississippi. We swam, sailed, motored, water skied, scuba-dived and fished many days of summer, skated or played hockey on the frozen rink that appeared on the little bay behind our house each winter, enjoyed the huge flocks of waterfowl that migrated through the area each

Spring and Fall, even joy-riding ice cakes downstream with the current flow in the Spring, demonstrating the foolishness of boys vividly.

Birds were a part of my life long before birth when I was but a gleam in my father's eyes. In 1927, my 18 year-old father convinced the bird banding office of the Department of Interior to grant him a bird banding permit. That first year he banded 162 birds of 16 species and was rewarded with 2 recoveries. A young bobwhite quail he banded was killed six months later by a golf ball on a Lansing course, and a mountain man killed one of his bronzed grackles for food in a Kentucky cornfield that November. By the date of Dad's death in March, 2002 the family had banded over two-thirds of a million birds of 214 species, more than one percent of the total of all birds banded in North America by all banders, even including those paid to do it by the governments! More importantly, the family would accumulate over 9,800 recoveries and 29,000 return or retrap records for 64 of those species, about 2% of all banding return and recovery records accumulated by all North American bird banders through 1995. Most banding was done on Great Lakes colonial water bird species or North Pacific albatrosses.

At first, grandfather Ludwig and Uncle Claude were quite skeptical of Fred's bird banding hobby, but by 1929, it was a family affair—especially annual June and July treks to various bays and islands of Lakes Huron and Michigan to band terns and gulls. Usually, the family would find a local fisherman, lighthouse keeper or coastguardsmen to ferry them to islands where they would band as many chicks as possible in one day. Throughout the 1930s, islands in Saginaw Bay, Thunder Bay, the Straits of Mackinac of Lake Huron and Grand Traverse Bay or the Beaver Islands of Lake Michigan were visited annually. During World War II, all colonial water bird banding ceased. Yet, the intrepid trio had banded 121,000 birds already, mostly of four species—common and Caspian terns, ring-billed and herring gulls—before WWII interrupted their compulsive banding hobby. Dad was already sharing his data with many others like Dr. Oliver Austin whose Cape Cod Massachusetts common tern banding work was already legendary, even writing technical papers in ornithology with mentoring from Josselyn Van Tyne at the University of Michigan (F. E. Ludwig 1943).

In 1934, Dad and his betrothed Jane were chaperoned to the Beaver Islands by Dr. Max Peet, a well-known pioneer neurosurgeon, ornithologist and University of Michigan medical school faculty member. There they banded and collected birds for a glorious week. Well before my brother Ted appeared in 1939 followed by myself in 1941, we were a family thoroughly inculcated in a serious hobby of banding Great Lakes water birds. If it could fly eventually, a Ludwig would clamp on a band. It was just a part of our growing up every year between American Memorial Day and early July. Banding trips were our camping trips. We learned far more about the outdoors through wet days and seasickness on those trips than through scouts or summer camps. One of the by-products was to visit the same places on the Great Lakes when they were still largely intact biological systems and to see the immense changes that followed WW II in these places year after year. My interest in the lakes began with banding and later matured into formal research. The following are some of my memories of what such places were like, and then how these were damaged so fundamentally in the five decades after I became a professional Great Lakes ecologist.

June 13, 1947 on the Straits of Mackinac. The family was finally reunited after the war and resumed banding. Dad and his father banded gulls on Thunder Bay islands and then we trekked to Mackinac City in the company of all four grandparents. Ted (age 8) and I (age 6) had been left out of the Thunder Bay trips, so we whined and wheedled as only persistent children can to be in on the next banding trip. Grandfather Ludwig and Dad found an old fisherman at Mackinac City who would let us use his old steel hulled boat of 15 feet to get to Green Island, four miles across the straits. Dad had an ancient 1929 ½-horse Champion 'one lung' outboard. Early one lovely, warm and quiet June morning we four set forth to cross the Straits in what could be called charitably a 'steel can'. At the stately pace of two knots, we made our way to Green Island, a speck of land just south of the Upper Peninsula and a quarter mile west of the north end of the Mackinac Bridge and the elders began to band the herring gull chicks. Ted and I were too small to band, although we could catch some smaller chicks.

I remember eating salami sandwiches at lunch and then falling asleep in warm sun, only to awaken when the wind changed to a northwest blow and it began to rain. We all huddled against the hull, now beached and turned sideways for a windbreak until the squall passed, leaving a stiff 20 knot northwest wind in its wake. Dad and Grandpa went back to banding, Ted and I to mischief. Ted found a can of blue paint lost from a passing freighter and we finger-painted just about everything in sight, especially ourselves. The elders waited until the wind largely subsided before we set out to return, but the residual waves were large in a stern-quartering sea running boisterously down the Straits, the typical residue of a northwest blow.

Fortunately, the old boat was mostly unsinkable with welded steel bulkheads, for we took on water with every following sea that broke against the transom. Grandpa, Ted and I bailed with everything from our hands to Granddad's hat and a cup from the thermos that had held coffee. Halfway across, a particularly large wave wetted the exposed spark plug and the old Champion stalled. In the ensuing battle to dry the motor enough to run, the handle broke off. Somehow, Dad got the old Champion going again. I remember him steering by holding the gas tank, occasionally getting a high voltage shock when his hand would bush against the exposed spark plug. It was my first experience with a storm event, compounded by equipment failure and bad luck that makes Great Lakes fieldwork difficult and dangerous. When we finally got back to Mackinac City three furious women and the other grandfather chastised the elder Ludwigs roundly for taking such risks with their 'babies'. That was the last banding for two years for Ted and I.

My memory of this day, eleven years before the great Mackinac Bridge would be finished, was of clean air and cold water, the small number of people around, black coal smoke spewing from the stacks of the car and rail ferries moving to and from the Upper Peninsula, the steam-powered Mackinac Island ferries, the high waves, how we had cooperated to survive and the vigor of the gull chicks. That a chick just hatched was already fully aware and could walk about the nest seemed absolutely magical to me.

July 4, 1952. St. James, Beaver Islands, Lake Michigan. I was furious. Ted got to go on the coastguard boat to Shoe Island to band Caspian terns, but they said I was too small. Two days before I helped band herring gulls on Pismire Island and tagged more than Ted. It seemed unfair that he got to go on the plum trip, but I did not. I was small for my age, for Ted was easily twice my weight and eight inches taller. I seethed all day, fished for a while off the old dock where the ferry from

Charlevoix moored, and finally went exploring. Poking around behind the old King Strang hotel where mother and dad had stayed under the benevolent eyes of Dr. Peet eighteen years earlier, I stumbled over the cover to the cesspool and fell in. In retrospect, this was likely one of two incidents in the Beaver Islands that set me firmly on the path to become a Great Lakes ecologist. I vowed that day never to be left out of banding trips again, and never was—probably because I almost always caused too much trouble when left to my own devices.

June 5, 1955. Black River and Bellow's Islands with Uncle Claude. The whole family of banders—Grandad Ludwig, Uncle Claude, Dad, Ted and I had spent the day banding Black River Island and the south Black River Shoals working on herring gulls and common terns. I saw my first cormorants. Two of their peculiar ground nests held blue eggs, and just-hatched naked black chicks were in two other nests. Compared to gulls, cormorants laid smaller eggs in larger nests. Several hundred tern nests held only a few chicks big enough to band. Even so, it was a good day with nearly 1,100 herring gull chicks banded. Granddad, Ted and Dad left to return home, leaving Uncle Claude and I to do Bellows Island in Grand Traverse Bay on the other side of the state.

Now, I shared a problem with Claude: we were far smaller people than our older brothers and had always lived in their intimidating senior shadows. Claude was possibly the most jovial, kind and wise person I have known. He saw that I was struggling, as had he, with the reality of being small with a larger than life big brother so he gave me a very precious gift this day and the next. I was 14 and had just received my first restricted drivers license. Although I had been driving farm tractors since the age of 9, I had driven little on highways. Claude had a brand new, powder blue Oldsmobile 88 with 238 miles on the odometer. As we made to leave for the three-hour drive to Northport where a local fisherman would run us out to Bellows Island, he got into the passenger side and handed me the keys. He told me to drive us there, for he would navigate. Actually, I drove there, then all the way back to Port Huron from Traverse City two days later—nearly 500 miles and over 13 hours in those days before freeways. The adventure of those three days around banding and driving was our little secret; neither of us ever said a word to any of the family of what I did with Claude's kind guidance and that beautiful Oldsmobile. We did boast a bit about the 1,604 herring gull chicks we banded at Bellows when we got back. This day and bird banding on the Great Lakes was integral to my growing up and learning responsible driving habits, thanks to a very kind and wise uncle.

June 6, 1959. Scarecrow Island, Thunder Bay Lake Huron. Dad and I ran the six miles from Black River Island north to Scarecrow Island in Thunder Bay in a small outboard boat to band gulls and any herons we could find in the tall ash trees there. When we landed Dad exclaimed at the sight of a sizeable ring-billed gull colony on the southwest tip of the island. Ring-bills had nested there before WW II, but we had not seen them in the previous three years of banding at Scarecrow. I was enthralled by their high-pitched calls, the density of their nests, but especially how near the adults came to us as we banded their chicks. One landed on the other side of a grass clump as I knelt to tag three of the 1,009 chicks we banded this day. I caught it with a quick lunge. The bright yellow feet, intensely red eye-rings and gape were quite beautiful. Dad banded the furious bird; I felt a genuine kinship to the species as we released it.

Nine years later I would finish a doctoral thesis based on studies of the ring-billed gull population explosion that was about to sweep over Lakes Huron and Michigan. I had no idea then that the fundamental technique of the thesis would depend on the art of cannon-netting adults in their colonies in order to retrieve banding data. Before I finished with the species, my teams of researchers would capture 9,226 adult ring-bills in all of the lakes except Superior on 29 different islands and would catch 806 birds banded as chicks (Ludwig 1968, 1974). Nine of those would be birds we banded this day. Later, I would adapt the technique to Caspian terns and begin a 27-year long study of their population (Ludwig 1979, 2013). But, another root of my commitment to ecology and the lakes sprouted when I caught and admired this magnificent gull on Scarecrow Island.

JAMES P. LUDWIG, Ph.D

A cannot net caught group of ring-billed gulls captured at Chantry Island, near Southampton, Ontario on Lake Huron, May 21, 1967.

Ring-billed Gull colony at Grassy Island, Thunder Bay Lake Huron, June 10, 1961. Starting with 560 nests in 1961, this colony grew to over 8,300 nests in 1967 during their immense population explosion; 377 adults were captured here in 1966 and 524 more were caught in 1967 by cannon net.

July 7, 1959. Gray's Reef, Beaver Islands, Lake Michigan. The Coast Guard patrol boat slid down a sickeningly steep trough, plunged headlong into a massive nine-foot wave off Gray's Reef, east Beaver Island in northeastern Lake Michigan. The boat slewed violently, seemingly close to capsizing; we were all drenched in frigid water again. Two coastguardsmen, my father, 73 year-old grandfather, and I held on for dear life to the back edge of the small cabin of the single-engine thirty foot Coast Guard patrol boat. I wondered again what had impelled me to join my father on this expedition to band Caspian tern chicks on Shoe Island. We got another tremendous jolt as we tunneled through another wave. My father smiled when grimly reminding me this boat was equipped with self-bailers and unsinkable—unless we turn over—for then we all drown or die with hypothermia. The Chief at the wheel muttered another foul curse, grandfather grimaced his Victorian disapproval and I moved to the rail one more time to puke. The icy water ran down my back, followed my spine like a river's bed, ran past my waist, and dripped into my pants. I was utterly miserable.

Even in this violence, as I feared for my own life while the unpredicted 45 knot westerly gale assaulted us in our wild ride back to St. James on Beaver Island, we were surrounded by phenomenal beauty. To the west, Hog Island was a potential haven denied to us by many reefs there. Eleven miles further around Gray's Reef was Beaver Island that could give shelter, but only if we smash our way through these huge waves for another seven or eight miles. The day was absolutely gorgeous— enormous waves, bright sun on a cloudless day with visibility over 15 miles, the wind cold and crisp and the water indescribably beautiful as the wind tore brilliant white spume from the wave tops to wet us continuously, chilling us to the very marrow of our bones.

Little did I realize that this day would be a seminal experience for a young man trying to figure out what to do with his life. I had just finished my freshman year at the University of Michigan in premedicine, was frankly bored and somewhat wary of being a practicing physician. I had watched my father and uncle pursue their careers as family physicians, working 16 to 20 hour days, having little time for their families, always exhausted, and thought there has to be a better way to live. Medical research was not an interest, so what was I doing in premedicine?

Another huge wave broke over the bow smothering us in green water. The 6-71 diesel faltered briefly, then picked up and rumbled on. The Chief at the wheel cursed again, asking his seaman, "Did you drain the goddamn fuel filter again like I told you to? If we get water in the fuel we are going to jam an injector shut on that son-of-a-bitch 6-71 again." The harassed seaman sheepishly replied, "Yes." We plowed onward, inching toward safe haven at St. James.

Gulls and terns raced by us, confident in their abilities, perhaps even amused at our plight. They flew on wings designed for speed and grace, even as we floundered and smashed about in the lake below. Somehow, it was fitting that this is how it is. On Shoe Island this day, we banded an immense number of young Caspian Terns, just over 700, the best day of banding Caspian terns my father can remember since 1929. "Something new has happened," he claimed. "There's a fish out here I've never seen before." That fish that none of us recognized would prove to be the soon-to-be ubiquitous alewife. The terns, responding to the abundant new food source, had produced a bumper crop of young, perhaps the best ever seen on the Great Lakes. We happened to be there at just the right time to band the maximum number of young.

The waves subsided when we tucked into the lee of the 12-mile length of Beaver Island. Now we experienced only the remnants of rollers that snuck around the ends of the island, dissipating much of their energy by bending around land. The Chief slowly eased the thirty footer up to faster speed; finally over the last three miles we roared into the harbor as if on wings. The doughty little thirty-footer had regained her pride, speeding into the harbor with a sort of elitism as if to say 'I survived another one out here'. Later, as a boat-owner who took on these lakes enduring regular beatings by storms, I would find great ecstasy when surviving the unexpected gale.

As we rounded the last buoy entering the harbor, I watched the Chief. He had an almost maniacal grin on his face as he looked over at me, the seasick landlubber as his seaman smirked. And, I felt acutely embarrassed, as if caring could cure motion sickness. And yet when I looked deeper into their eyes I saw the residue of fear they felt when those nine-footers smashed into us off Gray's Reef and almost turned us over. All of us were thankful to be back. With sudden insight I realized that I would be impelled like my father and his father, to revisit these islands and birds again and again for my entire life. Risk will be no consideration for I am now as much in love with these waters as with the most desirable woman imaginable. They will be a life-long obsession. I know that suddenly, with absolute clarity.

These then are the terms set by the lakes for us. They are beautiful. They are violent. They are constant in some ways, but change and are incredibly vulnerable, just like the mate you marry. There are times you are ready to kill because of what has been done to them, and always your soul cries out for better ways to care for the lakes. So it is with all those who are privileged to sail on the Great Lakes. We must try to understand what the lakes mean and what their values truly are. We cannot live here and be whole if we fail.

June 1, 1960. The Lady Jane begins eight years of population surveys. Dad finally gave in and bought a decent-sized boat capable of getting us to Great Lakes islands reliably, even if woefully slowly at 10-11 knots. The Lady Jane was a 33-foot steel-hulled rather unpretentious craft, under-powered by two small diesel 4-53s. She was reliable, but slow and always wet, spraying water and wallowing like an obese elephant in all but the lowest seas. For the next 13 years, this will be 'Dad's boat', and for the next eight she will do yeoman's service getting all of us to islands throughout Lakes Michigan and Huron. She will get us to over 130 islands in these years from the Beaver Islands in Lake Michigan to the east end of Georgian Bay in Lake Huron. Until 1966 when I will buy my first boat, the Lady Jane will be the platform from which I do much of my doctoral research on ring-billed gull and Caspian tern populations.

September 2, 1960. In Dr. Storer's office, University of Michigan Museum of Zoology. Bob Storer was a quiet, wise and accomplished man of classical ornithology. I was a mere bird bander, not even a competent birder in the Audubon sense as an identifier of local birds. For almost an hour we spoke about his 'Birds of the World' graduate level course. He wanted me to take basic ornithology first, but I finally cajoled him into allowing me to register for the graduate level course as an ill-prepared Junior undergraduate, only because he saw my determination to learn as fast as possible and catch up with life-long birders who already knew basic bird taxonomy and distribution. I will never work harder for a C grade than I did in his course, but it opened my eyes to the diversity of birds and their ecology. Bob also taught scholarship by example, and I was always humbled in his presence. He was an exacting, but always fair, taskmaster, representing the best of the careful and precise old-school academicians, a type of scholar once revered and honored for their accuracy, now almost extinct.

September 4, 1962. Rackham School of Graduate Studies at the University of Michigan. I graduated with a BS in Zoology in June 1962 after a thoroughly undistinguished undergraduate academic career, marked mostly by parties, good times and slowly developing interests in zoology, birds and population ecology. Today I was called in by the dean of the Rackham Graduate College who told me pointedly that while I would be admitted for the fall classes, it was only because I had done well in summer courses at the university's Biological Station and someone with a very good record from Columbia who was supposed to enroll declined at the last moment. I was the very last student admitted into graduate studies in zoology in the fall, 1962. The dean let me know he thought I would be flunked out within a year, two at most, based on my undergraduate record. I thanked him for the chance, even though I feared he might be right about my far less than stellar academic achievements.

The Michigan graduate program in zoology in 1962 was still rooted in a belief that a competent zoologist had to have a fundamental mastery of all branches of zoological science from vertebrate anatomy to ecology, evolution, cellular biology, genetics, developmental biology and the various taxonomic specialties—vertebrates, invertebrates, parasitology, etc. before one was allowed to specialize. Sadly, this requirement for breadth has given way to earlier and earlier specialization. When admitted to graduate school a student had two years to gain a fundamental broad mastery of zoology and was allowed into a doctoral program only after passing the dreaded graduate exam. If the student failed to pass in two tries, then they could earn only a master's degree at Michigan and must go elsewhere to pursue a doctorate. It was a brutal Darwinian system of academic selection that used three consecutive mid-January weekends to test students in nine fields of zoological competence.

I took the exam in January 1963 with 121 other candidates. A 'perfect score' was 9 in each field or 81 for the whole exam. In the previous three decades, the highest score ever achieved by a student was 59, the mean score was 28, and usually just 20 to 23 of those students taking it would pass with the basic competency score of 40 and at least a 3 in every field. First year students, regardless of their undergraduate records, passed the exam infrequently with about 85 percent of successful Ph.D. candidates using both chances and a year of remedial study to qualify for a doctoral program. Furthermore, it was an old school essay exam where writing skills and organizing answers under pressure were important. I was not expected to pass and even discouraged from taking the exam by my advisor who felt it would be a waste of time for the faculty to grade my drivel-like efforts. I passed with a score of 45, placing 8th of the 122 who took it and the 23 who passed in 1963, ranked second among 68 first year students taking the test.

My status among student peers changed instantaneously. Faculty members who knew me best were astonished. I had spent the entire fall reading everything I could and auditing three advanced courses in fields where I had minimal training or understanding. While my peers coasted with the hubris of those who earned four points as undergraduates (I had a 2.47 average), I pounded hard all that first semester. For once, parties were not important. The academic focus paid off handsomely. I felt like Bobby Thompson, the diminutive infielder who barely hit .200, but did hit the home run 'shot heard round the world' that won the 1951 World Series!

Peers and faculty began to listen attentively to my views on issues, including the strange inexplicable changes I was seeing in Great Lake bird colonies. After the 1964 field season I reported the first overt signs of the toxic chemical debacle of the lakes in herring gulls nesting at Bellow Island to the graduate seminars. Important people in the Great Lakes community of scientists listened, considered, offered sage advice on what to look for next, what constituted a cause-effect linkage and how to structure my research. Whether deserved or not, I had some instant *gravitas* and it felt damned good!

March 18, 1963. *The Smithsonian sojourn.* Dr. Storer called me into his office. The Smithsonian was recruiting young ornithologists for a special program on seabirds in the leeward Hawaiian Islands. He recommended I take a year or two to go and learn about true marine seabirds, possibly do a thesis study on one of them. He pointed out that I was narrowly focused on the lakes with its simplified water bird fauna and needed a more diverse experience to be able to put the lakes into context. I thought about it for several weeks, then agreed to go. The Zoology Department chairman assured me that I could take a year or two for professional development and finish within the seven-year time limit for doctoral candidates. Their excellent advice gave me perspectives on what I would see in the lakes over the next 45 years. I came close to doing a thesis on black-footed albatross populations, but the pull of the lakes was just too much. I was back in Michigan in ten months, just in time for the 1964 Great Lakes field season and more UMBS courses.

May 16, 1965. Bellow Island, Grand Traverse Bay, Lake Michigan. Hired by Dr. Joe Hickey of the University of Wisconsin for my first paid consulting job, I was to do control studies parallel to those of his Masters student, Tony Keith, on the performance of herring gull colonies in Michigan. Carl Tomoff and I were marking and assessing eggs in herring gull nests. In 1964, I saw a large decrease in the number of young and many eggs with crushed shells here. Joe's bander friends had seen the same thing in two Green Bay, Wisconsin colonies. It looked like this might be another DDT problem, similar to the crash of eagle numbers in Florida reported by Charles Broley. However, herring gull reproduction seemed to be perfectly normal at Pismire Island in the Beaver Islands of the open lake. So, Tony would study three Green Bay colony sites while Carl and I would examine nesting at Bellows in Grand Traverse Bay, a bay surrounded by over 20,000 acres of heavily sprayed cherry and apple orchards (a positive control) and Pismire Island in the Beaver Islands archipelago surrounded by open lake (a negative control).

The day before we had assessed 1,009 eggs and marked 344 nests at Pismire, finding little breakage and everything apparently normal. But, 28% of the Bellow eggs were broken and leaking contents. Later only a fourth of eggs laid hatched and few chicks fledged from Bellows compared to Pismire. We also found the Bellows gulls far more aggressive towards each other and us. Six adults were found tremoring violently, a specific neurological symptom of DDTr poisoning. The nesting population at Bellows had decreased by 32% compared to 1963, the last 'normal' year. We collected eggs and eggshells for Dr. Hickey and reported our field findings.

The effects in Green Bay in 1965 reported a year earlier by the banders were similar but not as stark (Keith 1966). When analytical data were returned for the eggs and dying adults, it was abundantly clear that DDTr was at concentrations known to kill chicken embryos. Brain concentrations in the six tremoring Bellows gulls were sufficient to kill the adults we found. The eggs from Pismire birds had about two-thirds as much DDT group compounds as those from Bellows (Ludwig and Tomoff 1966).

Rachael Carson's warnings in *Silent Spring* were confirmed. This was something never seen before in wildlife feeding from a body of water this size; no one had thought it was possible. And, we were even more surprised to find sizeable DDT concentrations in the birds at Pismire. Did this mean the whole lake was polluted? How could this be so far from the places DDT was being used? If so, how did it get there? This was my first experience with a phenomenon common to ecology: Field research rarely provides neat and clean answers, but far more often an abundance of complex questions, never anticipated when the research project was designed.

June 24, 1966. Botulism in Ring-billed Gulls of Saginaw Bay. Denny and Cathy Bromley working with my new bride, Kay, finished piling 427 ring-billed gull carcasses of those that died at the Charity Islands Reef colony in just one week by late afternoon as I collected blood samples from dying birds. Contracted by the U.S. Bureau of Commercial Fisheries, we were studying the factors involved in the huge gull kill on Saginaw Bay. In the two summer months from June 16 to August 15 we found almost 3,000 gulls and several hundred other birds killed at the reef colony from eating type E botulism-contaminated dead alewives. For the three years 1964-1966, a massive spring mortality of alewives unable to adjust to food shortages and cold winter waters owing to poor osmotic control segued into massive bird kills when botulism type E toxin developed in the dead fish that were scavenged by the gulls (Ludwig and Bromley 1988).

Over the middle five years of the decade of the 1960s, well over 10,000 ring-billed gulls, 5,000 common loons and hundreds of ducks—even blackbirds and sandpipers—were killed in Lakes Michigan and Huron by the potent toxin acquired by eating dead fish or through secondary transfers. Blackbirds, sandpipers and ducks eating fly maggots from rotting fish or bird carcasses were killed too. These were unprecedented mortalities, linked specifically to the annual kills of the invasive alewives. Three outbreaks of type E botulism in humans and nine deaths from 1961 to 1963 traced to consumption of cold-smoked Lake Michigan chubs raised public interest in this bird mortality.

May 13, 1967. Redux at Bellows Island. We finished catching 15 adult herring gulls from the Bellows Island colony by noon. Eight were sacrificed to provide baseline concentrations of DDTr compounds in their fat and tissues. Seven were moved to a large outdoor cage at Dad's home in Port Huron where he would watch them for a week to see if fasting that long would mobilize fat-stored DDTr and then initiate poisoning symptoms. All seven developed the classic DDTr tremors within eight days and died, the first just 70 hours after capture. I had inveigled Dad to apply his surgical skills to autopsy any dying birds because I had to capture ring-bills that week in Lake Ontario colonies for my doctoral thesis research. Between 1963 and 1967 the nesting gull population at Bellows had plummeted by 80%.

Throughout the three decades of 1933-1962, the Bellows Island herring gull colony had been the most productive of all colonies in Lakes Michigan and Huron that the family banded annually. Thirteen banded gulls from this colony had been found dead in Lake Huron colonies in the previous two decades, but no banded birds from other colonies in either Lakes Michigan or Huron were found at Bellows over the same period (Ludwig 1963). Suddenly, it was the least productive colony (Ludwig and Ludwig 1969). As the seven experimental birds died, each mobilized the DDTr stored in their fat. When the brain concentrations reached about 90 parts per million, the tremors began and each bird died within hours. Dad did the autopsies, collected the tissue samples that we sent to Dr. Hickey's lab and photographed the symptoms by 16 mm motion pictures.

This film was shown at the annual Great Lakes Research Conference in 1969. In the audience were representatives of three DDT manufacturers who asked many disruptive questions about the data and criticized the study's design vehemently. All three fled the room during the screening of the film and were nowhere to be seen when the lights came back on. Specific symptoms speak directly to cause and effect and mark disruptive questions as harassment. It was a lot harder to argue with images of birds dying in agony exhibiting the tremoring symptoms of DDT poisoning than a young ecologist. I learned how significant visual images of pollution could be to make the case for action against pollution. DDT was banned in 1972. I was gratified to be asked to provide a legal deposition in support of the decision through the Environmental Defense Fund.

June 12, 1971. High Island, Beaver Islands Caspian tern colony. My sixteen-month old daughter was running down the south shore of High Island toward her mother with some difficulty; her diaper had fallen down around one ankle just after the cannon net was fired. I decided to start my kids on banding even earlier than Dad was able to do for Ted and I. Dad, Dr. Tom Boates (a colleague from the Bemidji State University Chemistry Department) and I were finishing our last cast of the cannon net propelled by black powder 12 gauge shells in the Caspian tern colony. We recaptured terns to see how the population replaced itself and if birds moved between colonies. Of 76 adult terns trapped, 14 had been banded as chicks. Surprisingly, eight were raised in Canadian colonies, different than the samples caught during 1966 and 1967 when most birds nesting in Lake Michigan colonies had been raised in nearby US colonies (Ludwig 1968). I wondered why recruitment had changed? If this was a real change, then what could be causing this recruitment shift for the larger population? Or, was this an artifact of small sample size and limited to just one colony? Twenty-one more years of recapture work would follow before these questions were answered (Ludwig 2013).

June 1, 1978. Gravelly Island, northern Green Bay, Lake Michigan. My son Mark and I had come to net terns here and found the first confirmed Michigan nesting by 22 pairs of cormorants since the species was extirpated from the state in 1959! No chicks were hatched yet, but we were thrilled to see this extirpated species return to a Michigan Great Lakes site after an absence of 20 years (Ludwig 1984). We returned in early July and banded 38 cormorant and 704 tern chicks.

June 12, 1978. The Cousins Islands, North Channel, Lake Huron, Canada. The Canadian Wildlife Service evaluation team counted all Caspian tern nests covered by our cannon netting in one of their colonies. CWS staff were concerned the technique may be too disruptive, so we agreed to a test of the technique in five colonies of the North Channel and Georgian Bay by them. No significant damage or effects on tern productivity were found by their study; we were allowed to continue to mass trap adult terns for the next 15 years by cannon net in Canada (Blokpoel 1981). We recaptured 105 previously banded terns on this trip to five Canadian colonies. Sixty-one were banded as chicks; 60 were raised in Canadian colonies, but only one in a US colony. Subsequent trapping in the US colonies demonstrated that nearly half the birds nesting in the US in 1978 were hatched and raised at Canadian sites (Ludwig 1979). What could be causing this population shift? Why were US sites so much less productive of recruits than Canadian colonies? Although the US colonies were growing, all of their growth was from reproduction in the Canadian colonies. Why? What was so different between these two regions that drove this profound shift in the recruitment pattern (Ludwig 1979)?

A cannon net cast over nesting Caspian terns at Elm Island, North Channel, June 14, 1978.

Stan Teeple, a Canadian Wildlife Service biologist, with an adult Caspian tern caught by cannon net at Papoose Island, Georgian Bay, June 15, 1978.

July 6, 1981. Deer Lake, Ishpeming, Michigan. My consulting company (ERS) was hired in the spring by Callahan Mining Co. to do an environmental impact study of their proposed reopening of the Ropes Gold Mine in the Deer Lake watershed that drains to Lake Superior. This mine was operated from 1882-1897. In June we had sampled lake and streams sediments of tributaries looking for residual heavy metals from the old mine and tailings piles. Because this was the first place in the world miners had used mercury coated copper plates to capture gold dust, we were concerned mercury might still be there after 84 years, especially in Gold Mine Creek that ran right through the tailings of the old mine. Surprisingly, we found very little mercury in those tailings or that creek but twelve times more in the Deer Lake sediments and 27 times more in the Carp River sediments below the city's sewage plant. We came back in July to resample the sediments to be sure our preliminary findings were not a sampling error, and to seine for sport fish to see if the mercury in lake sediments was moving into them as well.

Deer Lake, with very high perch productivity from the sewage nutrients, was a favorite ice-fishing spot of local fishermen. Six weeks later, the results came back, confirming the mercury was coming from the sewage plant and the fish were just loaded. A steady diet of 8 parts per million was the estimated lethal dose for 50% of adult humans; the relatively small fish we caught for samples were all very contaminated, ranging from 0.6 to 1.8 ppm. Published data indicated perch of legal size should exceed 2 ppm, and could be as high as 3.5 ppm in old individuals. The hazard could be especially high in northern pike. The FDA recommended eating fish at 0.5 ppm no more than once a week by men and once a month or less by women of child-bearing age. Present recommendations are to eat fish with less than half the mercury concentrations advised in 1981. Kurita (1987) found concentrations of mercury as high or higher in pike and perch than we projected from 1984 and 1985-year samples taken four years after mercury discharges ceased.

Without waiting for permission from the client, I contacted the Michigan DNR and the Michigan Environmental Review Board with our findings and stepped into a political maelstrom. When the dust settled, the DNR did its own investigation and traced the source to the largest employer of Marquette County and Upper Peninsula, Cleveland Cliff International's analytical laboratory in Ishpeming. CCI had been using an average of 26 kilograms of mercury every year since 1967 as mercurous chloride for quality control analyses of their iron taconite pellet product, but just flushed the spent reagents with the mercury into the town sewer. Deer Lake was elevated to the IJC list of 43 Great Lakes contamination "hot spots" (AOCs). Once the impact study was finished, it was the last work ERS or I would do for Michigan's metal mining companies for I had become a *persona non grata* to the industry. It would be 24 years before mercury concentrations would drop to below the FDA action levels in fish from natural dilution and attenuation and Deer Lake could be considered for removal from the IJC list of AOCs. Much recent research on the impacts of mercury ingestion in humans shows a strong causal link to cerebral palsy, particularly in human males (Gilbertson 2008, 2009), and poor cognition in children exposed *in utero* before birth (Tassande *et al.* 2005).

January 17, 1982. The Michigan Audubon Society. Dr. Sylvia Taylor, Endangered Species Coordinator of the Michigan DNR, called to ask if she could nominate me to serve on the Michigan Audubon Society Board of Directors. My Upper Peninsula consulting company, ERS, had just completed a very successful project to reintroduce the extirpated pine marten to Michigan's Upper Peninsula from Ontario in exchange for wild turkeys. In the previous two winters we had captured 148 of those magnificent arboreal weasels in Algonquin Park in Ontario and brought them to their new Upper Peninsula homes. Sylvia, our MDNR technical project officer for the effort, had become a good friend and mentor on many endangered species issues.

I agreed to stand for election, beginning a decade of volunteer work with MAS, the second largest environmental group in Michigan with about 10,000 members. Eventually, MAS would play a prominent role in my colonial water bird research work and would make a valiant attempt to bring industries together with environmental groups trying to find common ground on Great Lakes issues. I would be elected president of MAS in 1989 for the next two years. This was the start of my environmental activism on Great Lakes issues. It came when effects of the persistent organochlorine pollutants (POPs) became obvious in the bird populations. My maternal grandfather's volcanic temper, and the lack of patience I inherited from Dad were about to become important.

June 29, 1983. Little Gull Island, northern Green Bay, Lake Michigan. Mark and I motored the 14 miles out here from the tip of the Garden Peninsula in an eleven-foot long aluminum skiff to see how the cormorants were faring. Part of me said we had to be nuts to use such a flimsy craft over such a distance of open lake, but we did and were lucky when the weather held. We only had to row in the last mile when we ran out of gas. We banded 455 cormorant chicks but found five with crossed bills, a very rare developmental defect in wild populations (Fox *et al.* 1991a, 1991b). Back at my office, I checked the literature and found very few reports of this defect in wild water birds, never at this rate.

I called Glen Fox of the Canadian Wildlife Service who had seen this defect in Lake Ontario birds when dioxins and PCBs were very abundant in herring gull eggs there in the mid-1970s. Glen suggested I talk with

Mike Gilbertson who found similar defects in gull and tern chicks from 1971 to 1974 and very low hatch rates in the Lake Ontario colonies. Mike described something he called 'chick edema disease', a complicated syndrome associated with dioxins and co-planar PCB congeners (Gilbertson et al. 1991). I had never heard of chick edema disease, co-planar PCBs or PCB congeners. As far as I knew then, all PCBs had the same toxic effects. I had a lot to learn.

Mike suggested I talk with Tim Kubiak of the US Fish and Wildlife Service Green Bay office. Tim was experimenting with Forsters terns from PCB contaminated Green Bay and Lake Poygan (a clean inland lake) to see if eggs exchanged between sites have the same viability and if fledging success was the same. If not, Tim wanted to know whether PCBs that were abundant in the Green Bay terns were associated with their poor survival and productivity and if these exposures correlated with poor incubation behavior. He would soon publish research that correlated the presence of the dioxin-like co-planar PCBs with egg death, poor adult incubation behavior and low fledging rates for the Green Bay birds (Hoffman *et al.* 1987, Kubiak *et al.* 1989).

I experienced the *déjà vu* of the herring gull failures at Bellows Island from 1964-1968: Is this bill deformity epidemic the same or a similar phenomenon to that? If it is owing to contamination from PCBs, then why is this happening as the population is recovering and PCBs are supposed to be disappearing? If not PCBs, what is the cause? Or, is this a new chemical, poor genetics, a virus or heavy metal exposure? Frustrated, all I had was an ever-lengthening list of questions, but no answers. Regardless, this was crystal clear: a rate of hatched crossed-bills greater than 1 in 100 was not normal. The published literature suggested a rate of 1 in 20,000 to 40,000 is about the normal range of crossed bills among wild water birds in uncontaminated regions. The rate in these cormorants was far more than two orders of magnitude (100 fold = 10^2) higher.

June 23, 1985. St Martin's Shoal, Straits of Mackinac, Lake Huron.
Today Mark and I finished looking at the cormorant colonies from Green Bay through northern Lake Michigan to the straits area—six colonies in all. In the banding of 700 chicks we found six more crossed

bills to add to the eleven collected since 1981. Thirteen have come from Green Bay sites, three from the Beaver Islands colonies and one from a Straits of Mackinac Lake Huron colony. Published contaminant data from the fish cormorants eat suggested a gradient of total PCB contamination from high in Green Bay to low in the Straits area. Twice I had spoken with Michigan Department of Natural Resources wildlife and fisheries officials and been blown off. They say total PCBs are going down so this must be something else, probably genetics. With prompting from Tim Kubiak and the literature I asked if the dioxin-like PCBs are disappearing at the same rate as the other PCBs. But, they had no answers because fish were never analyzed for the dioxin-like congeners, only for total PCBs. It was abundantly clear they were unwilling to find out, for this was one of those nasty inconvenient truths that cannot be fixed easily or cheaply.

Now furious at their blasé—even cavalier—dismissal, I secured a spot on the agenda of the next Natural Resources Commission meeting agenda for a public presentation in July, a meeting that just happened to be scheduled for Gaylord, Michigan, a few miles from my Boyne City office. As I spoke, Mark went to each commissioner and placed a dead cross-billed cormorant on a towel in front of them as I made a pitch for funds to find out what was happening to the colonial water birds of Michigan. In retrospect, I recommend this technique to gather and concentrate the attention of public officials who would rather deal with arcane policies that cost little than to deal with real problems that are expensive. Well covered by the media, this problem could no longer be swept under a bureaucratic rug of simple indifference. Corpses that present unassailable evidence of graphic damage for unknown reasons are among the most powerful motivators for public officials—especially when presented in full view of the press. Our proposal was accepted and we were funded for a pilot study in 1986. One senior DNR Conservation Officer pulled me aside to suggest pointedly that I really should be somewhat more circumspect when speaking to authorities. I chose to ignore his advice then and for the next decade. This was not something that demanded politesse and deference to entrenched authority: rather, it demanded careful research to find the cause or causes.

JAMES P. LUDWIG, Ph.D

A few of the herring gulls and cormorants nesting at St. Martin's Shoal on June 18, 1986. Most cormorant chicks in this view are 14-24 days old, an ideal size for banding.

June 25, 1986. The Beaver Islands archipeligo, northern Lake Michigan. Today Dr. Gordon Guyer, recently appointed director of the Michigan DNR, and two assistants joined our assessment team to visit three cormorant and two Caspian tern colonies we were evaluating with MDNR funding in the Beaver Islands. Interestingly, 21 years earlier, I had written Gordon to obtain information on DDT use on the Grand Traverse Bay cherry orchards when herring gulls were poisoned at Bellows Island. Even though he was an Agricultural Extension Service entomologist for Michigan State University working in Traverse Bay regional orchards and actively supported the use of DDT, Gordon supplied data on DDT use there quickly. Thus, I knew him to be an ethical man in search of the truth, and not a blind adherent to convenient policy.

Our team and the DNR staff had a grand field day visiting Hat, Ile aux Galets and Pismire Islands. For once, the weather cooperated. We encountered no cross-bills hatched, banded nearly 360 cormorant chicks and opened 63 of their dead eggs that failed to hatch. In those eggs we found dead embryos with seven specific developmental defects characteristic of the same chick edema disease Mike Gilbertson had reported from Lake Ontario herring gulls in 1973. Eleven cormorant and three tern embryos with crossed bills had died in their eggs. The following January when I submitted a request to MDNR for continuation funding for 1987, the second year's grant was approved quickly.

When Gordon left the DNR to become President of Michigan State University later that year, MDNR support evaporated, replaced by indifference and great reluctance to proceed with any research involving contaminants, birds or other top predators. Unknown to me, just before Gordon left the DNR, he contacted the Michigan State University Environmental Toxicology Program and asked Dr. John Giesy to measure the contaminants in bird eggs to determine if our theory that the dioxin-like compounds were the cause was valid. Although still not convinced and harboring the skepticism that all good scientists have, Gordon wanted answers to the questions our work posed, regardless of the impacts on MDNR policy. Were the dioxin-like chemicals still a problem in the Great Lakes? If so, what did that mean for MDNR policies and programs?

JAMES P. LUDWIG, Ph.D

September 9-20, 1986. The great flood of toxins into Saginaw Bay.
Returning to Bay City (where ERS was now located) from a mine reclamation project where we had just hydroseeded 76 acres of taconite mine tailings at Black River Falls, WI, we drove in torrential downpours for two days. At home, we found everything just drenched with fields flooded and many crops ruined. On average, the 22-county Saginaw River watershed received 11.8 inches of rain in 30 hours—3.9 inches more than the 100-year storm event, marking this as the most intense deluge ever recorded in mid-Michigan. In the next week the river increased its discharge more than 300 fold, scouring PCB-contaminated sediments from the most polluted reaches of the river and spewed the toxic mess into lower Saginaw Bay. Caspian terns nesting there would require more than five years to resume a normal fledging pattern for Saginaw Bay colonies (Ludwig *et al.* 1993b; Yamashita *et al.* 1991; Figure 1).

Effective reproduction leading to breeding adults raised from chicks hatched in these colonies would not occur again until the 1989 year-class, and even that modest recovery would be at less than 5 per cent of production by the year-classes raised from 1987-1994 in Canada. Deformity rates in Saginaw Bay chicks increased 23 fold in hatched chicks in 1987 compared to 1986. Even adult survival was compromised; birds nesting in Saginaw Bay lived half the life spans of those nesting in Canada (Ludwig *et al.* 1993a, Ludwig 2013; Figure 3). An angry mother nature had just established the experimental conditions for a test of the theory that dioxin-like contaminants were responsible for deformities and poor reproduction we saw in Great Lakes bird colonies even as total PCBs were declining.

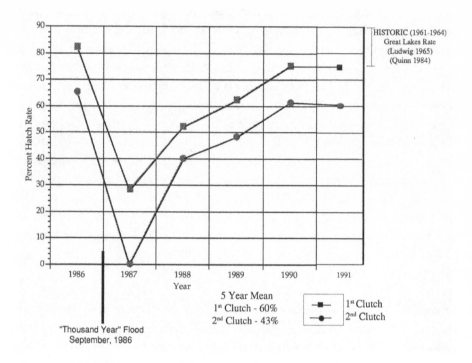

Effect of PCBs released from sediments on Caspian tern eggs after the thousand-year flood in the Saginaw River watershed.

April, 1987. Testing the dioxin-like chemical effects hypothesis. I was seated at my desk planning the next step of the taconite reclamation project when the telephone rang. Don Tillitt asked if I would come to East Lansing and the MSU toxicology lab for a meeting with him, Tim Kubiak of US Fish and Wildlife Service and Dr. John Giesy to discuss a research project on water birds the MDNR had requested at Dr. Guyer's insistence. We met and designed a combined field and laboratory program to look into the question of causality by the dioxin-like chemicals.

I was to supply egg samples from water birds in different colonies having different expected exposures with a sample code number known only to me. Dr. Giesy's team would analyze for the dioxin-like contaminants blind, using an innovative enzyme-induction technique that measures the total burden of contaminants as equivalents to TCDD (TCDD-EQs) as well as total PCBs (Tillitt and Giesy 1991a). Our field team would collect data on egg hatching and chick fledging rates in the field and learn what we could from dead eggs that failed to hatch by assessing embryonic deformities. Once the field and laboratory data sets were complete, we would meet and match up the locations, colony performance, egg viability and deformities data with the contaminants data. The analysts would not know where the samples had come from. Our field team would have no role in the analyses. This was sound interdisciplinary science practiced blind, just as it should be, to prevent bias.

The lab got four samples of Caspian tern eggs from four colonies and three of cormorant eggs from three colonies, identified by number only. I selected the field samples based on total PCB contamination reported in forage fish samples near each colony, hoping to get a gradient of exposures in the bird eggs. Contamination analyses gave a minimum contamination of 141 dioxin equivalents (TCDD-EQs) in cormorant eggs from a Lake Superior colony up to 414 TCDD-EQs in tern eggs from a Saginaw Bay site. When contamination was correlated with hatch rates, there was an obvious strong relationship with a correlation coefficient (r value) of 0.94 and a coefficient of determination (r^2 value) of 0.88. In statistical shorthand, these data indicated that 88 percent of the variation of egg viability between colonies was explained by the burdens of TCDD-EQs in the eggs alone (Tillitt *et al.* 1991b, 1992).

However, these data were for two species, so we agreed to repeat the experiment in 1988 using cormorants only. In 1988, we included a very clean Lake Winnipeg colony, with help from Chip Weseloh, Glen Fox and the CWS, and tripled the total number of Great Lakes cormorant colonies sampled. The teams assembled in January, 1989 with data on nine Great Lakes' colonies, an exposure range of 35-382 TCDD-EQs and an egg hatching rate ranging from 92% in Lake Winnipeg down to 63% in Wisconsin waters of Green Bay (Figure 2).

Figure 6

Cormorant Egg Mortaility in Colonies

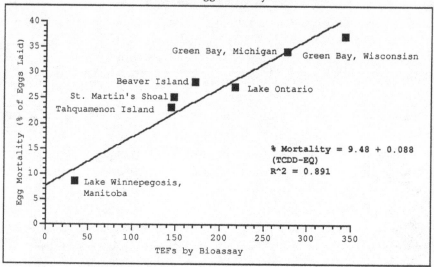

Cormorant egg mortality in 1988 correlated with toxic equivalent factors to dioxin (TCDD-EQs) measured by EROD bioassay.

In one of the more quaint moments of all the research I have been part of, Giesy's associate Paul Jones left the meeting room to run the statistics on a computer. Paul soon returned with a graphical plot (Figure 2) showing an r value of 0.95 and an r² of 0.891, an almost unbelievably high correlation for real field ecological studies. With a straight face, John pretended to criticize Paul because the correlation was just far too low and demanded a recalculation! These data were published in 1992 when results from four other years were added. The coefficient of determination decreased to r² 0.71, probably from inter-year variation in weather causing random egg death in five different years. The inter-year variance confounded the results slightly compared to all data from a single year. Even so, the probability that the results of all years pooled were a random variance was less than one in ten thousand (Tillitt *et al.* 1992). It should be noted that when the MDNR chose to abandon this research in 1988, the Dow Chemical Company, the Upjohn Company and the McGregor Foundation all stepped forward to grant research funds for the project through the Michigan Audubon Society. The corporate support was

JAMES P. LUDWIG, Ph.D

especially noteworthy because this research had potential to damage their interests.

March 28, 1989. The National Geographic Special. Joe Seamans, a producer of National Geographic specials from the Pittsburgh National Public Television affiliate, telephoned to inquire about our research. Joe had heard about the rash of deformed birds appearing in the more polluted parts of the Great Lakes and dug up my 1979 paper on Caspian tern reproduction that found the more contaminated US colonies were half as productive as the cleaner Canadian sites (Ludwig 1979). We discussed these data for nearly an hour; then Joe asked if he could incorporate our work into a National Geographic Special on the effects of toxic chemicals on Great Lakes wildlife. Astonished at the interest, I agreed readily.

Three months later Joe and his film crew of four joined my team, Mike Gilbertson of the International Joint Commission and Loraine Campbell (another MAS director) for a two-day visit to Green Bay cormorant colonies. We banded close to 1,700 young cormorants and found seven more crossed-bill and three leg-deformed birds. We also opened 156 dead eggs and found 69 more deformed dead embryos, again with all the characteristics of the chick edema disease Mike had reported in birds from Lake Ontario in 1973-1974. A decade later, our team assembled all of the deformity data collected on cormorant and Caspian tern eggs from 1986-1995 and related those findings to the TCDD-EQ analyses of eggs provided by John Giesy's team over the same period. Those data would show an exceedingly high correlation (r^2 = 0.71) of *in ovo* exposures from PCBs as TCDD-EQs to the rate of deformities of embryos in eggs that died before hatching (Ludwig *et al.* 1996b).

The National Geographic special appeared on television many times in the following fall and winter. Soon our field team was deluged with requests to film our research. In the next three years, film crews from Chicago, Flint, Traverse City, Detroit, Toledo, Boston, Buffalo and Tokyo television stations and a half-dozen newspaper reporters would join our field crews. Many journalists and dedicated environmental activists learned what it was like to walk around guano-covered islands, get insect-bites, wet and seasick, brush against stinging nettles, and spattered with feces from birds—not to mention nauseous—when we opened dead (mostly rotten) eggs that failed to hatch to record the deformities of those dead embryos. All of them experienced the pungent hydrogen sulfide stench of rotted eggs. One documentary, done by Sue Zelenko of WJRT in Flint titled 'Summer Among the Flock', won the United Press International second place award for Best Documentary in Michigan in 1989.

However, NHK, the national network of Japan, spent more time with us than any other media group, covering the stories about effects of Great Lakes toxic chemicals for eleven years. In this time span, the NHK reports made the cross-billed cormorant Cosmos an international star. NHK followed with a second documentary on the subtle effects of toxic exposures on development and endocrine disruption in 1996, and completed their 'trilogy' of specials by filming a delegation of Japanese organic farmers visiting our Kingsville, Ontario organic farm in 1999 for an exchange of ideas and techniques on the best means to grow crops without chemicals.

In fact, Cosmos would become the symbol to Japanese children of the dangers of unregulated toxic chemical use. She was the cover image on the fifth grade textbook for all Japanese public schools on pollution and climate change. The visceral reaction of Japanese people to a deformed cormorant, made so by PCB exposure in its egg, has always stood out as the most vivid example of cultural programming I have ever experienced. The Japanese revere their tamed fishing cormorants that live in the homes of fisherman as honored working pets—identical to working dogs that protect sheep and cattle in the western provinces and states. But, our North American fishermen have lobbied successfully for massive public spending to kill cormorants under the guise of protecting sport fish populations.

July 23, 1988. Cosmos. Today was the shakedown cruise of our new-to-us, but well used, research boat, an unpretentious fourteen-years old 24-foot fiberglass tri-hull. We tried it out for our last trip across Lake Michigan in 1988. Mark and I had inspected several islands in Northern Green Bay and Northern Lake Michigan for PCB-induced deformities in cormorant chicks. It was a bad year. We found numerous leg deformities, eight cross-billed birds, five in colonies of Green Bay, two in northern Lake Michigan, and one in Lake Huron (Fox *et al.* 1991a,

1991b; Ludwig *et al.* 1996b). We finished a long run on this beautiful day from Mackinac City to Naubinway Island, a tiny speck of land, the northernmost discrete island in Lake Michigan. We found a crossed-bill chick there two weeks ago and were back to band the late-hatching chicks. This was a small cormorant colony of 42 nests, on a drab island distinguished only by its navigation light. Nothing marks it as unusual among small Great Lakes bird colonies.

As we glided in to anchor, a tired Mark asked the inevitable question, "How many more islands tonight, Dad?" "Probably two." I answered.

This colony was growing. There were seven new nests in addition to the 42 that were here last month. We moved along, banding quickly, while counting fish dropped by adults or regurgitated by the chicks, accumulating data on over 14,000 fish captured by cormorants for food between 1986 and 1995. The data showed these birds were eating alewives, not sport fish, when nesting (Ludwig *et al.* 1989; Ludwig and Summer in Belyea *et al.* 1999). In the next to last nest, a bird with two normal nest mates had one of the most grotesque bills I have ever seen. Still largely naked, this bird was just growing body feathers to be able to regulate its body temperature. The lower bill, or mandible, projected from the skull and suddenly turned downward 90 degrees and slightly to the left. The maxilla, or upper bill, projected outward, immediately turned about thirty degrees to the left and completed nearly a full circle, looking vaguely like a boars tusk.

How this bird ate at all was a mystery. Young cormorants typically get food from their parents by reaching into the parent's mouth to grasp regurgitated fish. This bird must have been fed directly to grow to this size, since it could not grasp anything. With a sigh, I placed her in a carrying sac and moved along. Angry thoughts boiled through my mind like the smoke from a dampened fire. This made the total nine cross-billed birds from Lake Michigan and Green Bay in 1988. The rate of hatched deformities was not decreasing appreciably, even though the total PCBs in their eggs was dropping slowly each year. Meanwhile the pace of regulatory action in this free market era had faltered again, with the Michigan DNR avoiding the issue and their fisheries biologists criticizing our work whenever possible. Worse, certain Republican Wisconsin legislators were trying to set ridiculously high standards for PCBs discharged by its paper mills. The politicians and agencies continued to demand more studies before cleanups can begin: Such incredible stupidity! At the boat, I put the young cormorant in with another found earlier in the day with a deformed leg. They nestled together—two freaks in a milk crate lined with newspaper. I resolved to deal with these specimens later in the day.

We moved out from Naubinway, striking a course for the Pismire Island colony on the south side of Garden Island in the Beaver Islands archipelago, about 25 miles south. As the boat speed lifted onto a plane, my thoughts were in turmoil. I hid them from my son, not wanting to upset him. But, I certainly wanted to get my hands on the sons of bitches that discharged the PCBs that have caused these problems. If I had their necks in my hands this moment I would most certainly be indicted for assault, at the very least a sharp left jab followed with my best right hook to their normal bills.

A drawing of Cosmos' head done in the summer of 1989 by the late Wayland Swain, Ph.D., toxicologist and human health specialist. Wayland was especially interested in the effects of PCBs on human health and cognition.

JAMES P. LUDWIG, Ph.D

That evening at anchor in lovely Hog Island harbor, I dispatched the leg-deformed bird and placed the body with other the deformed specimens in the cooler. It would be frozen and later dissected in the winter to ascertain the exact nature of this deformity. The crossed-bill chick was a different matter. Since 1981 I had seen and collected 41 other crossed-bills like it in colonies—28 from Green Bay, 8 from northern Lake Michigan, 4 from northern Lake Huron, but just one from Canadian sites on Lake Huron and none from Lake Superior. I had also seen numerous hatchlings with eye deformities, leg and hip deformities, even birds missing cervical vertebrae. The pattern was always the same: the most deformed birds came from Green Bay colonies, then the colonies of northern Lake Michigan, then northern Lake Huron with fewest from the colonies in US Lake Superior and Canadian Lake Huron.

This victim did something quite unusual—*it studied me* with its coal black eyes, shivered violently, begging plaintively for food. For perhaps ten minutes we watched each other as I delayed the decision to dispatch her again and again; then, an unusual idea emerged. Could this bird survive with hand care and become the 'poster child' for the movement to clean up the lakes? The National Geographic special certainly stimulated academic and public interest, just as Tim Kubiak's stuffed crossed bill cormorant 'Henrietta' did at meetings. But, a deformed *live* bird that people could see and touch would grab the attention of common folks in a way that no television show, film or stuffed specimen ever could, just as dad's movies of DDTr-poisoned herring gulls had done 19 years earlier.

So, I made a bargain with this damaged bird, something a dispassionate scientist should never do. I would do everything possible to keep her alive, and she would handle the PR for the movement to ban toxic chemicals and clean-up Great Lakes' AOCs with high contamination. I fed her some of the extra fish samples. She quieted, and I took her onto my lap. We watched the sunset together, bonding in the beauty of a lovely Lake Michigan evening as I kept her warm. Finally, she dozed off. Earlier that month I had been reading one of Carl Sagan's books on the formation of the universe. As the sun disappeared, the name 'Cosmos' just seemed to suggest itself, for she was an accurate reflection of the Great Lakes cosmos in agony from persistent chemical toxicants.

Thus began a strange and wonderful thirteen-month friendship and partnership. Cosmos made 16 different television appearances, testified by her presence in legislatures or legislative committees in Lansing, Madison and Washington, DC as I gave verbal testimony at various committees in these capitols between October and May. She accompanied me to 27 different evening presentations to environmental and teachers groups in five of the Great Lakes states and even appeared with Reid Collins in a live interview on the CNN morning news when we were in Washington. One March evening after a five hour drive from Green Bay toward home after a talk she scared the daylights out of a toll taker at three AM on the Mackinac Bridge when her black visage squawked loudly from her customary travel perch on my left shoulder.

I remember vividly three days spent with Jane Elder of the Sierra Club and other environmental activists in their annual 'Great Lakes Washington Week' in March, 1989. In the mornings we planned our lobbying of indifferent congressmen and senators in the basement of the Sierra Club's Washington office, Cosmos at hand, grunting encouragement to the committed activists from NGOs who would fan out every afternoon to spread their messages across the Hill. In the afternoons we met with legislators or agency officials, or gave testimony in hearings.

Among the attendees was Wayland Swain, a man of great *gravitas* who had quit the USEPA when Reagan emasculated, then closed, the USEPA Grosse Ile Great Lakes research laboratory he directed. Wayland had found the aerial transport pathway for chlorinated pollutants by testing fish from inland Lake Siskiwit on Isle Royale where there was no connection to Lake Superior and only the air could be the source of toxicants like the PCBs (Swackhamer 1988). He would brook no nonsense on the issue because humans were being damaged, notwithstanding the politics of the day. One afternoon we attended a committee hearing arranged by a Minnesota congressman, Jerry Sikorski. I spoke briefly and Cosmos was quiet, just as she always was whenever I spoke. I believe Cosmos thought of me as the largest, most alpha, cormorant in the room. But, as I left the podium to turn the hearing over to Wayland, Cosmos began her antics, for she had developed into an absolute ham. All through Wayland's testimony and the congressman's concluding comments, Cosmos paraded herself up and down the balustrade that separated the people from the lawmakers, preening and grunting, drawing attention to her rather than those who testified and summarized their scientific findings and political concerns.

Later, and only half in jest, Wayland would berate me for her antics and declared that we should have given credence to W.C. Fields' famous remark never to share the stage with children or animals, especially 'a deformed, godforsaken water chicken'! But, that was Cosmos. She seemed to understand that her role was to be seen and she relished human attention. Actually, Wayland had a soft spot for Cosmos, for two years later he produced a beautiful rendering of her that has an honored place on my office wall (cover and previous drawing).

When people saw her they were invariably curious. We traveled in my Aerostar van. I gave her free rein to wander wherever she chose to go, covering the seats with a tarp. Often she would perch on my left shoulder on long drives and attempt to nibble an ear, even though her deformity made that impossible. Drivers passing inevitably slowed down to 'check her out'. We became friends and colleagues on a mission. On the return trip to Michigan after 'Washington Week', I stopped at an Ohio Turnpike rest area as a busload of school children pulled in. An hour and fifteen minutes later I finally was able to go into the rest area only to find a new busload of Japanese tourists gathered around the van gesturing animatedly when I returned with fresh coffee in hand. The interpreter/guide asked if this was the famous bird—Cosmos—NHK had filmed the previous summer? When I confirmed it was, virtually the entire busload exclaimed and many of them actually bowed to honor the crippled cormorant. What a refreshing difference these were to our fishermen who were starting to try every political dirty trick to have cormorants killed and change public policy from protection to destruction! One culture revered Cosmos' kin and respected the message her deformity made real. The other had many who loathed cormorants enough to commit avian genocide on a massive scale. I was deeply ashamed to be part of the wrong culture.

I think it safe to claim Cosmos in her single short year of life did more to propel the issue of toxic chemicals to the forefront of political agendas in Michigan and Wisconsin than all the other environmental activists and scientists were able to achieve through lobbying or explaining their findings. When she appeared in Madison at a state senate hearing on the bill to loosen the rules for paper company discharges of PCBs, the

Republican senators attempting to force the rule change through the natural resources committee and legislature fled the room as Madison television station cameras filmed her. It was Cosmos that destroyed their credibility, not me. Their proposal was defeated, even though it had seemed certain it would pass only a few weeks earlier. Appropriately, at the end of that event Cosmos deposited a rather immense poop on the great mahogany table of the senate hearing room, a pungent and apropos comment on the politics of contamination in Wisconsin's AOCs. That amused assemblyman Spencer Black, who had asked us to come and testify, but left me with a large clean-up.

Sadly, Cosmos was never a fully healthy bird and suffered numerous recurrent bacterial infections. She died of natural causes August 6, 1989 and is buried on the eastern point of High Island in the Beaver Islands where her spirit can see each sunrise and mingle with the cormorants of the day. She was a colleague and honored partner. I still miss her. My good friend Loraine (Rainy) Campbell was part of our research team at the time and sensed my deep sadness at Cosmos' premature death. Rainy touched me deeply when she produced a lovely pen and ink drawing of Cosmos' head and transcribed the insightful comments by Henry Beston from his classic work *Outermost House* onto a parchment in calligraphy at Christmas, 1989. It has hung in my office ever since, warning me against the hubris so common to scientists while reminding me gently every day of the remarkable creature that shared my mission for thirteen months.

"We need another and a wiser and perhaps a more mystical concept of animals. Remote from universal nature, and living by complicated artifice, man in civilization surveys the creature through the glass of his knowledge and sees thereby a feather magnified and the whole image in distortion. We patronize them for their incompleteness, for their tragic fate of having taken form so far below ourselves. And therein we err, and greatly err. For the animal shall not be measured by man. In a world older and more complete than ours they move finished and complete, gifted with extensions of the senses we have lost or never attained, living by voices we shall never hear. They are not brethren, they are not underlings; they are other nations, caught with ourselves in the net of life and time, fellow prisoners of the splendor and travail of the earth."

Quotation from **Outermost House** by Henry Beston.

May, 1988 to October, 1990. New sources of support emerge. Support for our research from the Michigan DNR disappeared in 1988 with the arrival of a new director and pointed criticisms from the MDNR fisheries group. He simply did not believe that bad news should be reported during his tenure; moreover, influential DNR fish biologists were furious over the findings we made and released to the public. These data made it more difficult to convince some people to buy fishing licenses that supported their programs. Politics and economics had trumped truth. Interestingly, four new sources stepped forward in 1988 and 1989 to support our research. Three, Dow Chemical, Upjohn (pharmaceuticals) and the McGregor Foundation were mentioned earlier.

The substantial funding by both corporations was noteworthy since the research we were doing could have damaged their interests. Each made, or used and discharged, a wide variety of chemicals that some activists posited had similar effects to the dioxins and PCBs. Even so, both corporations stepped forward because ethical persons in them, Randy Croyle at Dow and Mel Visser at Upjohn, wanted the truth and convinced their administrations we were on track to find it. A third source was the McGregor Fund of Detroit that granted unrestricted monies to allow our team to continue our broad scale research across the upper three Great Lakes.

The fourth major source was the Consumers Power Company. They hired ERS to determine the concentrations of chemical residues in fish and potential effects on the wildlife resident in the watersheds of three of Michigan's major rivers with dams. Importantly, they funded research to measure the uptake of contaminants by nestling cormorants around the Great Lakes in order to provide a baseline for measuring the extent of hazards from the dioxin-like contaminants to inland wildlife that fish could bring inland if the Consumers-owned dams were removed or they were forced to install fish ladders. The research was performed with analytical support of the Giesy toxicological group at Michigan State and substantial help from Bill Bowerman, one of Giesy's doctoral students working on Great Lakes' bald eagles.

Ultimately a set of six landmark peer-reviewed ecotoxicological studies (published 1992-1996) emerged from this complex interdisciplinary work. The most significant finding was that the dams actually protected inland wildlife that ate fish (Giesy *et al.* 1994 a,b,c). Fish of the same species above dams were 10 to 100 fold less contaminated with the dioxin-like chemicals than fish below dams. Dams prevented the inward migration of highly contaminated Great Lakes fish, especially the introduced salmonids, protecting the inland wildlife species (Bowerman *et al.* 1994, 1995; Freeman, 2003). With these studies, the Federal Energy Regulatory Commission relicensed the hydroelectric dams but refused to allow inward passage of Great Lakes fishes until the fish had toxicant concentrations below thresholds of effects on sensitive inland wildlife, including eagles, mink and otter.

The cormorant uptake study found Green Bay cormorant chicks acquired burdens of the dioxin-like chemicals eleven times faster that the cleanest Lake Superior birds (from the Apostle Islands, WI), while herring gulls from Saginaw Bay accumulated these contaminants 27-fold faster (Jones *et al.* 1993a, 1994b). In many ways, these six studies solidified the cause-effect linkages of dioxin-like contamination with wildlife damage and bioeffects to an unassailable certainty. No longer were speculations that effects had to be genetic, viral or from something unknown credible. However, in this window, Michigan and Wisconsin elected doctrinaire neoliberal Republican governments. Both states lost all interest in understanding or control of toxic chemicals in the Great Lakes for years. More bad news was the very last thing these regimes would tolerate on their watch. Instead, they would fund public relations efforts to 'Celebrate the Great Lakes' while hoping we would just disappear.

December 29, 1988. The Karn-Weadock Consumers Power Plant Headquarters, Essexville, Michigan. For the previous three years ERS had been contracted by the Karn-Weadock Power Plant of Consumers Power Co. to plant and establish vegetation on its flyash mounds at the mouth of the Saginaw River to prevent wind erosion. I came to appreciate the savvy of the Karn-Weadock plants manager, Paul Elbert. We had a natural point of contact: Paul was the inveterate Buckeye, I the resolute Wolverine. Football, specifically the greatest collegiate gridiron rivalry of all time—Ohio State v. Michigan, Woody Hayes v. Bo Schembechler— was our point of reference. We had exchanged genial insults and engaged in friendly repartee on the classic rivalry for three years.

On a chilly December afternoon between Christmas and New Years I dropped into Paul's office to chat and share a clandestine dram of the good stuff. Eventually, we got to the subject of how an environmentalist (me, by then the Vice-President of Michigan Audubon Society) had done effective work for Consumers Power (Paul). He wished there were other ways to cooperate between the corporate and environmentalist worlds and produce practical solutions to real environmental problems. Over the course of an hour (and several more drams of distilled inspiration) we brainstormed. Soon the concept of a private council of corporations and environmental groups dedicated to solving the environmental problems of the Great Lakes region, completely independent of public agencies, emerged. Paul asked what a council might cost. I doodled for a bit and came up with $30,000. per year. Paul astounded me by offering to provide half from Consumers Power, provided Audubon could raise half as a match. A month later, I took the concept to Maureen Smythe, Executive Director of the Mott Foundation that soon agreed to provide the match. Thereby, noble experiment was born—The Great Lakes Regional Corporate Environmental Council [GLRCEC].

GLRCEC was specifically a joint venture of Great Lakes environmentalist organizations and corporations. We excluded all media and public agencies to be able to discuss our disparate agendas without the temptation to slant our views for public consumption. For a time, the concept worked splendidly. We produced a report that strengthened recycling by closing the loop to stimulate demand for recycled products that was promptly adopted by Michigan. We dealt with many issues including air pollution, toxic chemicals and climate change. As an environmentalist I saw substantial change within several of the corporations that participated, not just public relations intended to placate critics. We learned how to find solutions when posturing for our constituencies was banned.

Interestingly, it was the activism of the IJC that set the conditions of failure by GLRCEC. The IJC adopted a call to sunset the use of synthetic chlorinated compounds and some chlorine uses after 1991 as the only solution to the problem of toxicant contaminants in the lakes (IJC 1991b). Simply put, this proposed action was too great a step for society to take, and GLRCEC atrophied after trying to find a common ground on this issue for more than four years. Even so, this experience taught me the lesson that some corporations are directed by those who want to do the right thing every bit as much as environmentalists. The truth is that corporate leaders are constrained to serve shareholder demands for profits first in our neoliberal free market economies. But, if corporate leaders move too fast, then they are replaced by other leaders who forget environmental concerns. Sadly, that is how our capitalist system works.

Cause-Effects Linkages I. February, 1989. Steady progress of researchers interested in the effects of legacy toxic chemicals on wildlife produced astonishing data rapidly in the late 1980s. Researchers studying fish (Mac and Edsall 1991), herptiles (Bishop *et al.* 1991), birds (Kubiak *et al.* 1989; Gilbertson *et al.* 1991) and mammals (Wren 1991; Hornshaw and Aulerich 1983) all reported identical deformities and poor reproduction in the predators they studied correlated to the presence of the dioxin-like chemicals. The fact that the same deformities (homologies) occurred in all taxa and were reproduced readily in laboratory populations after exposure to the dioxin-like substances helped seal the case for effects owing to the sum of the dioxin-like chemicals, mostly co-planar PCBs (Kannan *et al.* 1988; Smith *et al.* 1991; Summer 1991).

Mike Gilbertson of the IJC organized the first Cause-Effects Linkages conference (IJC 1989b) among researchers and agency administrators only. Data sets were exchanged and evaluated in a two-day session closed to the public. Only the most skeptical or biased scientists could continue to deny the case for extensive damages caused by these substances. Yet, even with these powerful, consistent replicated data, most fisheries scientists and some ecologists (Cooper, 1995) continued to discount the effects of contaminants, clinging stubbornly to a belief that the poor reproduction and health of many Great Lakes species (especially fish) had to have many causes. Contaminants were not high on their list of causes, probably because these chemicals were not disappearing fast enough.

May 1989 to August 1992. Assisting immune suppression research of Keith Grasman. One of the joys of field studies is the opportunity to work with talented and energetic young people. Some call this mentoring. But, when you have a chance to work with an innovative talent like Keith, it is really just the opposite, for you learn far more than you teach. Simply put, I had the boats and could give the logistic support required to get Keith out to bird colonies. There, he compared the performance and development of the immune systems of wild herring gull and Caspian tern chicks from cleaner with more contaminated colonies of the lakes. Keith and his bride Suzanne joined our team for three full field seasons. We exchanged labor for each other's projects, had wild adventures with the weather, got blood and tissue samples through customs, banded large numbers and interfaced with skeptical officials in both nations.

The author (left) assessing cormorant embryos in dead eggs with help from Keith Grasman (right) at UMBS, June 30, 1989.

Keith's basic research design was to collect a sample of eggs from colonies for TCDD-EQ and PCB congener-specific analyses to measure the embryonic exposures to those chemicals. After chicks grew to three weeks of age, he challenged their immune systems with sheep red blood cell antigens or an inflammatory plant protein. The intensity of immune responses could be measured as antibody induction, by inflammation and counts of immune system cells. Then, Keith correlated these markers of immune function to contaminants. He found statistically significant reduced immune responses that tracked contaminants inversely: the greater the TCDD-EQ embryonic exposure, the poorer, more delayed and more compromised were the immune responses (Grasman 1994, Grasman *et al.* 1996). In Green Bay and Saginaw Bay, immune competence was less than half what it was in the cleaner Canadian colonies of Lakes Huron and Lake Superior. Sadly, 20 years later Keith has determined the same reduced immune responses in the birds from these AOCs; very little has changed (Grasman *et al.* 2013).

The beauty of Keith's work was how well it fit with the long-term recruitment data for the Caspian tern population that I had been collecting since 1966 by trapping nesting adult terns banded as chicks. Finally, a plausible mechanism explained why recruitment was so much less from the more exposed US colony sites compared to the much less exposed Canadian colony sites. The contamination gradient was always greatest in Saginaw Bay > Green Bay > Northern Lake Michigan > North Channel & Georgian Bay Canadian colonies. Tern immune responses were depressed inversely to contamination; recruitment from contaminated sites followed the same pattern as immune competence.

In essence, Keith handed me the smoking gun that provided a mechanism for what I had measured as tern recruitment during 27 years of trapping (Ludwig 1968, 1979, 2013) and others had correlated to circulating blood concentrations of total PCBs in Great Lakes Caspian terns (Mora *et al.* 1993). Further, Keith's work was among the first field demonstrations of many animal laboratory studies that had shown huge deleterious impacts on the immune system after exposure to the dioxin-like contaminants (Kerklviet *et al.* 1990; Birnbaum 1993). And, gentleman that he is, Keith has always given me far more credit for his work than was warranted by including me as a junior author his landmark paper (Grasman *et al.* 1996). In truth, Keith provided the genius and did the meticulous hard work. I just drove the boats, helped with the sampling, cooked the meals, handled the logistics and learned from him.

October, 1989. The Biennial Meeting of the IJC with the public, **Hamilton, ON.** For two decades the IJC had presented their evaluation of the state of the Great Lakes and reviews of the governments' responses to the damages caused by eutrophication, toxicant pollutants and invasive species at a public meeting held every other year. Usually, these meetings drew several hundred people, mostly scientists, activists and a few from the public in the local area where the meeting happened to be held, but not this time. The 1989 meeting was held in the Copps Auditorium in Hamilton. It was packed to standing room only. People came from every corner of the Great Lakes, Ottawa and Washington to demand clean-ups of legacy chemical contaminants. These IJC commissioners were acting to protect the Great Lakes, and they encouraged full public participation.

The US commission co-chair Gordon Durnil, a conservative Indiana Republican fundraiser for George H. W. Bush, was rewarded with an appointment as chair of the US delegation. Surprising to many, Gordon studied the toxic chemical debacle carefully, then lent his considerable *gravitas* to the debate, leading towards substantial clean-ups (Durnil 1995). The public responded with strident calls for action. The conservative politicians on both sides of the border, George H.W. Bush and Brian Mulroney, were caught out by the integrity of their own commissioners. Each appointed independent persons who would encourage full disclosure and vigorous public debates over legacy contamination in the next four years. Gordon was at the epicenter of all this effort.

This was the exact outcome the politicians did not want. It violated the most practical 'principle' of the modern American and Canadian neoliberal governments, to wit: *One must never allow bad news to be publicized during their administration!* If that happened, they might actually have to do something to remedy the damages they (and predecessors) had allowed to persist. Soon, the question would be reduced to this: Would the governments act to clean-up contamination of the worst hot spots? Or, would they encourage a counter movement in order to derail clean-ups by demands for further studies? Or, would they divert focus away from AOCs and contamination issues? Or, would clever shills employed in the neoliberal governments find ways to change the subject to something else? The heat was on and the temperature was rising very rapidly. Something had to give. Suddenly, a great many people in regulatory agencies and the industries that had discharged contaminants were most uncomfortable (Visser 2007).

September, 1991. Cause-Effects Linkages II & the Traverse City Biennial meeting of the IJC. Cause-Effects Linkages II, with the organizational support of the Michigan Audubon Society, especially Rick Campbell (MAS 1991), was held concurrent with the 1991 IJC biennial public meeting at Traverse City, and chaired by Dr. Theodora Colborn whose landmark book *"Great Lakes—Great Legacy?"* had just been published (Colborn *et al.* 1990). In many ways, this meeting was the high water mark of the movement to ban persistent toxic substances from the Great Lakes and get clean-ups started (IJC 1991a; MAS 1991). New research was thoroughly reviewed; the data showed common effects of the dioxin-like chemicals to all vertebrates.

Head of a typical crossed bill cormorant. Snake Island, Bay de Noc, northern Lake Michigan July, 1990.

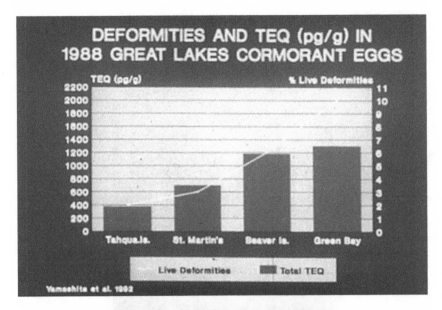

DEFORMITIES AND TEQ (pg/g) IN 1988 GREAT LAKES CORMORANT EGGS

Caspian tern embryo that died just before hatching showing severe gastroschisis with yolk sac and organs outside body wall, Gravelly Island, Green Bay, July 16, 1990.

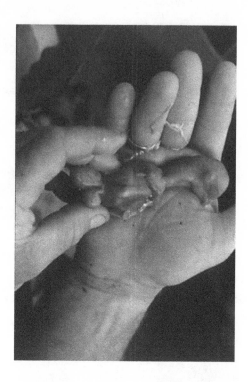

Cormorant embryo that died just before hatching with severe head and neck edema and gastroschisis. Gull Island, northern Lake Michigan, July 13, 1990.

For the first time, studies of human health effects were given equal time and weight to wildlife reports. The previous cause-effects conference had reviewed data related to human health effects, but only between research scientists and agency administrators. But, CEL-II dove headlong into these emotion-charged waters. This time the public and the media were in the room. Dr. Helen Daly and the Drs. Jacobson reviewed their data from their respective Great Lakes human cohorts of children born to fish-eaters and companion studies of surrogate mammals (Jacobson *et al.* 1990 a, b.). Their data showed very large, troubling and permanent effects on cognition and reasoning from *in utero* exposures acquired through eating Great Lakes salmonids. Wayland Swain updated his review of all human studies around the world that showed many effects on people exposed in different ways (Swain 1991).

Their impact was tremendous. No longer did reporters or politicians have to ask what a disturbing wildlife study meant to people and then listen to scientists hedge their answers to protect themselves. The data were out, front and center, that said we humans were very little different from all other vertebrates. The dioxin-like substances damaged us in exactly the same ways our kindred vertebrate cousins were afflicted. Only the sensitivities were different between species. It was the scientific echo of Henry Beston's literary commentary on animals as equal nations to us, sharing a world of Great Lakes splendor, degraded insidiously by effects of toxic POPs contamination.

March 1991-August 1992. The Great Lakes Protection Fund experience. The eight Great Lakes states were faced with a rising tide of public demand to improve pollution controls and management of these resources by the late 1980s. An aroused public encouraged by the IJC (IJC 1991) and many NGOs all demanded state and federal agencies address long-avoided problems. Public quiescence was over, replaced by intense agitation for genuine change. The states' response was to create a research and management fund (GLPF) to stimulate targeted research and find new ways to solve old problems. At the outset, there were two basic goals to the GLPF program. Serious problems, like the legacy of toxic chemicals, were to be thoroughly researched to understand the mechanisms producing damage. Processes, especially at the macro and watershed level, that exacerbated damage were to be studied to make cost-effective reforms to management programs of Great Lakes resources.

On the research side, the ERS proposal to search for biological markers (biomarkers) of exposures and effects in cormorants was selected for funding. A pilot study and other preliminary work were accomplished in 1991 with a huge effort scheduled for 1992. Similar to the Giesy-Tillitt-Kubiak-Ludwig studies of 1987-90 when exposures to the dioxin-like chemicals were shown to relate to egg death rates (Tillitt *et al.* 1991b, 1992), this research studied cormorants. We sought to monitor biomarkers that would predict contaminant effects but cost far less to measure over many years than the actual chemical analyses of samples. A congener-specific analysis of a single egg, fish or tissue sample cost upwards of $2,000, an H_4IIE bioassay for TCDD-EQs about $600. But, biomarkers such as thyroid hormone or vitamin A in blood that also respond to the dioxin-like contaminants could be analyzed for $20 each. If these biomarkers were proven to predict effects as accurately as detailed chemistry, then the potential for heightened surveillance using small blood samples from many individuals was huge. Sample sizes could be increased greatly at far less cost.

The design called for marking nest and egg contents of 21 different cormorant colonies with widely varied exposures to the dioxin-like chemicals. Then, we were to measure hatching rates, deformities in live and dead eggs, and the selected biomarkers of vitamin A and thyroxine in blood from older chicks. The logistics of work on colonies from the Apostle Islands in Lake Superior in the northwest, south into central Lakes Michigan and Huron including Saginaw Bay, and east into Georgian Bay were daunting. Three research boats supported two field teams. We began by collecting eggs in the first two weeks of May. Blood sampling for biomarkers and related survival data were to be accumulated from mid-June to August, with the expensive detailed analytical chemical analyses done on the eggs and the much cheaper tests to be done for the biomarkers in blood as the chicks grew large. Once all the data were available, the results could be correlated to determine how accurate biomarkers were to predict effects of the dioxin-like chemicals. Four visits were planned for each colony site over this 120-day period with more than 500 hours of boat travel time; 2.1 person years of work were required to sample the colonies spread across 450 miles.

All egg samples were collected and undergoing analysis by May 24. Egg hatching rates were determined by June 18. The third visits to collect blood and band chicks were scheduled to start in the last week of June. But, Newcastle disease virus (NDV) broke out among all North American cormorants unexpectedly, with the greatest damage done to embryos and chicks that have no acquired immunity to the disease (Glaser *et al.* 1998). We found the first dead and dying chicks at Snake Island in northern Green Bay on June 23, then confirmed the presence of the highly contagious disease in all 16 colonies of cormorants we visited from Green Bay to Lake Superior and the North Channel by June 26. We learned from the National Wildlife Disease Laboratory at Madison that NDV had broken out simultaneously all across North America from Alberta to the Canadian Maritimes, a true North American pandemic. East of the Rocky Mountains, all cormorant populations were affected. There was huge concern the highly pathogenic NDV could spread to domestic poultry farms.

The effects on the research design were catastrophic. In addition to the dioxin-like chemical exposures, NDV was present in all study areas, but apparently at different levels in local populations. The worst affected colonies lost more than 40% of their hatched chicks and hatched just 52% of their eggs. The least-affected lost 7% of chicks and hatched 78% of their eggs. The distribution of colonies most affected by the disease seemed to be random, and the effects of the viral infections on the biomarkers were large which combined to destroy the research design. With the potential that our research teams could vector the disease inadvertently from colony to colony, or worse, to domestic fowl, our research was cancelled.

This was the only case in my career where a research design was destroyed by a random variable that appeared without warning. Unfortunately, the greatest expenditures were at the front end of the work to set up the study of 21 widely-spaced colonies and to pay for the expensive analytical chemistry work on the egg samples. All this effort yielded no publishable results on biomarkers except a description of the epidemic (Glaser *et al.* 1998), and a substantial debt for ERS. Naturally, the principals of the GLPF were extremely discouraged too. A significant outcome for me was to see research funding for effects of POPs chemicals on Great Lakes' birds evaporate after 1992. I learned the truth of the saying "A success has many fathers, but a failure has just one".

November 9, 1992. North Pacific albatrosses and the dioxin-like toxins: Focus on a worldwide perspective using Midway's albatrosses. In April, 1992 Theo Colborn assembled a group of marine researchers to look into the worldwide distribution of synthetic dioxin-like compounds and related endocrine disrupting chemicals in marine species. Theo led a team to prepare a very large research proposal with a worldwide reach. I was invited to participate as a 'bird person', arguing successfully to include albatrosses as well as whales and dolphins in order to monitor oceanic POPs pollution. With predictable migrations and surface-feeding habits, albatrosses were expected to have different exposures than marine mammals. Much to my surprise and delight, the albatross component alone was selected by the USEPA for a pilot project using unspent FY-92 funds granted to the World Wildlife Fund where Theo worked.

I found myself alone on Midway Island, 5,950 kilometers west of San Francisco in the middle of the North Pacific Ocean the third week of November, 1992 working to start a project modeled on our many Great Lakes studies of the previous five years. Albatross nests were marked, eggs collected and blood samples taken for analysis by the Giesy team at Michigan State. We were astonished to find black-footed albatross egg PCB concentrations higher than continental cormorants from prairie colonies in Manitoba and carrying more DDTr compounds than still present in Lake Michigan eagle eggs in the 1992-year samples. Worse, about 40 percent of the total of DDT congeners (DDTr) was 'parent compound', meaning that most of it was recently used (Jones *et al.* 1994a). Less than 2 percent of the DDT_r in Lake Michigan's eagles by 1991 was still parent DDT compounds; over 98 percent had decomposed to DDE (Giesy *et al.* 1994a).

This meant the North Pacific albatrosses were encountering fresh DDT pollution, not the legacy pollution we had been studying in the Great Lakes! The mixture of the dioxin-like compounds was also different with much more furan and the aerially transported congeners of PCBs. This all suggested recently made Asia-sourced fire-formed toxins and atmospheric transport had delivered the chemicals into albatross foods (Jones *et al.* 1994a; Ludwig *et al.* 1997a). Since DDT was banned in North America in 1972, this DDT had to be coming from new Asian sources. It was another example of emerging countries ignoring UN conventions to reduce uses of POPs to the practical minimum (e.g. the Stockholm Convention), and an excellent example of what happens when globalized trade and commerce are unregulated. In essence, both the sources of POPs contamination and industry had migrated to Asia as North America developed 'service' economies.

The author (left) and Cheryl Summer sampling a Laysan albatross' for blood, Sand Island, Midway Atoll, Hawaii, January 24, 1994.

Black-footed albatross chick with a severely-crossed bill, Sand Island, Midway Atoll, Hawaii February 17, 1994.

Black-footed albatross embryo with severely-crossed bill, missing right eye and gastroschisis, all typical signs of dioxin-like chemical exposures. Eastern Island, Midway Atoll, February 11, 1993.

Two black-footed albatross eggs with exceptionally thin shells, a typical effect of DDTr exposures. Sand Island, Midway Atoll, Hawaii, November 30, 1994.

Over the course of three years, we documented increasing DDT_r and PCB concentrations in the albatrosses and significant biological impairments in the black-footed albatross. We found the same suite of deformities seen in the Great Lakes birds (photos 11 & 12), but at lower rates, plus slight egg-shell thinning (photo 13) in black-foots from their DDT_r burdens (Ludwig *et al.* 1997). Interestingly, eight years later, Myra Finkelstein as a doctoral student at University of California Santa Cruz repeated the sampling we did in 1992-93. She found a 408 percent increase in DDT_r, about the same ratio of parent DDT:DDE compounds and a 170 percent increase in the total PCBs above what we had found (Finkelstein *et al.* 2006). The Pacific Islands National Wildlife Refuge managers at Midway reported a decrease in the nesting population after 2005. In 2008 the black-footed albatross was placed on the ICUN globally threatened populations list. Contamination by dioxin-like chemicals and DDT_r were prominent candidates for the cause of this population decline.

The USEPA continued to support the Midway work through FY-1995 until Newt Gingrich's "Contract with America" destroyed all extramural research of that might damage the conservative pro-business neoliberal political agenda then ascendant in America. The impacts of research on POPs done on the Great Lakes in the late 1980s had stirred up a veritable 'hornet's nest' of reaction by North American industry that wanted no more contaminants research funded *ever again anywhere in the world.* Their lobbyists went to work, and the neoliberal Republican congress responded to their lucrative blandishments. All extramural ecological research of the EPA was curtailed. Federal US support for Great Lakes university research was reduced drastically and a freeze on virtually all new Canadian research combined for a 36% reduction in funding from FY-95 to FY-96 (IJC 1996). Most federal support for research on contaminants in wildlife and people vanished abruptly in both countries. It was another vivid illustration of the law of *realpolitik*—'No bad news is to be allowed on our watch. Heaven forbid, we might be held responsible and then have to do something about this!'

Summer of 1995: Perch and Cormorant Research. In the early 1990s the perch populations in most of Lakes Huron and Michigan experienced one of their periodic crashes. This time cormorants were there to be blamed, and intense pressure was put on the Michigan DNR to 'prove' a cause-effect relationship of cormorants with drastic perch population declines after 1988. A small pilot study was accomplished in 1994 and a full-scale attempt to test this hypothesis by a large fish tagging and cormorant collection program followed in 1995 in 'the snows' (Les Cheneaux) island group of northwestern Lake Huron. Cheryl Summer and I provided data on the cormorant nesting population of the region, current and historic banding data and the food items regurgitated by cormorants during nesting. We found no perch, perch fish tags, salmon smolts or salmon tags in cormorant nests, but we did find 168 salmon tags in threatened Caspian tern nests in the Beaver Islands.

A set of talented fish biologists from the University of Michigan led by Jim Diana and Susan Maruca joined with DNR biologists Glen Belyea and Richard Clark, Jr. to examine the impacts of cormorants on the perch population. They concluded that cormorants consumed perch infrequently, except during spring spawning, and were responsible for about 1% of the total annual perch mortality in the 'snows' region. Sport fisherman accounted for 2.5 times more perch killed than cormorants. The sum of both cormorant and sport fisherman-caused mortalities was far below the annual loss (45%) of perch in this locale; over 90% of the annual mortality remained unknown. They also noted that cormorants were exploiting competitive alewife and even ate some northern pike that prey on perch, actions that could even benefit the local perch population. Regardless, this study was soon touted by some MDNR fisheries biologists as unassailable evidence that cormorants damaged the perch fishery seriously. Thus, the cormorant holocaust became official policy of several states and the federal government; Michigan and the USFWS would soon spend $350,000 per year on this dubious control program (Diana 2010).

January, 1996-June 21, 2002. An organic farmer's perspective. My personal life had undergone a huge transformation in 1991 when my first marriage dissolved. I married again in June, 1993 to a lovely Canadian woman, Alison Kilpatrick. Since I was working on albatrosses for the next two field seasons, we elected to move to British Columbia to be closer to Midway Island, but still in Canada. I took the first steps to Canadian citizenship that would be granted in 2005. But, the USEPA funding ceased in October, 1995. We had to decide what to do with our lives. My old friend Steven Apfelbaum, who had once worked for me at ERS eighteen years earlier, offered me a half-time position with his Wisconsin ecological firm. I began there in January 1996.

Alison and I debated where to move to and settled finally on the rural area of Kingsville, Ontario about 35 kilometers south of Windsor on the north shore of Lake Erie. We found an old 44-acre farmstead with 18 acres of young apple trees and moved in May 1996, spending the first summer assessing our lives and directions. Consulting held promise of a decent income. With a half-time commitment to Steve, I could pursue Great Lakes related work, do more consulting for other clients, or pursue farming. We found no funds to restart the Great Lakes colonial water bird studies (IJC 1996). So, we elected to try organic farming, specifically a community supported agriculture (CSA) venture and organic orchard. Starting with 23 families in 1997, our CSA grew rapidly to 122 shareholder families in 2001. The orchard venture became the only certified organic apple and cider operation of southwestern Ontario in 2000.

November, 1994-1998. *The pernicious effects of neoliberalism begin to strangle Great Lakes restoration and clean-up efforts.*

From my perspective, my time as a research ecologist studying Great Lakes problems had been as rewarding as possible to someone interested in birds and legacy POPs. But, the energies of the public had waned under unremitting pressures, starvation of regulatory agency budgets, and tactics of some in the government agencies striving to serve their neoliberal masters (Gore 2007; Alexander 2009), even by outright misrepresentation of science-based findings (Cooper 1995).

Although I could not attend the 1993 Windsor IJC public biennial meeting because I was on Midway, I have learned that it was a raucous confrontation of those supporting the ban of all chlorinated substances and industrial representatives defending all chlorine uses with equal passion. Agency attendees hid from view as much as feasible, having no effective programs to offer the aroused public. The meeting was barely controlled. It would be the last of the biennial IJC meetings with an unscripted agenda. Many in agencies refused to attend thereafter, responding to the rapidly emerging conservative neoliberal political climate. Mel Visser's recent book 'Cold Clear and Deadly' offers an industry attendee's view of this meeting, and is must reading for anyone interested in Great lakes issues, especially POPs contamination and one man's evolution of an understanding of their pernicious nature (Visser 2007).

In essence, the IJC commissioners had committed the cardinal sin of an agency with only advisory powers. Under Gordon Durnil's enlightened leadership, the IJC had allowed—even actively fomented—criticisms of government programs on toxicant chemicals and the lack of real clean-ups (IJC 1991). The answer of the governments was simple and effective: Shut down or control all meaningful public input through the IJC by exerting tight control of the biennial public meeting agendas and substitute 'State of the Lakes Environmental Conferences' [SOLECs]. Only technical and research persons would be invited to present on the politically acceptable topics at the SOLECs, although anyone could attend. Agendas of all future meetings would be tightly scripted by the agencies to avoid any appearance of ineptitude or inter-agency conflict. Clean-ups of AOCs would be deemphasized by promoting 'the ecosystem approach' (Allen *et al.* 1993). The once vaunted USEPA Great Lakes Initiative that had addressed contamination from a water quality perspective and proposed stringent water quality standards for many POPs was abandoned quietly, then buried by every agency that had been involved with it.

The first of the SOLECs was held in 1994 focused on Lake Michigan; others have followed on each of the lakes. By having SOLECs on each lake, fewer people would attend and criticisms would be muted because the public would appear to be less interested. In the meantime, the structure and membership of the three Great Lakes IJC technical advisory boards was being altered substantially (Ludwig 1995, appendix 1). It was a bald-faced attempt to change the direction of the IJC from a focus on the BWT and subsequent GLWQA-mandated remediation criteria that address the damages from excess nutrients and POPs to the vague 'ecosystem approach' that is very difficult to use to develop testable scientific hypotheses since it has no theories of causality.

The proponents of the ecosystem approach maintained that everything had to be managed at once to improve the Great Lakes, because the essential problems of the system are interrelated, something that is true as far as it goes. However, in law, the IJC and its authority were derived from two documents—The Boundary Waters Treaty of 1909 and the agreements embedded in the 1972 Great Lakes Water Quality Agreement (GLWQA) and the codicils of 1978 and 1987. None of these legal documents focus on an ecosystem approach. Instead, they addressed damage by toxic substances, pathogens and excessive nutrition, specifying numerical criteria in order to achieve good water quality. The treaty was especially relevant as damage, and commitments to prevent damage between the two nations were the specified goals of article 4. Control of pollutants was to be achieved through enforcement of numerical criteria and 'virtual elimination' by the GLWQA until the ecosystem approach was adopted that allowed the focus to shift to processes.

It was the damage focus of the BWT and GLWQA that had the governments and industry spooked: Who would pay? How would governments determine that fairly? The ecosystem approach was the perfect cover to sound good and engaged while actually doing nothing substantial to clean up contaminants and repair damages. And, because the ecosystem approach would continue to support calls for relatively inexpensive academic research compared to the monumental costs of clean-ups, many in the academic and research communities would go along to get along in their careers.

However, others in the scientific community were outraged by this attempt to hi-jack the legal agreements with the ecosystem approach that could ignore concrete goals to clean-up contaminated areas of concern (AOCs) and substitute 'comprehensive management' (Allen *et al.* 1993). The strategy of the parties was to substitute this warm and fuzzy public relations approach to critical lake issues while simultaneously controlling public participation carefully through the IJC and SOLEC meetings. Criticisms of the government parties and programs could be controlled, while the neoliberal governments on both sides of the border would neither have to do clean-ups, or wrestle with the contentious issue of who would pay.

Even though I was now focused on North Pacific albatrosses and living far away in British Columbia, I saw the particularly egregious changes to IJC advisory boards as a sure signal of political control of the IJC by the parties to the GLWQA. I chose to express my opinions in a pointed editorial for the Journal of Great Lakes Research (Ludwig 1995a; appendix 1). After publication, many friends in the research community wrote to thank me privately for the candor. Several colleagues opined that I had just black-listed myself for any more research funding on the Great Lakes; their pessimistic assessment was spot on.

When the last research report on the albatrosses was finished for the World Wildlife Fund and USEPA in December, 1995, it was apparent there was simply no option to return to monitoring toxic chemicals effects on

Great Lakes wildlife. My bridges to government agencies were burned and would smolder for a very long time. But, with restricted research funding and tight control of all controversial research, these were bridges to nowhere in a neoliberal world, unlikely to produce relevant research on POPs dynamics. The regulatory agencies were castrated by the deadly combination of tax cuts and indifference of their neoliberal governments toward the commonweal of the Great Lakes: It was a North American version of 'The tragedy of the commons'. I wanted no part of it.

All of this played into the decision of Alison and I to go into organic farming and for me to return to reclamation consulting for income. From the narrow perspective of personal finances, it was a sound decision. I sold my three research boats between 1996 and 1998, reinvesting the proceeds in an organic farm venture. Over the next seven years Ali and I built a substantial organic farm into a rewarding business based on the ethic of growing people clean local food, produced to organic standards. We provided food to well over 200 Canadian families in the six years of our CSA venture. A very substantial vegetable, apple and cider export business to the United States was built, principally with the Whole Foods Markets and other natural foods stores in southeastern Michigan. With farming occupying more of my time each year, our lives grew more complex, even as demand for my unique consulting specialties of large-scale land reclamation and waste management grew. Soon, I had no time to pursue Great Lakes work, even if funds were available.

I was also coasting as a professional researcher. Many research reports and publications on Great Lakes cormorants and terns, plus the North Pacific albatrosses were completed even though I was no longer doing field research. By 2001, most of these professional contributions were published. Alison and I were ever more focused on organic farming as the way we would address the life goals of reducing human exposures to toxic chemicals to the absolute minimum in a callous neoliberal world. Given the disputed election of George W. Bush in November, 2000, we were certain that would mean an even stronger suppression of the truth about toxicant chemicals. Organic farming was the only viable choice for us to continue to address human exposures. Great Lakes wildlife would just have to fend for itself. Outside of the stress to fit everything into the time available, it was a deeply satisfying life on the edge of Lake Erie, but I was now relegated to the fringes of current research.

JAMES P. LUDWIG, Ph.D

June 21, 2002. Disaster and migration to Nova Scotia. I was on a consulting project in Northern, Virginia evaluating contaminated military lands proposed for redevelopment when the cellphone rang with an emergency call. Alison had not gone to work that day because a fire in Kingsville factory had blanketed the farm with dense choking smoke overnight and her asthma had flared up. Although there was no immediate threat to her, she was concerned for the impact on the farm's crops. It did not seem reasonable there would be a problem from a small fire, so I reassured her.

I was completely wrong. The fire consumed a plant that manufactured plastic pots and trays for the local greenhouse industry. The night it began, two million pounds of plastic pellets were stored in the old steel-roofed industrial building. During the fire, the roof collapsed into the molten mass of burning plastic bringing catalyst metals—iron, zinc and copper—into intimate contact with the flame zone, but dampening down the fire to moderate temperatures. Winter road salt was also stored in the burning building. It was the perfect set-up to make large quantities of dioxins, furans and PAH contaminants. The plastic pellets provided the phenyl rings, the road salt the chlorine atoms, and the metals the catalysts for rampant chemical syntheses of dioxins and furans while the collapsed roof provided the perfect moderated flame temperatures. Worse, the first two days of the fire were almost windless. This allowed the heat of the fire to move the fire-formed toxins up into a mushroom cloud-like formation until they cooled at the edge of the cloud and fell back to the soil or into Lake Erie. The zone of heaviest deposition was centered right over our certified organic farm.

When I returned from Virginia late the next evening, the fire was still burning because the collapsed roof prevented the fire departments from foaming the burning mass to smother the flames for three full days and nights as our land got many doses of toxicants. On the following weekend I sampled the vegetation and found soots and PAHs over the leaves of all trees, even on the lettuce and vegetables growing for CSA customers. When I reported our situation to our organic certification specialist, we agreed that our hard won certification as a clean organic operation must be revoked immediately. We no longer had an organic farm and would have to wait for four years even to attempt to requalify the farm. Requalification would depend on there being no detectible dioxins or furans in the soil. It was the most ironic experience of my life.

Having chosen to move into a new career direction and to grow clean food for the public through organic means because we knew exactly what these substances could do to wildlife and humans, it was our clean farm that was crippled by fallout of those very same toxicants. Nearby conventional farms that used pesticides, herbicides and synthetic fertilizers were not affected. No one would test those crops sprayed with all sorts of pesticides for this type of cryptic contamination.

Over the next two weeks I monitored the farm, watching carefully for the tell-tale symptoms of POPs poisonings in the farm's robust wildlife. On June 26, I found the first dead short-tailed shrew. Shrews are among the most sensitive wildlife indicators of toxic chemical pollution. In fact, nearly every regulatory agency in Canada and the US models expected impacts of contaminants at polluted sites on wildlife using shrews as the top predator. Shrews feed at the soil surface on insects and earthworms, bioconcentrating toxicants deposited on soils very quickly owing to their intense metabolism. Before the mortalities finished, 13 more shrews were found dead in our driveway along with two Ontario-threatened common eastern moles, another insectivore species. In the previous six years I had seen a dead shrew on the farm once, that one run over by a vehicle!

We had a complex network of 45 bird nest boxes placed in and around the orchard as one natural way to reduce fruit insect pests. Before the fire, 19 boxes held eggs or young of tree swallows, two had house wrens and nine house sparrows. All young of all species were dead and all nest boxes abandoned within a week. Three robin and two barn swallow nests on and around the house and farm buildings also failed in the ten days following the fire. The effects reverberated throughout that summer, but were obvious only to a trained biologist's eyes and ears. Even the vigorous praying mantis population of August and September did not appear in 2002. The population of every predatory species that ate herbivorous insects or worms was devastated. It was eerie to step outside and hear no birdsong or insects, but that was the reality of our summer of 2002 until the fall migrants reappeared.

From the organic farmer's perspective, we went from a very successful certified organic farm, growing rapidly with a loyal customer base that took everything we could grow as fast as we could grow it to a destroyed enterprise with contaminated crops and land, literally overnight. And, knowing that

JAMES P. LUDWIG, Ph.D

the half-life of dioxin in the soil is 9.9 years (Schecter 1994), we were certain this land could not be recertified organic for several decades at the very least, probably far longer. Organic farming was no longer possible. There was no option but to search out a new location if we wished to continue an organic farming lifestyle. It was a bitter irony for a 61 year-old man to confront the realities of a neoliberal world that just did not care.

The economic impact on us was huge. A large amount of consulting business income—$83,000—had been diverted into the infrastructure of the farm over the previous six years. The organic operation had been conceived as both our retirement income and a passion held in common, not Canadian RRSPs or other retirement investments. That was gone. All CSA memberships had to be refunded when we had used most of the annual CSA income to plant the crops for the year and support the orchards. A bank loan that was to take three years to repay allowed us to reimburse CSA shareholders their membership fees. Our commitments to Whole Foods Markets in Michigan and Toronto were broken; we were out of business. But the worst aspect was that the land we had cherished, nurtured and brought into clean productivity along with our well-laid plans for the rest of our lives were just gone and irretrievable at this site. Our lives had changed in an eyeblink, just like an accidental car-crash, terminal cancer, or a weather event like Hurricane Katrina or the Calgary flood has done to many other families.

Within two weeks we decided our only option was to move and try again somewhere that a similar incident was most unlikely. Ironically, Alison and I had planned our first real vacation in seven years for the Canadian Maritimes that July. By the time we left for the trip, she had already downloaded descriptions of 24 properties in the agricultural Annapolis Valley of Nova Scotia and contacted a realtor. Utterly determined not to become victims, we bought a house with five acres on Porter's Point between Canning and Port Williams, NS on July 26 and moved the following March. We left the Great Lakes behind, chased out by the very same toxicants I had spent a professional life helping other scientists expose as the serious threats to healthful human life and wildlife that they are in the Great Lakes.

June 2005 & 2006. The Beaver Islands archipelago and Green Bay, Lake Michigan. Contemplating retirement and reminiscing with brother Ted on Easter weekend, we decided to revisit the bird colonies of the Beaver Islands in northern Lake Michigan. Ted had never banded much in this area, leaving it to my team. I had not been in a Great Lakes bird colony for a decade. Our intent was to restart a regular water bird banding program in the areas where I had worked annually from 1959-1995. I was feeling mildly guilty that I focused all my energies on consulting and organic farming the past decade, foregoing the unique family legacy of banding. Ted had soldiered on, keeping the legacy alive. None of our children are able to follow it up, so we are probably the last of three Ludwig generations of compulsive bird banders. By stretching our busy professional schedules we found a three-day weekend each year for banding.

Our first trip into the Beaver Islands in 2005 aroused concern, but the second into Green Bay the following June left me absolutely flabbergasted at the huge changes in the decade of my absence from this Sweetwater Sea. In the Beavers we landed at Ile aux Galets first to find only a small group of cormorants, much reduced Caspian tern and ring-billed gull colonies and a very few herring gull chicks to band. The few gull chicks we found were scrawny. Tern nesting was late. The number of eggs laid per nest (clutch size) was as small as I could remember at 1.85 eggs to the nest. In the 1960s when alewife abundance was at the peak, the mean clutch size was 2.83 at nearby Hat and Shoe Islands. Most disturbing was the nest count of just 134 attempts, less than half the number present every year here from 1986 to 1995. All observations suggested a widespread food shortage for all species and steep population declines for all water birds.

We moved on to Grape Island where there were 2,600 cormorant nests and 3,100 ring-bill nests in 1995 to find those colonies abandoned. The next day we ran out to High, Gull and Whiskey Islands all of which had Caspian tern colonies in the early 1990s; all those colonies were gone. Except for the Hat Island colony, now off-limits to us as a new part of the Seney National Wildlife Refuge, Caspian tern nest numbers in the archipelago were down by more than 60% in a decade. At Gull we visited the cormorant colony on the northeast tip where an average of 480 cormorant and 225 herring gull nests were present in the 1990s to find barely 220 cormorant and 115 gull nests. Most significantly, we found just two scrawny gull chicks alive when we expected 150 healthy birds.

Moreover, we watched the adult gulls devastate cormorant nest contents. Herring gulls have always attacked undefended cormorant nests during investigator visits, usually breaking a few percent of cormorant eggs and gobbling up a few of the smallest young. But, it was rare that more than a few were eaten. These frenzied attacks were unprecedented. Every cormorant chick less than two weeks old and every egg was broken or eaten whole by the gulls. All this suggested a widespread collapse of the gull's food web. Each place we landed we saw the same evidence on the beach—mussel shells in windrows where there were none in 1995, sparkling clear water and thick new mats of *Cladophora* algae growing on the rocks and bottom.

In 2006 we went into northern Green Bay only to find two of six cormorant colonies abandoned and both Caspian tern colonies gone. The Gravelly Island tern colony dated back to at least 1875 and had 660 nests in 1995, still apparently normal then. The satellite Little Gull Island colony that I had counted every year from 1984-1995 with about 400 nests was gone too. We spent two days in the area and neither saw, nor heard, a single Caspian tern. It was one of the most gut-wrenching experiences of my professional life—observing a decline of just about 80% of the Michigan population of threatened Caspian terns nesting in northern Lake Michigan in a single decade.

Again, we saw the evidence on the beach of a wholesale change in the ecology of the region—windrows of mussel shells, exceptionally clear water and *Cladophora* mats washed onto the rocky beaches. Interestingly, in the two cormorant colonies visited we found fewer young per nest and fewer nesting attempts than a decade earlier. The size of alewives being fed to their chicks was far smaller and there were significant numbers of sticklebacks in their regurgitations. Sticklebacks were not common in 1986-1989 food samples from Green Bay sites but some were found in the 1990s; clearly, the local food web had changed drastically.

Of all the waterbirds, only the foot-propelled diving cormorants can reach forage fish well below the surface. Our observations indicated only cormorants were getting some of the food they needed; all other birds were just starving. Seefelt and Gillingham (2008) would soon publish data on cormorant diets in the Beaver Islands from a 2003 study. They found radical changes in cormorant diets compared to our findings of the previous two decades when alewives had been over 90 percent of cormorant foods in the Beaver Island archipelago. Finally, Ted and I spent two days searching for herring gull chicks to band. We found 12 at Gravelly when we expected at least 300, 46 at Gull Island when we expected 400; all were scrawny. This was no longer the productive, recovering Green Bay and northern Lake Michigan I had left a decade earlier.

November, 2006. The 'Cold Clear and Deadly' manuscript by Mel Visser arrives. My physician father used to say you never know whether your efforts to treat someone will have important impacts. For him, there was always a cadre of grateful patients that showed up at his door, unannounced and uninvited, simply to thank him for treatment. They often revealed how Dad helped them to recover and prosper. Today I experienced something similar when a draft book arrived from a man I had come to know and respect deeply for his commitments to the clean-up of Lake Superior and the Arctic.

I had worked for Upjohn on the reclamation of some of their lands at Kalamazoo in the late 1980s, and later to estimate the effectiveness of their wastewater management ponds from 1994-1997 in a study co-designed with USEPA and Tim Kubiak of USFWS. I reported to Mel Visser, UpJohn's Vice-President for Environmental Affairs. In the 1989-1991 period, Mel and I had served on the GLRCEC group. He represented Upjohn and served as the GLRCEC Chairman; I represented the Michigan Audubon Society. I remembered Mel as deeply concerned to do the right thing. He became very concerned about POPs, especially how these chemicals moved through the air to reach his beloved Lake Superior. Mel was one a very few that worked for industries that took two days from busy schedules to attend the Cause-Effects II conference in 1991.

I did not realize it at the time, but that conference made an abiding impression on Mel. Thoughtful man that he is, even though skeptical, Mel quietly set out to study the literature on toxicant effects and especially how aerial transport had transported so many POPs to Lake Superior. We had lost touch for almost eight years after his retirement in 1998 until he sought me out to discuss Lake Superior and new Asiatic toxaphene sources. He was thinking about writing a book on the continuing pollution of his beloved Lake Superior, especially by toxaphene. He had found the very widely scattered literature on airborne contamination of the Arctic and high mountain lakes on his own.

Cladaphora algae and mussel shells on the shore of Naubinway Island, June 21, 2013, indicators of grossly altered ecologies since the mussel invasions.

A courier brought me a final draft manuscript of Mel's book *'Cold Clear and Deadly'*. It is marvelous scholarship written from the perspective of a man who could look at everything and produce an accurate understanding. He did no chemical analyses for POPs, nor any ecological or epidemiological fieldwork. But, reflecting the engineer he was trained to be, Mel doggedly searched out everything available in the peer-reviewed literature, obscure reports buried in libraries and on the internet in his search for the truth of what was happening. He made trips to the Canadian Arctic and found an appalling disconnect how the Canadian government dealt with aerially-transported chlorinated toxicants contaminating Arctic wildlife and the Inuit diet. Here all of it was in a manuscript ready to be published by Michigan State University Press, a singular triumph of an exceptional man. With no small sense of pride, I thought this morning about how Mel found a path through GLRCEC and the crazy idea Paul Elbert and I had for a cooperative organization of Great Lakes environmentalists and industrialists. Dad was right. Scatter the seeds of ideas, help others to cultivate them and a valuable crop will emerge—the hybrid vigor of melding different perspectives into new understandings.

May to June 2008. IAGLR and the USEPA botulism meeting. As the years have passed since I ceased banding, the banding office continued to accumulate recoveries of the birds tagged in the previous forty years. Longevity records of 21 years for a cormorant, 25 for a common tern, 26 for a herring gull, 31 for a Caspian tern, 36 for a fairy tern and 44 for a black-footed albatross arrived by early 2008. I had waited for at over a decade since the last Caspian tern banding of 1995 to look at relative recovery rates to see if their survival to the age of first breeding was related to their embryonic exposures to the dioxin-like chemicals. Finally, by January 2008 I was retired from regular consulting and could assemble all recoveries of terns banded as chicks from 1922 through 1995 and adult trapping data from 1966 through 1992. This immense data set included seven thousand adult retrap and recovery records. In it I found exactly the same response at the population level that Keith Grasman had documented with his immune studies sixteen years earlier. Birds raised at the most contaminated colony sites in Saginaw Bay and Green Bay had 20% and 38% survival to adult age, respectively, compared to the birds raised in the Canadian colonies. The intermediately contaminated chicks from northern Lake Michigan had 59% survival of the terns raised in

Canada (Ludwig 2013). More interesting yet was the finding that birds banded as nesting adults in Canadian colonies survived twice as long as adult birds banded at Saginaw Bay colonies, five years longer than those from Green Bay, and 4.2 years longer than those from northern Lake Michigan indicating that continued sublethal exposure to the TCDD-EQ toxins damaged adults just as the embryonic exposures damaged the chicks. Adult birds nesting the three Canadian colonies had a third of the PCBs in their blood as those nesting in Saginaw Bay or Green Bay colonies (Figure 3; Mora *et al.* 1993). And, these data confirmed my suspicions that contaminants could control the demographics of water bird populations on the Great Lakes (Ludwig and Ludwig 1969; Ludwig 1979).

Figure 3

Average Total PCBs in Adult Caspian Tern Blood Sera vs. Average Age

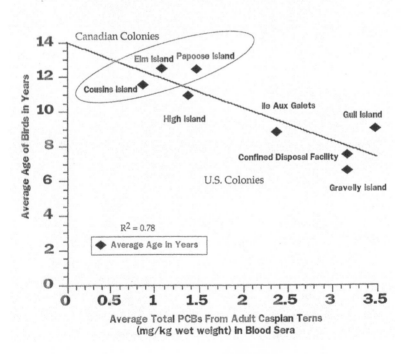

These findings were presented at the 2008 International Association for Great Lakes Research conference in Peterborough, ON. After the presentation I chanced to meet two young women from the USEPA Great Lakes National Program Office in Chicago. We discussed the emerging problem of widespread type E avian botulism in the lower four Great Lakes since 1998. Similar to the 1960s outbreaks in Lakes Huron and Michigan (Ludwig and Bromley 1988), the new outbreaks were centered on locations where extensive blooms of blue-green algal species had occurred in the same years before, or coincident with, the botulism outbreaks. The 1960s outbreaks had been shown to be caused when birds ate alewives dead long-enough to develop type E toxin in their bodies. But, the new outbreaks seemed to be linked to sick gobies that were eaten by cormorants and loons when the fish were still alive. This suggested that the recent botulism may be actually an artifact of initial sublethal poisoning of gobies by blue-green toxins, similar to a link suggested by Murphy *et al.* (2001) to type C outbreaks in waterfowl feeding on dead algae. Certainly, the appearance and distribution of the blue-green algal species largely matched and usually preceded these new botulism outbreaks (Becker *et al.* 2006).

In June, 2008 I was invited to participate in a USEPA-sponsored workshop to discuss the problem. We reached no firm conclusions, but the possibility of direct acute toxicity of the blue-green microcystin toxin to humans from drinking Great Lakes-sourced water is a large concern. The workshop was useful but very troubling, for it revealed how the loss of institutional memories among Great Lakes scientists can cripple understandings. I met a number of highly dedicated administrators, agency personnel and talented young people who will—if given the training and opportunity—contribute much to our knowledge of the Great Lakes through their own research.

Yet, there was almost a universal ignorance of the research and observations reported on the botulism outbreaks of the 1960s and earlier, along with the lessons in those historic reports. This stimulated me to reflect on the dangers of loss of institutional memory that is held in the minds of the people of our agencies and universities. The classic remedy for this affliction is thorough familiarity with the historic literature, breadth of training, mentoring and experience. Each element of institutional memory is correlated positively to the age and diversity of service of those that control access to information. Obviously, institutional memories are lost as the 'old salts' of agencies and institutions retire or die. But, in the last decade there has been a concerted effort to delete easy access to much historic information on the Great Lakes, justified by the tenuous claim of cost savings. Both GLNPO and the International Joint Commission's Windsor Great Lakes Office closed and disposed of their libraries, decisions that anyone with a classical training should find utterly reprehensible. I recalled vividly Dr. Storer beating into my thick head the immense value of studying the literature. The famous dictum 'Those who refuse to study history are condemned to repeat it' came to mind during these meetings.

Participant after participant spoke of the avian botulism as something unique when—in fact—type C was reported as a suspected cause of duck mortalities as early as 1937 from western Lake Erie and confirmed to occur in ducks from Lake Erie and Saginaw Bay in 1948, 1957 and 1961 as well as the type E outbreaks of the mid-1960s in loons and gulls in northern Lake Michigan. The only thing unique about the new outbreaks was that the new generation of researchers had not seen this! As far as I could tell, only three of the 84 persons attending the workshop had actual field experience with the historic outbreaks and perhaps five of the participants had a reasonable grasp of the historic botulism literature. When it is the policy of agencies to destroy or discontinue libraries, this kind of loss of institutional memories can only get much worse. Each new generation is likely to be forced to 'reinvent the wheels' of their science when libraries disappear.

In the long run, every decision related to historic information should be to enhance access to it. The argument that the Internet has replaced libraries is hogwash. It has not and will not for the foreseeable future. This is especially true of information contained in the historic literature and archived notes or specimens, because these historic studies and records are rarely uploaded comprehensively to the web. Somebody would have to pay for that. Moreover, most Internet search engines have not been designed to find the nuances of scientific endeavors; it is these subtleties that typically lead to the formation of new testable hypotheses that sound science requires.

Another troubling aspect to emerging problems like the new botulism outbreaks and the significance of blue-green algae is the tendency of every regulatory agency to model everything to get answers rather than actually go into the field to observe and test hypotheses. Fieldwork is expensive and slow. Modelers can sit at a desk with a modern personal computer and generate model answers to many questions in a few days of work. Models are very sexy because they give you plausible simplistic answers to very complex problems. For example, in my field of ecotoxicology there are dozens of models used predict the behavior of PCBs (e.g. Clarke *et al.* 1987; Braune and Norstrom 1989), several of which were applied to the uptake of contaminants by birds using the bioconcentration (BCFs) and bioaccumulation (BAFs) factors developed from caged animal studies.

Early in the landmark Canadian herring gull monitoring program of the Canadian Wildlife Service (CWS) models from pesticide exposure data were applied to predict expected uptake rates by water birds nesting in the Great Lakes after the decision was made to use herring gulls as the key monitor species. The modelers of PCB and pesticide contaminants concluded that only the year-round resident herring gulls were an acceptable species to monitor the lakes because it would take too long for migrants to pick-up the contamination, supporting the decision to focus long-term studies almost exclusively on the herring gull. Yet, within a decade the CWS researchers Chip Weseloh and John Struger assembled all of the early monitoring data for migratory Caspian terns that the PCB models said would not be suitable species. They found comparable contamination in eggs of the terns and the gulls (Struger and Weseloh 1985).

Later, some of the work I did on Saginaw Bay terns in 1988 with Yamashita and Tanabe from Ehime University in Japan found total PCB uptake rates deposited into their eggs greater than 2.3 ppm per week when the prevailing models predicted the rate would be 0.28 ppm per week (Yamashita *et al.* 1991). Substantially, the early stochastic models of PCB behavior were inaccurate by almost an order of magnitude probably because caged animals expend no energy to find their food or defend their territories as free-living birds must do. The later models are largely unverified by careful field studies, although a new dynamic model for Herring Gulls developed by the late Ross Norstrom may remedy this.

If there is one thing true of models it is that they are only as good as the field data used to calibrate them and the assumptions of the model itself. Models obey the GIGO principle: Garbage Input = Garbage Output. The only way to be certain one is not using 'garbage' observations or false assumptions is to do careful fieldwork to calibrate the model. The rub is this: Fieldwork is very expensive, but model runs are very cheap. Would you care to guess where agencies put their money? Models of course! And, when this *modus operandi* persists long enough, the agencies accept model results *preferentially* to real field data. After all, real data are very likely to provide unwelcome answers, and model results rarely get published if they threaten conventional wisdom based on expediency or economic growth.

Real field data are definitive rarely, can be confounded by unanticipated conditions, take time to acquire, and nearly always produce results unacceptable to the politicians of the day. This is especially true of biological communities as unstable and unpredictable as the Great Lakes are today. It is far easier to model answers to get a 'preferred or acceptable' result because all one has to do to get an 'acceptable' answer is to tweak model assumptions or change the input parameters. The practice of GIGO modeling is alive and well in Great Lakes agencies. It goes a long way towards explaining why agencies are often ineffective protectors of resources.

I also found myself reflecting on the immense value of long-term data sets for the Great Lakes vs. the typical two to three-year study done for the normal doctoral thesis. I looked at my own work and thought about a banding return and recovery data set for Caspian terns that went back to the first bandings done in 1922 and extended 74 years through the 1995-year class. It was work begun by Fred Lincoln and my father as volunteer bird banders who paid their own way! The immense power of this work done over decades is because it spanned many unanticipated changes to the Great Lakes. Banding data for the terns bracket the introductions of the smelt, alewife, gobies, zebra mussels, losses of whitefish diversity, the lamprey and spiny water fleas, and the hugely complex series of introductions of toxicants among many other large changes that have affected the biota.

Here was a data set for a species sitting atop the food web that has been forced to integrate the impacts of all these biotic changes plus the widespread contamination by POPs, the dioxin-like chemicals and now the changes following zebra mussels and blue-green algae dominance of the food web. It is a powerful means to understand the system because of the length of time it covers, and how the tern population responded to change. However, governments operate on a much shorter time frame, usually less than a decade, most often until the next election. In part, this is an artifact of the usual way Ph.D candidates are trained. University academicians insist on studies of 'clean' small problems by their Ph.D candidates; very few Ph.Ds gather data more than 2 or 3 years.

The longest term of intense monitoring work on a species by a government are the long-term studies on lake trout and the landmark work of the Canadian Wildlife Service to monitor herring gulls at the same sites (including some US sites) for the last 39 years. Simply put, we know more about the real-time behavior of legacy contaminants of the lakes from this work than any other monitoring programs in the Great Lakes. Yet, twice in the last 15 years federal neoliberal governments in Canada of both conservative and liberal parties attempted to delete the herring gull program without substantive objections from US agencies. Only great public Canadian outcry (much of it orchestrated by the celebrated Canadian environmentalist David Suzuki) has preserved this program. I regard the penchants of all governments (federal, state/provincial), especially those federal agencies focused on the Great Lakes, failing to conduct well-designed *long-term* monitoring programs as the principal scientific failures of the last five decades.

Finally, I met seven very motivated young people in these two meetings who worked at three different agencies; each delayed their education to get experience in government and was ready to return to some university doctoral or masters program in Great Lakes research. The commitment of governments and agencies to train new students presently is abysmally low, even as university costs rise inexorably. This has happened before. I commented on the problem of employment for young biologists in 1982 near the end of that severe recession (Ludwig 1982). The IJC explored the problem of diminished funding for university research in 1996 (IJC 1996). Somehow, this must be changed. Agencies will need a whole new crop of well-trained professionals to replace retirements by the 'baby-boomer' generation. I have no idea how training these recruits can be accomplished if our parsimonious neoliberal governments, their agencies and corporate sources continue policies that ignore training of new professionals.

Furthermore, the need is not just for more bodies. Rather, it is for bodies and minds with particular training in field research methods. We need people who will get their hands dirty and feet wet gathering real observations far more than we need new policy gurus, modelers or agency administrators. Modern research should acknowledge three truths: The most valuable research for management is long-term, multidisciplinary and developed from real field data, not models. Models should be used only as broad guides, never as definitive information. Fieldwork should be incorporated into every training program, even though this will cause faculties to change the way they mentor and teach students. Some faculty disinclined to work in the field will have to get their feet wet and hands dirty too. Getting academic institutions to change their ways is never easy. Neither are reforms of the way governments implement policy. Clearly, there is much to be done in academia and government if we are ever to restore health and sustainability to the Great Lakes.

II.

The legacy
of persistent contamination.

HUMAN COMMERCE IS very sloppy. Spills were 'cleaned-up' often by washing materials—even hazardous substances—into the nearest storm drain or sanitary sewer that flowed into the Great Lakes. Pollutants costly to dispose of were clandestinely discarded outside the view of regulators and the public. Effective pollution control and regulation of wastewaters is only about 50 years old, even less for storm waters that often go into the lakes without treatment. Many egregious pollutants were cleaned from point source discharges only in the last four decades. One of the unexpected effects of wastewater pollution abatement by end-of-pipe permit regulations was to divert many pollutants into airborne discharges. But, many substances are much more difficult to control in air. Some substances like dioxins, furans and mercury are created or mobilized by burning. Airborne pollutants from far distant as well as local sources enter the lakes continuously. Interestingly, Lake Michigan is still so contaminated that it is among the most prominent *sources* of hydrophobic PCBs to the regional Great Lakes air shed through PCB evaporation from its surface, especially in the warm summer months.

Biogeochemical cycles of sedimentation, rock formation, weathering and recycling are the dominant forces of geology and control natural water quality. On the geologic time scale, the recent history of the Great Lakes after European settlement is a blip. These lakes have existed in one form or another for about 10,000-14,000 years. Their water levels and discharge points have varied greatly with the rebound of the earth's crust following the melting of the mile thickness of glacial ice that covered them four times by glaciers in the last million years. Glacial rebound was not completed substantially on the north shore of Lake Superior until about 500 years before the Christian era (BCE) and it still proceeds very slowly. One or more of the lakes have discharged through the Mississippi drainage via the Illinois River, through the French River to the Ottawa River, the Trent Severn Waterway to Lake Ontario and finally through Lake Erie and the Niagara River into Lake Ontario. The modern pattern was not in place until about 1,500 years BCE, and the present levels of Lakes Superior, Michigan, Huron and Erie were not fixed until the Niagara Gorge stabilized about 0 BCE, roughly 20 centuries ago. In geologic terms, the Great Lakes we know have existed for the smallest eye blink of time.

The geochemistry of Great Lakes' waters comes from two great bedrock provinces. The unusually stable Canadian Shield forming the heart of the North American continent is the north half of exposed Great Lakes bedrock. The shield is made of hard metamorphic rocks (especially granites), igneous and sedimentary rocks as old as 3.8 billion years. Iron formations are especially abundant. The southern edge of the shield forms most of the Lake Superior watershed, a tiny part of the Lake Michigan watershed and about a third of the Lake Huron and Lake Ontario watersheds. Shield rocks include remnants of old geological systems from the Penokean orogeny and volcanism between one and two billion years before present (BP). It has been one of the most stable areas on earth for the last billion years, roughly half the time complex life has existed. Precambrian shield rocks are very hard and erosion resistant; they generate nutrient poor, thin and acidic soils. Waters flowing through shield soils and over these rocks are soft with a low bicarbonate-carbonate balance and nutrient-poor, supporting low natural productivity lakes (oligotrophic).

The southern bedrock province is defined by the great Niagara Escarpment, the lip of an immense limestone basin that was formed under a tropical equatorial sea in Devonian and Silurian times, roughly 350-400 MYBP. This ancient sea bottom accumulated the bodies of countless trillions of tropical sea organisms, principally corals. Now it is a massive limestone basin over the southern edge of the Canadian Shield where the shield dips into the earth's mantle. Thick evaporite deposits of salts and gypsum under the limestone were created by an entrapped hypersaline tropical ocean that existed between the shield and Appalachian Mountains when this part of the world was near the equator, far warmer and wetter than today.

Niagara limestones are relatively soft, easily fractured, erosion-prone, and very rich in calcium and magnesium, two elements required for high plant productivity. Soils derived from this bedrock are mildly alkaline and often very productive. Waters that enter the Great Lakes from these areas have substantial carbonate-bicarbonate buffering capacity with good supplies of calcium and magnesium ions. These constituents make lakes from the Niagaran watersheds well-suited to high productivity (mesotrophic or eutrophic) when key plant nutrients, especially phosphorus and nitrogen, are added as pollutants.

The Niagara Escarpment, essentially the outer perimeter of the ancient limestones, rides up on the shield at Niagara Falls. It completes two-thirds of an immense circle that cuts through the center of Lake Huron separating Georgian Bay from the main body of this lake, then turns west to bisect the North Channel of Lake Huron, to form the north and west sides of Lake Michigan, ending at Chicago. Lake Erie is surrounded completely by limestone bedrock, as is about a quarter of Lake Ontario on the west and southwest. The remainder of the Lake Ontario watershed is either on the shield or soils derived from the shield by the passage of glaciers that deposited them on the northwestern flank of the Appalachian Mountains (Table 1). Overall, the Great Lakes as one immense watershed are just about evenly divided between shield bedrock and limestone bedrock. This geology helps explain the original patterns of natural productivity for these lakes. Lake Superior, with its immense size, depth and shield geochemistry, was the least productive system. Lake Erie was the most productive lake, and the remaining three were intermediate before European settlement.

The water residence time, depths and temperature also influence water quality and lake biota. Deep lakes are colder and less productive. Superior with a maximum and average depths of 1331 and 385 feet respectively, can sediment and remove nutrients acquired from watersheds far more effectively than Erie with a maximum and an average depth of 212 and 58 feet, respectively. The abyssal depths of Superior mean that a

JAMES P. LUDWIG, Ph.D

far lower portion of those waters warm seasonally compared to Erie. A low residence time for Erie also means that water borne pollutants can pass through this lake much faster than the other lakes—provided these pollutants stay in solution or suspension. From the perspective of an average North American human lifetime of 78 years, the water in lake Erie will be exchanged and replaced about 30 times, Ontario 10 times, Huron three times, Michigan slightly less than once: But, Superior requires 2.7 average human lifetimes to exchange its water. On physical criteria alone, Erie should be most prone to damage and Superior the least likely to be harmed. Conversely, POPs are likely to have greater long-term effects on Lakes Superior and Michigan owing to the long residence time of water.

Conventional management wisdom emphasizes physical criteria, limnological processes, physical damages to habitats, nutrients and alien species as the critical factors in control of these ecological systems. This is not surprising because these are readily understood factors, seen and researched easily. It is easy to establish a cause-effect linkage of lowered oxygen levels in the hypolimnion of a lake from sewage discharges containing biological oxygen demand (BOD), with elevated phosphorus and nitrogen driving productivity. Observing, measuring and calculating damage from BOD is straightforward: biotic change with oxygen depletion is predictable from data on many similar aquatic systems.

However, pollutants have not come into these lakes one at a time; rather, they have entered these lakes in groups, overlapping one another, appearing in various waters at different times and concentrations. Worse, the biological pollution of invasive species has arrived coincident with chemical and nutritional pollutants. The ever-changing mixtures of alien species and pollutants have altered the lakes profoundly. No competent scientist would ever design the massive experiment that has been proceeding on these Sweetwater Seas. Scientists traditionally do research by manipulating a single variable in order to establish a 'clean' cause-effect relationship with that variable.

The task facing policy makers and politicians who set priorities to fund projects to rehabilitate the lakes is to tease out of this immense complexity which factors caused the most damage, and in what order of importance. When a factor controls the outcome of a system or survival of a species, ecologists term these 'limiting factors'. If a limiting factor is overlooked or misunderstood, then massive sums may be spent without beneficial effects. Worse, many unintended consequences may follow.

So then, what are the key limiting factors for the Great Lakes? How can these be recognized? Justus Liebig, a German nutritionist, experimented with animal diets and formulated his law of the minimum in 1848, to wit: 'There is a minimum concentration of every substance necessary for life that, if not provided, will cause death'. Fifty years later Victor Shelford extended Liebig's 'law' by stating 'There is a *minimum and maximum concentration of every substance and condition necessary for life; life exists only within these boundaries*'.

Shelford's law is one of the foundations of ecology. It is the basis of the niche concept and a cornerstone of the cause-effects paradigm of toxicology. For example, brook trout die in water with ~ 4 ppm or less oxygen or more than a trace of dissolved iron. By comparison, the central mud minnow prospers in water with virtually no oxygen or more than twenty times the dissolved iron the trout can tolerate. The same pattern of a specific range of tolerance applies to every species and substance. Critical concentrations and the range of tolerances are different for every species. This example explains why the trout thrive only in fast-flowing oxygenated streams, but mudminnows prosper in stagnant waters with little oxygen, lots of iron where no other fish competitors can survive.

Organisms employ a host of mechanisms to acquire the substances they need through feeding and selective retention. If you catch a walleyed pike in Green Bay where there is about 28 ppm of calcium dissolved in the water and analyze the whole fish for calcium content, you will discover the walleye has about 12,000 ppm of calcium in its body, essentially five hundred times above the concentration in the water. Similarly, for essential trace minerals like selenium, iodine, copper and zinc the difference between the concentration in the fish and the water may exceed a million (10^6) to a billion fold (10^9).

Organisms evolved to bioaccumulate the substances required for growth and reproduction from their foods and habitat. Complex life forms do not thrive without bioaccumulation. Eating is the usual route of bioaccumulation, and for larger organisms a food chain is usually involved. For the pike, the food chain begins with sunlight, the essential 'food' of phytoplankton that convert light energy into more green algal biomass. Phytoplankton are food for zooplankton like water fleas, or alien species like the zebra mussels. In turn, the zooplankton are eaten by small fish or insects that are eaten by larger fish until biomass and energy finally reach the walleye. Several things happen along this pathway. Each time the energy is transferred to the next consumer, 90% or more is lost to metabolism or wastes, and bioconcentration of essential micronutrients and fats occur. By the time the energy reaches the walleye, commonly 99.9+ % of energy the phytoplankton captured from sunlight was used by lower links in the food chain, while many essential and non-essential substances were bioaccumulated.

This pattern of energy transfer and bioaccumulation is universal in the animal kingdom. All communities follow the same principles. Green plants always are the most abundant organisms; predators are rarest. Green plants have the lowest concentrations of mineral substances and fats. Predators have the highest concentrations. Almost all essential natural substances have the potential to become a pollutant when moved through a food chain, or if naturally abundant. Consider this example: Mono Lake, California receives agricultural drainage from soils rich in selenium. Selenium is an essential micronutrient, sufficient at very tiny concentrations in the fractional part per billion range (ppb). An animal diet deficient in selenium (typically, just 50-500 ppt is required) will affect two essential liver enzyme systems and can cause death or deformities in offspring. However, if selenium is bioconcentrated into the 10-25 ppm range, this essential micronutrient becomes toxic to adults; worse, the embryonic dose causing birth defects in a wide range of bird and mammal species is about 1-2 ppm. When agricultural discharges to this system increased in the 1960s and '70s in backflows from irrigated fields, selenium increased markedly in the Mono Lake food chain. This led to birth defects in many duck and grebe species that fed on small fish and insects from this system causing many resident water bird populations to crash. Similar situations occur with almost every essential element (e.g. zinc, copper, boron), and a wide variety of non-essential metal elements and toxicants as well (e.g. mercury, cadmium, arsenic, PCBs, etc.) when natural or sources or pollution provide high concentrations to aquatic biological systems.

Table 1. The approximate distribution of bedrock types by lake watershed and water residence time in the five Great Lakes.

LAKE	% SHIELD	% NIAGARAN	% OTHER	RESIDENCE TIME in Years
SUPERIOR	86	0	14*	191
MICHIGAN	6	94	0	99
HURON	47	53	0	25
ERIE	0	100	0	2.7
ONTARIO	48	26	26**	7.8
Total for all Watersheds	47	48	5	-

* There is a small area of Cambrian-aged sandstone that outcrops in the Munising Michigan region, forming the Pictured Rocks area. This is a small finger of the sandstone sequences that underlie most of the central United States. There is also an outcropping of unique precambrian-aged volcanic rocks about 1 billion years old represented by the Keweenaw Peninsula and the 'Copper Country' of Michigan in Lake Superior.

** The areas of New York state that form the southeastern part of Lake Ontario's watershed have soils derived largely from the shield, but much of the basement rock is actually the buried western flank of the Appalachian Mountains dominated by sedimentary shales.

* * *

This reality represents an interesting conundrum for resource managers. For example, the agricultural soils of the Great Lakes region, especially those derived from the Niagara limestone, are exceptionally poor sources of iodine (essential for thyroid hormone production) and selenium. Farmers around the Great Lakes add both elements to cattle, sheep and horse feed to keep their animals healthy: but, if they use too much, they will poison their animals. Water quality managers face the same dilemma.

JAMES P. LUDWIG, Ph.D

Ideal waters will have some of all the essential micro and macronutrients present for a healthy biological system, but never too much of any element. Either over, or under, supply of any essential element or substance will eliminate species from a biological system.

Presently, watershed managers are moving to adopt a system of regulation that seeks this balance through implementation of the 'total maximum daily limit' concept (TMDLs) for streams that enter the lakes. The concept is simple—Provide enough for the resident biota to thrive, but never too much to cause toxicity or eutrophication. This is very difficult to achieve when human effluents, aerial and natural sources blend to create a particular stream water quality. In the blending process, the bioavailability of potentially deleterious substances may change when pH or the concentration of oxygen varies.

There are also instances when natural sources cause dangerous conditions; fortunately, these are rare. One example involved the Flambeau River in northwestern Wisconsin near Ladysmith. There a native sulfide metal deposit actually outcropped into the river releasing mercury and other heavy metals. Mining the deposit was beneficial to river water quality. Mercury that often exceeded 1.5 ppm in walleyed pike from the Flambeau River in the 1970s fell to less than the 0.5 ppm FDA action level in the same sized pike in 2006 after mining removed the source. There are a few source areas for geological mercury in the Great Lakes including shield regions around Georgian Bay, the Keweenaw Peninsula and north shore of Lake Superior. Fortunately, Great Lakes waters are generally fully oxygenated and somewhat alkaline. These conditions lower the bioavailability of many metallic elements by precipitating them into sediments as carbonates or hydroxides, effectively sequestering them from the food web.

Pollution abatement becomes a very complex regulatory task when the phenomena of bioaccumulation and bioconcentration occur with non-essential substances and human by-products. Mercury is one non-essential metal with high potential to damage animals neurologically, especially predatory animals. Presently, about 80% of all mercury in flux across North America is released to the air by burning fossil fuels, especially coal; this mercury then returns to earth in precipitation. There were periods when elemental mercury was discharged directly to Great

Lakes waters from industrial processes, particularly chlorine production cells using caustic soda and mercury anodes, certain types of paper mills, tanneries and even analytical laboratories.

The mercury pollution of the Carp River tributary to Lake Superior caused elevated mercury concentrations in the Deer Lake fish. The smallest fish were far above the FDA action limit of 0.5 ppm, and the larger pike were contaminated enough to impair adult survival and decimate reproduction of mink, otter, and raptorial birds that fed from the lake. The Deer Lake pair of eagles failed to reproduce for the 15 seasons after the discharge began (1968-1982), the worst performance of all occupied eagle territories in Michigan over this period, even those Great Lakes shoreline territories highly contaminated by PCBs. During 1982 no mink or otter were seen in this watershed when they were abundant throughout the rest of the Michigan's Upper Peninsula.

Other non-essential elemental metals in human use that have similar potentials to create severe problems include arsenic, cadmium and tin. Tin is especially hazardous when in the form of tri-butyl tin (TBT), once used as bottom paint for ships and boats. TBT devastates reproduction of various mollusk species at low ppb water concentrations by altering their sexual differentiation. TBT is one example of many man-made substances that caused serious damage. Unfortunately, there are many others. The most prominent synthetic toxic compounds have a backbone of phenyl rings of six carbons. The phenyl ring is a common component of many amino acids and proteins in animal bodies. Among critical natural substances are several halogenated phenyl ring compounds; the most important is thyroid hormone, essentially iodinated diphenyl ether. Halogenated chemicals do occur in nature, but their widespread use and release is always man-made.

Among the pollutants are the polycyclic aromatic hydrocarbons (PAHs). The first substantial PAH releases by humans came with widespread wood, coal and oil burning. These are condensed ring structures that may be chlorinated or fluorinated. They are heavy hydrophobic chemicals associated with soot and partially burned coal, wood and oil. Many are carcinogens if applied to skin or ingested. They adsorp to sediments, particularly those with clays, silts and organic matter. Fortunately, few

JAMES P. LUDWIG, Ph.D

PAHs dissolve readily and bioaccumulate only slightly. However, if PAHs are in sediments, they damage invertebrates and bottom-feeding fish severely. Bullheads and catfish species in the Black and Cuyahoga Rivers that flow into Lake Erie develop tumors and lose sensory organs when exposed to PAHs in sediments. PAHs are believed to be a prominent cause of species loss and community simplification in many Great Lakes harbors and bays.

There are a huge number of polyhalogenated diaromatic (two phenyl rings) contaminants that have caused great damage. These are compounds with two aromatic phenyl rings linked covalently, by oxygen, nitrogen or a short chain hydrocarbon. They are chlorinated, fluorinated or brominated, have very low water solubility and bioaccumulate strongly. They are hydrophobic, adsorp to sediments, and accumulate rapidly in fats of predators. Many resist metabolic degradation strongly. Well over a thousand congeners of synthetic diaromatic halogenated pollutants are known from Great Lakes sediment, water and biotic samples. The general chemical types are shown in Figures 4-7 and their general effects described below.

- **Dioxins.** Dioxins have a double oxygen bridge between the two phenyl rings. There are 75 different congeners each of the chlorinated and brominated dioxins. The most potent congener is 2,3,7,8 tetrachloro-di-benzo-*para*-dioxin (TCDD). TCDD attaches to nucleic receptors and interrupts the translation of codes for protein synthesis from DNA to RNA, modifies gene action and causes many effects simultaneously. The dioxins are co-planar, substantially two-dimensional molecules because the oxygen atoms between the two benzene rings create a rigid flat molecule. The length of TCDD and the substitution pattern allow it to bind with certain transport proteins in the blood that move hormones and vitamins from source organs to tissues, especially thyroid hormone and vitamin A, allowing dioxin to initiate very complex effects at tiny concentrations. Other chemicals that mimic the pattern, size and shape of TCDD also degrade biological systems (Figures 5-7). Only human-sourced combustion and industrial processes create sizeable volumes of the dioxins that degrade very slowly (Schecter 1994).

- **Furans.** These are dioxin-like compounds with the two phenyl rings bound together by one oxygen atom and one covalent bond. There are 135 possible congeners each of the chlorinated and brominated families of the furans. Their biological activities are virtually identical to TCDD. Furans are very common byproducts of combustion processes, especially if plastics and other petroleum products are burned at moderate temperatures (~ 400-600 °C) in the presence of certain metals (Cu, Zn, Fe) acting as catalysts.

- **Biphenyls.** Polychlorinated biphenyls (PCBs) and polybrominated biphenyls (PBBs) have two halogenated phenyl rings joined by a covalent bond between the rings (Figure 7). There are 209 possible congeners of each halogenated group; 132 of the chlorinated biphenyl congeners have been found in Great Lakes biota. Unlike the dioxins and furans that are rigidly coplanar, biphenyl rings are free to rotate into a three dimensional shape depending on the placement of the halogens (Figure 7). When halogens occur in the next to the covalent bond (an *ortho* chlorination), the two rings rotate away from a coplanar dioxin-like shape. The *ortho*-halogenated biphenyls have little dioxin-like toxicity that causes birth defects and mixed function oxidase enzyme induction, but they depress the neurotransmitter dopamine in the brain. Biphenyls with *meta* and *para* halogens only are dioxin-like and coplanar. All biphenyls are hydrophobic and highly bioaccumulative. They tend to sort into different places in the environment according to their substitution pattern, molecular weight and degree of planarity (Burkhard *et al.* 1985; Oliver *et al.* 1989). PCBs are the most damaging chemicals to wildlife and humans eating Great Lakes' sourced foods. PCBs were manufactured and used worldwide from 1929 into the early 1980s in over 300 applications before banned in almost all developed North American and European economies. But, PCBs are still used commonly in China, Russia and elsewhere in the third world (Visser, 2007).

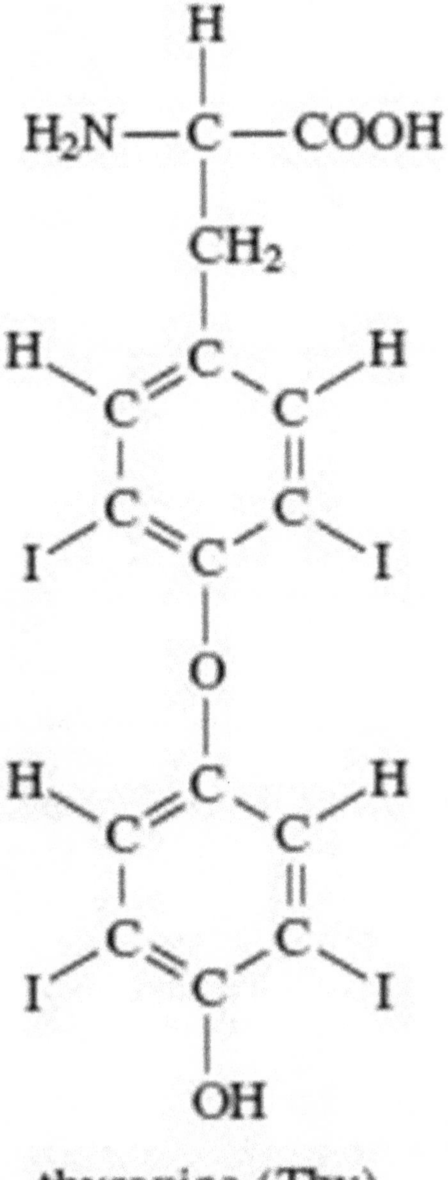

thyroxine (Thy)
occurs only in the hormone protein
thyroglobulin: I=iodine

Figure 4. The Structure of the T$_4$ form of Thyroid Hormone.

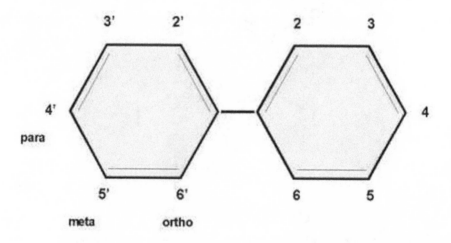

Tetrachlorodibenzo-*para*-Dioxin (TCDD). **Figure 5.**

Generic Structure of Polybrominated Diphenyl Ethers. **Figure 6.**

Structure of Polychlorinated Biphenyl (PCB) Molecule

Figure 7.

- **Diphenyl Ethers.** These compounds have two phenyl rings connected by one oxygen atom; both polychlorinated (PCDEs) and polybrominated (PBDEs) congeners are found in the environment. They have similar toxic effects and material properties to halogenated biphenyls, dioxins and furans. Made as PCB and PBB substitutes, they are very widely used in computers, cellphones, other electronics, foams and flame-resistant fabrics. If you are sitting on a couch with a foam cushion made in the last 20 years, then your bottom is probably in intimate contact with PBDEs, as is your ear when you chat on your cellphone. In the 20 years between 1985 and 2005 the PBDEs increased in North American environmental samples by 100-300 fold. The brominated PBDEs appear to have even greater thyroid toxicity than the chlorinated PCDEs or PCBs. However, because they are not intentionally added to foods or used as pesticides, they fall outside of most US and Canadian federal regulatory programs, just PCBs once did. The failure of North American developed nations to ban production and use of the halogenated diphenyl ethers was an international disgrace for two decades, although belated USEPA actions in 2004 and 2008 did ban some PBDE mixtures. PBDEs are used in the developing economies and are in many products imported under free trade agreements. Generally speaking, there are no requirements in the US or Canada to disclosed the presence of the PCDEs or PBDEs in products imported for sale to North American consumers.

- **Atrazines.** This family of diphenyl compounds have two phenyl rings linked by two nitrogen atoms. Developed as herbicides, when the chlorination pattern mimics TCDD, the atrazines express dioxin-like effects. Fortunately, the—N=N—linkage between phenyl rings is much less stable than the oxygen bonds of dioxins, furans and diphenyl ethers or covalent bonds of PCBs and PBBs. This renders atrazines more easily broken into single ring compounds with much less toxicity. However, acute wildlife effects are well documented. Presently, Lake Michigan waters have ~115 ppt of dissolved atrazines. Some research has linked the atrazines to the global epidemic of deformed and sexually-altered frogs.

- **DDT.** DichloroDiphenylTrichloroethane is a notorious insecticide with widespread subtle biological effects. It is another diaromatic compound with two phenyl rings. However, most chlorines are on the ethane bridge between the two phenyl rings. DDT has a low acute animal toxicity and a relatively short half-life in the environment, averaging about 2.7 years in the Great Lakes. In the tropics, half-lives may be as short as 120 days; in the arctic half-lives can exceed four years. After WWII, DDT was touted as a miracle insecticide until insect resistance and very severe wildlife damage appeared. Even though DDT is not a dioxin-like chemical, DDTr congeners are included here because they attach to the estrogen receptor and act as an estrogen or antiandrogen. DDTr is a potent synthetic estrogen with a structure similar to the notorious diethylstibesterol (DES). The deleterious effects of DDT and other diaromatic chemicals that have this mode of action on the denizens of the Great Lakes are profound. Many wildlife species on the Great Lakes experienced estrogenic or antiandrogenic effects, especially eggshell thinning in birds and feminization of genetic male embryos (Ludwig and Tomoff 1966; Fry *et al.* 1987; Weseloh *et al.* 1995).

There are numerous other families of chlorinated and brominated organic compounds in the Great Lakes. Many of these are associated with paper mills and the pulping processes of paper production using chlorine and chlorine dioxide for pulp bleaching. For the most part, the toxicology of these compounds is not known. However, some have properties similar to TCDD. Others are endocrine disruptors or estrogen mimics like DDT.

The effects of the synthetic chemicals differ from most natural toxins and heavy metals that attack one specific metabolic or detoxification enzyme. These are direct actions, such as enzyme X is inhibited or stimulated, causing process Y to slow or increase markedly. Death may follow if metabolism is altered beyond the limits for survival. However, the dioxin-like and endocrine-active chemicals are different. These chemicals cause multiple subtle impairments simultaneously (Schecter 1994). This complexity makes it far more difficult to confirm synthetic chemicals as the cause of population changes compared to the obvious evidence of a parasitic lamprey attached to a lake trout. The more important modes of action by these synthetic chemicals include:

- The non-*ortho* halogenated (*meta* and *para*-substituted) congeners of dioxin, furans and biphenyls are potent inducers of the oxygenase enzymes that detoxify wastes and the natural toxins vertebrate animals ingest. These enzymes evolved to inactivate natural toxins safely and to break down certain normal by-products of metabolism. For example, several oxidases promote excretion of spent thyroid hormone through the liver bile and promote the removal of spent hemoglobin from blood by storage in the liver. When upregulated, the liver accumulates unwanted iron porphyrins leading to porphyria. The most famous historic example of genetic porphyria was King George III, portrayed in the movie '*The madness of King George*'. TCDD-like chemicals upregulate all of these enzymes indiscriminately, leading to many diffuse effects. Typical responses to the TCDD-like substances include elevated metabolic rate, excretion of important natural substances, hormone mimicry, birth defects, and neurological damage to embryos and young with fast-developing neurons. The neurological and hormone-like damages are insidious, diminishing the lifetime potentials of exposed individuals.

- The TCDD-like congeners of these chemicals are potent thyroid agonists with remarkable structural similarity to thyroid hormone (McKinney *et al.* 1985; Figures 4-7). They upregulate metabolism markedly. At high exposures, animal metabolism may be so accelerated that food cannot be consumed and digested fast enough to sustain the organism (Peterson *et al.* 1990). Some highly exposed organisms refuse to eat. Then, a wasting syndrome develops that ends in death, even if the victim is feeding at a normal rate. There is laboratory evidence that TCDD poisoning does not stimulate appetite (Birnbaum 1993). Wasting was documented in Saginaw Bay Caspian terns from 1987-90 (Ludwig *et al.* 1993a) and may have depressed growth of chicks in 2012 (Grasman *et al.* 2013).

- TCDD-like congeners and some of their partially-dechlorinated breakdown products bind selectively to the blood transport protein transthyretin (TTR), the mechanism that moves thyroid hormones and vitamin A from source organs (thyroid gland and liver) to the tissues (Brouwer 1989). Many essential substances, especially hormones and vitamins, are moved on blood transport proteins. Many natural hormone and vitamin compounds are structurally similar to the TCDD-like chlorinated compounds and insoluble in blood. Transport proteins are the essential 'train systems' that move these compounds. Like a commuter train, there are only a fixed number of 'seats' available. In the absence of the TCDD-like substances, this pick-up, transport and delivery system functions normally. But, when an essential natural substance is displaced by a dioxin-like chemical, then subtle impairments develop, partly because the upregulated oxygenases eliminate them from the blood. Target organ and tissue deficiencies may develop even when there are stores and an adequate amount in the diet. These are very difficult to measure because the mechanisms of damage are very complex. Conventional testing may even reveal concentrations of hormones and vitamins considered to be normal when the dioxin-like chemicals have blocked delivery to the target tissue. The damage is slight at onset and confused very easily with dietary deficiencies, even by trained personnel.

- The TCDD-like chemicals are potent teratogens (Latin: terato = monstrous, gen = growth). Some embryonic defects produced are characteristic, especially cleft palate in mammals (= crossed bills of birds), ascites (retention of fluid in tissues), defects in the long bones of the legs, failure of skull bones to knit together, and gastroschisis (Latin: split belly) where the body wall fails to enclose internal organs (Photos 6, 8, 9, 11, 12, and 14). Generally, embryonic effects begin at a tenth (an order of magnitude less) of concentrations that cause acute symptoms in adults. These complex conditions were described as 'chick edema disease' when first seen in chickens produced by PCB-contaminated hens fed fish meal in the 1960s, and later in water birds from Lake Ontario from 1971-1974 (Gilbertson *et al.* 1991). Terata often lead to embryonic death, and can be overlooked in wild populations if observers assess only the offspring born or hatched alive.

- The TCDD-like chemicals and some of their breakdown products have many impacts on cortico-steroid hormones, including all sex hormones (testosterone, estrogen, progesterone etc.). Some are estrogens; others are anti-androgens that elicit effects opposite to androgens like testosterone. Among the PCBs, there is evidence that some sulfonated or hydroxylated breakdown products have potent antiandrogenic effects but no other toxic manifestations (Klassan-Wheler *et al.* 1998). Thyroid hormone is the hormone trigger for metamorphosis in amphibians (McKinney *et al.* 1985). Exposure to TCDD and TCDD-like chemicals will initiate premature metamorphosis in many amphibians. The dioxin-like chemicals may well have played a prominent role in the catastrophic loss of amphibians worldwide since WW II. Early metamorphosis in amphibians has identical effects to premature birth in humans, often causing a quick death. Much research has linked TCDD-exposures to the development of type-II (adult onset) human diabetes and even obesity (Birnbaum 1993). Moreover, new research by many investigative teams has shown the dioxin-like chemicals and certain other endocrine disruptors actually turn genes on or off in exposed adults that then pass on the 'switched' genes to the next generation when they reproduce (Heindel 2010). This is an epigenetic (Latin: epi = on top of) effect and spreads damage across generations. One recent study found damages to female reproductive cycles from a single low dose PCB exposure to female rats were not expressed fully until the granddaughter generation matured (Steinberg *et al.* 2008).

- Virtually all of the TCDD-like chemicals effect large changes to the immune systems of exposed populations, especially if exposure occurs at the embryonic or fast growing immature life stages (Kerkveliet *et al.* 1990). At the cellular level, the beta, T and T helper cell populations are often reduced (Grasman *et al.* 1996), the same T cell populations devastated by the AIDs virus in humans. Then, the overall immune response to antigens or pathogens is markedly reduced. Major immune organs typically shrink after exposure, rendering animals less able to mount an effective immune response to a disease or parasite. Then, they may experience delayed mortality easily attributed to pathogens when TCDD-like chemical exposures predisposed them to diseases. At low concentrations, the TCDD-like chemicals have been implicated as agents that sensitize mast cells leading to type II human diabetes and asthma at later stages in life. Many modern 'quality of life' syndromes in human children like ADHD may well have roots in exposures to TCDD-like chemicals *in utero* or to fast-growing children.

- The PCB and diphenyl ether congeners that do not have a planar configuration do not elicit the bio-effects described above to any great degree but do cause subtle neurotoxicity (Seegal and Schantz 1994). The *ortho*-substituted PCBs depress the essential neurotransmitter dopamine, critical to normal brain function. PCBs are strongly associated with a wide variety of learning deficits and related mental processing disabilities in human children born to mothers who ate large amounts of Great Lakes fish (Jacobson *et al.* 1990a,b; Stewart *et al.* 2005, 2008). A PCB/Furan mixture produced the same damage in a Taiwanese poisoning incident with contaminated cooking oil (Rogan *et al.* 1979). It is very likely these neurological effects occur with exposures to the *ortho*-chlorinated diaromatic chemicals of all chemical classes discussed above (PCBs, furans, diphenyl ethers etc.) even though some these connections remain to be demonstrated.

The massive complexity of effects of environmental mixtures of dioxin-like chemicals bedeviled researchers for more than three decades. Many scientists recognized that all of these chemicals and chemical families were acting by the same mechanisms, eliciting the same damage but at vastly different potencies in the late 1980s (McFarland and Clarke 1989; Giesy and Graney 1989; Safe 1990; Tillitt and Giesy 1991a; Birnbaum 1993). For example, testing of individual PCB congeners against the TCDD standard revealed a million-fold difference in dioxin-like potency among the 132 PCB congeners that have appeared in wildlife and humans around the Great Lakes. Some mixtures were found to be antagonistic, with effects lower than expected from the potency of the individual congeners (Kerklviet *et al.* 1990; Silkworth *et al.* 1993). These complexities led to two new systems to evaluate the potency of complex environmental mixtures.

The first is to separate and quantify all of the individual congeners in a mixture from an environmental sample by very expensive gas chromatography. Then, the toxic potency of the mixture is then calculated relative to TCDD as TCDD-Equivalents (TCDD-EQs). This method assumes no potentiation or inhibitory effects occur in mixtures even though these are known. A second method is to use a living cell culture system to assay for potency of the whole mixture. This technique tests for induction of a multifunction oxidase correlated to TCDD and the environmental mixture. This method gives TCDD-EQs regardless of what chemicals are present and accounts for all interactions (antagonisms and agonisms) among all chemicals present. Both methods to assess the dioxin-like potency of mixtures are far more accurate predictors of effects than measures of the totals of chemical classes, especially total PCBs (Tillitt *et al.* 1991, 1992; Schecter 1994; Ludwig *et al.* 1996b).

Toxaphene and other pesticides: the other POPs. The chlorinated pesticides, especially toxaphene, atrazines, DDT, dieldrin, endrin, endosulfan, mirex, hexachlorobenzene are important pollutants. Collectively, these pesticides and the chlorinated diaromatic compounds are known as persistent organochlorine pollutants or **POPs**. Some, such as atrazine arrived principally in agricultural runoff from the watersheds of the lakes; others like toxaphene and hexachlorobenzene came in on the air. These substances stress the biota of the lakes in numerous ways. Several (e.g. atrazine) have some dioxin-like toxicity; others are hormone mimics with prominent reproductive effects. Others are exceedingly complex mixtures with an unknown set of biological effects (e.g. toxaphene with 670 congeners). Some have multiple modes of action.

These compounds move into the lakes in waters from a Great Lakes watershed where they were used, or on the wind, rain and dust that settle into the lakes from the air. All POPs prefer to dissolve in lipids (fats). When moved in the air, they behave essentially as distillates. The less chlorinated compounds are the most mobile; the most highly chlorinated congeners the least mobile. The smaller POPs move faster toward the geographic poles. In essence, this physical behavior fractionates the POPs so that chemicals discharged into the air have different destinations. Single ring camphenes (toxaphene) with a lower molecular weight end up in far greater concentrations in Lake Superior than Lake Erie; the reverse is true for the heavier diaromatic PCBs that maintain higher concentrations in Lake Erie compared to Lake Superior (Visser, 2007).

Once in the water, all POPs tend to attach to organic matter (detritus), silts or clays and move into sediments. The non-*ortho* PCB congeners have a rather pernicious habit that explains the persistence of PCB and dioxin-like toxicity in the face of declining totals of all PCBs. Samples of PCBs taken from the air tend to have far less dioxin-like toxicity than the original mixtures of PCBs and lower concentrations of the dioxin-like congeners but higher concentrations of the ortho-substituted congeners (Burkhart *et al.* 1985). Conversely, sediments and waters tend to develop higher concentrations of the most toxic non-*ortho* and more highly chlorinated *ortho*-congeners. Sediment PCBs often are more toxic per unit of total PCB than the original PCB mixtures were (Oliver *et al.* 1989; Jones *et al.* 1993a, 1994b).

Worse, as the PCB mixture moves into a food chain, it generally gets more potent with each transfer up the food chain. Upper level organisms may have a PCB mixture four to seven-fold more potent in dioxin-like toxicity than the parent mixture discharged decades earlier (Jones *et al.* 1993a; Ludwig *et al.* 1993, 1996) yet still retain some of the non-*ortho* dopamine depression capability of the parent mixture. The longer a PCB mixture is in the environment, the more likely it is to be dominated by the most highly chlorinated congeners that are the most toxic (Oliver *et al.* 1989). Kannan *et al.* (1987, 1989) measured the distribution of congeners in parent mixtures and marine mammals showing the enhanced toxic potential of weathered environmental mixtures. Stewart *et al.* (2005, 2008) found the more highly chlorinated PCB congeners dominated the PCBs found in placentas of mothers who ate Lake Ontario salmon. When all of these studies are evaluated, the phenomenon of environmental and food chain sorting of PCB mixtures *with selective retention of the worst congeners* becomes obvious.

One of the more interesting failures of all governments has been the almost universal unwillingness explain these environmental sorting processes to the public. Most egregious has been a stubborn refusal to acknowledge these truths in fish advisories. Virtually all governments have persisted issuing fish advisories on knowledge dating to the early 1970s when environmental sorting, modes of action including dioxin-like toxicity, hormone mimicry, and dopamine effects of PCBs all were unknown effects. Initially, PCB toxicity was estimated from the acute toxicity of the original mixtures to adult test animals only; offspring were not tested. Apparently, politically oriented agencies have preferred to reassure the public by failing to communicate these truths in spite of the crucial importance of this information.

There are no cheap answers to this legacy problem that will be horrifically expensive to remediate through contaminated sediment removal. Is the political wisdom to just ignore the threats? Virtually all Great Lakes governments have misled the public by stating truthfully that total PCBs have declined by 80 to 90 percent while implying the lie that the toxic threat was reduced proportionately. It is another of those nasty inconvenient truths for governments that the remaining PCB congeners in the food web and aquatic environment are far more toxic than the original mixtures were. It does make one wonder whether the real motive of governments is to promote the harvest of fish resources because that recreational activity generates money and taxes. One might even conclude that public and wildlife health are not, and never have been, genuine priorities!

Metals. Many metals that are toxic at moderate or high concentrations are actually essential micronutrients (e.g. zinc, copper, boron, selenium) and must be present at small concentrations to sustain a normal metabolism. The Great Lakes are notoriously deficient in two micronutrients, iodine and selenium. However, three metals are potential toxins of note. Cadmium from with natural sulfide metal deposits of the Canadian Shield and many industrial processes and products, is known to damage wildlife (kidney toxicant) in Ontario. Fortunately, the Great Lakes have sufficient dilution capacity and the alkaline pH to render cadmium inconsequential, except near deposits, smelters or highly acidified natural communities. Lead is a significant human neurotoxin that occurs from time to time in sufficient concentrations in some urban harbors to damage humans and wildlife. Lead sources once included paints, batteries and gasoline, but only lead-acid battery use remains common in North America.

Mercury is probably the largest human hazard of the metallic elements discharged to the lakes. The primary route to the lakes presently is from the air. The principle source is coal-burning power plants. Point source mercury pollution was significant at two sites. The manufacture of elemental chlorine by Dow Chemical at Sarnia, Ontario between 1953 and 1971 contaminated the St. Clair River and connecting channels down to Lake Erie. Mercury was used in the analytical laboratories of Cleveland Cliffs International at Ishpeming, Michigan that polluted the Carp River—Deer Lake watershed. In these cases, the local damage was severe. Sport fish accumulated mercury far above concentrations safe for human or wildlife consumption.

Fortunately, gross toxic behavior of metals in Great Lakes waters is usually buffered by the alkaline chemistry of these waters. This fortunate chemistry tends to create insoluble metal carbonates, hydroxides and oxides that precipitate or adsorp into sediments. Some heavy metals may be reduced to completely insoluble sulfides if the sediment is anaerobic. However, the behavior of mercury in anoxic sediments is very complex. Sometimes mercury is methylated creating the most toxic and bioaccumulative form. Once in the sediments, most metals are unavailable to biological cycles, unlike the halogenated organics that establish a dynamic equilibrium between the sediments and the water and reach the biota more readily.

Once point sources of mercury are eliminated, mercury disappears from local food webs reasonably quickly. In Deer Lake, 24 years after the source was eliminated, the high concentrations in resident fish and the hazards from eating those fish were largely gone. In the St. Clair River case where much greater flows were available for dilution and redistribution downstream, mercury in sport fish declined below the advisory level for most fish about eight years after the discharge stopped. Mercury is a very potent neurotoxicant with profound effects on developing human embryos (Tassande *et al.* 2005). At high concentrations, mercury leads to the infamous 'Minimata disease'; the Detroit River AOC has a human population that shows these effects (Gilbertson 2009).

It is important to recognize when these toxicants began to appear in the Great Lakes in quantities sufficient to initiate damage. Cores of sediments from Lakes Ontario, Michigan, Huron suggest that substantial *local* metal pollution began in harbors and connecting channels between 1880 and 1900 and peaked by the mid-1970s. Most of the areas with high concentrations of metals were contaminated by specific point sources that were shut off. Widespread dioxin, furan and PCB pollution, including the main body of each lake, began between WWI and WWII: but, their concentrations did not become toxicologically significant until the 1950s. Sediment cores suggest that discharges of most POPs peaked in the decade of 1966 to 1976 from many point sources and widespread uses in hundreds of products.

Chlorinated insecticides appeared in 1947, and then came on rapidly with DDT, then methoxychlor, lindane, chlordane, dieldrin, endosulfan, atrazine (mirex in Lake Ontario) and others. By the mid-1970s widespread damage to wildlife from pesticides and dioxin-like chemicals was documented in Lakes Ontario and Michigan and suspected in Lakes Erie and Huron (Ludwig and Tomoff 1966; Gilbertson et al. 1991). Some damaging pesticides were carried in on the wind and precipitation, the best example being toxaphene from use on cotton in southern states. But, most pesticides that caused great damage were probably from local use in the Great Lakes watershed.

A host of new, mostly replacement, chemicals for the uses made of traditional POPs have entered the lakes in the past 40 years. New insecticides, herbicides and material additives are in these substitutions. Some, like the diphenyl ethers, have virtually identical modes of damage to the traditional POPs they replaced; other chemicals, many in personal care products, present new toxic threats, especially endocrine and epigenetic effects. Unfortunately, regulation of these newer substances is often virtually non-existent, unless that substance is added to a food intended for human use. The present status of these substances is very complex worldwide. Most POPs are now banned in North America and Europe. But, the developing world is making all of the ecological blunders around POPs once made in North America and Europe (Visser, 2007). POPs moving in air get to the Great Lakes and Arctic reaches of North America, regardless of where they are used worldwide.

Most certainly, it would be in the self-interest of the United States and Canada to negotiate a worldwide ban on these substances. But, given the complete failure of the NAFTA nations to adhere to the Kyoto Accord on climate change, especially the withdrawal of Canada from the protocol, it is unlikely developing nations will have faith in the probity of the United States and Canada on POPs issues—even if America and Canada abandon their obstructions to addressing the causes of climate change. Regardless, taking steps to address these compounds by enforceable international bans is crucial; otherwise, the Great Lakes will never be 'clean'. Unfortunately, the Stockholm Convention on global use of POPs has been ineffective. Deleterious effects to humans and wildlife will always be present, blowing in on the wind, falling to earth and into the lakes in the rain we once believed was pure (Visser 2007). Now we know better, but whether we can, or will, do anything about it remains to be seen.

III.

Perspective.

E XPERIENCE, SUCCESS AND failure are the parents of perspective. Each of us brings our prejudices, culture and knowledge to bear as we develop perspective on any subject. When strong emotions are present, we should know our perspective is biased. I do not pretend to be immune from this constraint. I have strong emotions, especially anger, whenever the plight of our Sweetwater Seas comes to mind and how this tragedy came to be. Even so, perhaps some of my perceptions of just where we are, and what we can do to repair the damages, will be useful. Many concepts used to describe the lakes are misapplied. Meaning must be crystal clear for a discussion of perspective to be useful. A scientist must add the requirement to dissect and consider all peer-reviewed lake science without regard to authorship or personal opinions.

Ecosystem is a very sloppy concept. The Great lakes community has struggled with the ecosystem concept for decades. Jack Vallentyne discussed 'ecosystem' extensively in 1978, and the IJC commissioned a report on the 'the ecosystem approach' that served only to thicken the rhetorical fog around the idea (Allen *et al.* 1993). In classical ecology there is a clean distinction between the concepts of an ecological community and an ecosystem: but, these concepts are often used interchangeably. An ecological community is an aggregation of species that relate to each other in a particular place. The boundary of ecological communities is measured by the distribution of the living creatures. A lake community will include the species that live in the water, such as the plankton and fish species, plus those air breathers that live on the aquatic resources such as colonial water birds, mink and otter. However, the ecosystem concept includes a good deal more than the organisms in a place. A lake ecosystem includes the watershed, the water itself, the soils or sediments, dissolved substances, the gasses, the organisms themselves and all the processes that link them together.

Tansley (1935) first used the term 'ecosystem' in order to stimulate the use of more precise terminology for plant communities, especially research into ecological processes that link organisms together. The ecosystem concept was expanded to include processes and all aspects of habitat by Ray Lindeman, a Yale University limnology student (Lindeman 1940). He studied Minnesota bog lakes that isolate themselves from surrounding watersheds by retention of rainfall and processes that resist water losses and prevent inflow of groundwater. These lakes develop acid-loving plant communities with unique animal associates. They exchange only air, water and energy (light and heat) at their edges, maintaining unique communities inside boundaries defined by very strong acidification of their peaty soils and very soft waters with few dissolved substances over perched water tables.

Bogs accomplish isolation by creating the conditions for hard-pan formations that block out groundwater. Bogs have many plants with leaves adapted to reduce water use to the minimum, similar to desert plants, allowing bogs to export water. Their boundaries are razor sharp, water quality and fauna unique, and closure to import or export of all substances (except water and gasses) is close to perfect. Their habitat is limited precisely by water quality, especially acidic waters low in dissolved substances. Bogs are destroyed quickly if alkaline waters are allowed in (typical of groundwater). They maintain isolation by being perched above the local groundwater table and self-sealing their boundaries to all input waters, except naturally acidic rainfall.

Bogs recycle the few nutrients present and accumulate organic matter very slowly as peat because their strong acidity shuts down decomposition. The elegant technical term for bogs is ombrotrophic (Latin: ombro = cloud, trophic = fed). Unfortunately, the precision of Lindeman's process-based closed ecosystem concept has been diluted and lost by scientists and the public who apply the term 'ecosystem' willy-nilly to just about any biological association, even as they overlook the crucial importance of boundaries and isolation (Allen *et al.* 1993).

The ecosystem concept is relative. 'Good' ecosystems with high integrity resist alien species' invasions, have distinct boundaries difficult to penetrate, a unique association of organisms linked by specific processes and abiotic qualities that reinforce isolation by self-maintenance. They readily recycle and reuse substances within their boundaries, but export or import very little. In essence, a 'good' ecosystem is self-sufficient and self-regulating. 'Poor' ecosystems with low integrity have open boundaries, are forced to deal with inputs of nutrients, toxicants, sediments and invasive species, are unstable and cannot resist invasions. Clearly, the Great Lakes were once 'good' well-defined ecosystems that met the classical ecosystem concept, but have been transformed into very 'poor' ecosystems with our pollutants, especially exotic species, nutrients and chemicals.

The terms 'ecosystem management' or the concept of the ecosystem approach to management in fact borders on the oxy-moronic, since the essential characteristics of an ecosystem are antithetical to human manipulation or management. Good ecosystems are defined by recycling of substances, self-regulation and sustainability. But, management incorporates the idea of adding or subtracting substances, altering processes or introducing species to manage for a preferred outcome that may, or may not, be sustainable. If anything is clear from the history of the Great Lakes, it is that the abundance of damages now present all relate to unhealthful additions (boundary breeches) of nutrients, alien species, toxicants and sediments combined with deletions of native plant and animal species. In truth, we simply do not know enough to manage unstable communities like these with any assurance we can produce an outcome we want.

Therefore, I believe the 'Ecosystem Approach' for management of the Great Lakes is an intrinsically bankrupt concept. At the very least it is a thoroughly confused idea made obvious by the IJC ecosystem approach report (Allen *et al.* 1993). The principal value of an ecosystem approach can be only to organize and inventory the threats to the lakes: management by addition or subtraction of anything or any biota is simply antithetical to a 'good' natural ecosystem of high integrity. Only when barriers to toxicants, nutrients, soils, sediments, alien species etc. are kept intact by management, thereby materially strengthening ecosystem integrity, can 'the ecosystem approach' be valid at all. If barriers are absent, irreparably damaged, or processes are altered significantly, then 'the ecosystem approach' to lake management can be only a public relations gambit. Moreover, the ecosystem approach intrinsically provides no guidance on what to manage for or how to decide which threats are most important. However seductive the idea may seem, an ecosystem approach is not possible for the Great Lakes. However, when one speaks to its proponents, it is immediately clear they do not grasp the inherent contradiction of 'ecosystem' with 'management'. Some may prefer to confuse by intentional misuse of the concept. The hubris of managers is one aspect of this human problem of those seeking to conceptualize management of these resources, the crucial requirement of an ecosystem closed to exchanges and invasions is another, and the way humans interact with the lakes' watershed and airshed is yet another.

Every human action that adds or subtracts a substance or species to the natural waters or air of the Great Lakes lessens ecosystem integrity. Deleterious influences include an immense list of actions ranging from agriculture and development that release sediments, toxicants and nutrients, to sewage plants, invasive species, toxic industrial chemicals, airborne pollutants that settle into the lakes and many other actions. These ecosystem intrusions are properly called pollutants—even the alien species—because all ecosystem pollutants penetrate that ecosystem's boundaries.

The most important reason to understand what the term ecosystem actually means is to realize how it has been misapplied to the Great Lakes, and to connect that misuse of the term to the *de facto* state of government inaction. The GLWQA of 1972 was exactly what the name said: i.e. It was a specific *water quality* agreement that targeted specific substances and their deleterious concentrations for remediation. However, 'the ecosystem approach' has become the justification for doing nothing to remedy the ills of the Great Lakes. For, if everything must be managed at once, something clearly impossible for the modern Great Lakes, then how does one prioritize very critical factors like the toxic chemicals that cause immense sustained damage? Most importantly, how does one set priorities for management in the absence of enforced standards and goals?

The ecosystem approach permits governments to talk about 'improving the ecosystem', to spend small sums on more research and public

JAMES P. LUDWIG, Ph.D

relations, but avoid the very large costs to remediate damages measured by specific criteria. Interestingly, the Great Lakes Water Quality Agreement was developed specifically to control those substances that breech the Great Lakes ecosystem boundaries, including the classic nutrient and toxic substance pollutants, by actions to restrict the use of, and virtually eliminate, those damaging substances. Unfortunately, most of the real impact of 'the ecosystem approach to management' has been to dismiss the importance of these substances rather than to address them as the foundation of competent plans for Great Lakes recovery.

True remediation requires that specific goals and objectives are set and met to control these pollutants, the very centerpiece of the GLWQA when it was negotiated in 1972. But, the ecosystem approach specifically warns against this, to wit: '. . . our [proponents of the ecosystem approach] concerns go well beyond system alterations that are caused by chemical contaminants commonly called pollutants' (Allen et al. 1993). It is unfortunate that this nebulous approach to Great Lakes management has allowed the parties to shift focus away from specific criteria. Now dominated by the neoliberal philosophy of goal-less process management, as little government intervention and control of pollutants as elected officials and agencies can get away with, and the smallest expenditure of public money possible, the actual outcome of 'the ecosystem approach' has been to preside over inexorable deterioration of the Great Lakes. This is exactly what we have seen in the Great lakes for the last four decades. It has been all talk, little public money to meet standards or do research, and little or no vision.

Sadly, many scientists, managers and even environmental groups end up in a posture of de facto support of the ecosystem approach in spite of the failures of governments managing by this philosophy to deliver remediation for our crippled Sweetwater Seas. Former Vice-President Al Gore has commented on the effects of this cryptic neoliberal philosophy that led to the full emergence of these policies in the two George W. Bush Administrations 'It's not only that there was no vision; it's that there has been a misguided vision. The Bush Administration has appeared to be determined to weaken and diminish the ability of the federal government to do its job.' (Gore 2007).

Shiv Chopra reported cases intentional abuse of governmental regulatory powers derived from the same neoliberal deregulation and privatization philosophies in Health Canada during the Mulroney and Chretien administrations from the 1980s well into 2005 (Chopra 2009). Jeff Alexander has recently exposed the incredible pattern of avoidance of legal responsibilities by the USEPA, NOAA, USFWS, the Canadian and US Coast Guards and the Corps of Engineers in the long battle to prevent the invasion of the Great Lakes by alien species (Alexander 2009). The list of agency regulatory blunders and avoidance of assigned duties is very long. Virtually every agency at every level of government is part of the problem. Critically, every mismanaged problem is rooted in violations of Great Lakes ecosystem boundaries: Breaking those boundaries means breaking the ecosystem.

Changing the subject (also known as *diversionary reframing*) is a specialty of politicians unable to find solutions to society's ills because to do so would risk their reelection chances. The frequency and pervasiveness of this simple strategy applied to the Great Lakes is little less than astounding. Politicians thrive on mixed messages, especially messages that divert attention from root causes of problems to other issues that are irrelevant. A compelling case exists that management of the Great Lakes is not directed at root causes, but rather to the political expediency of market-driven neoliberalism.

Consider the unusual biology of the yellow perch, a small but very popular sport fish that had huge population fluctuations in the Great Lakes for as long as the species was studied. A decades-long cycle of alternating abundance and scarcity first was noted between the two World Wars. Further, local perch populations often defy lake wide trends, increasing or decreasing out of sync with greater lake wide populations. Sometimes, perch populations develop very unusual sex ratios of well over 90% males, for no apparent reason. The yellow perch has steadfastly refused to yield its secrets on why its populations have these large fluctuations in spite of a century of research, much to the chagrin of fishery biologists (Diana *et al.* 1987, 1997, Diana 2010).

Now, enter the resurgent cormorant population of the 1980s just about the time the perch was starting into one of its periodic population crashes in Lakes Huron and Michigan. Suddenly the fishery biologists and fisherman had a convenient scapegoat to blame for the decline of the perch—it had to be those goddamn black sea-crows! The inability

JAMES P. LUDWIG, Ph.D

of fish biologists to ascertain why perch numbers fluctuate so wildly was no longer a concern, nor were studies that pointed to overfishing and unknown sources of mortality (Diana *et al.* 1987, 1997). Furthermore, the last crash of perch populations happened thirty years earlier. Few living fishermen and fish biologists knew, or remembered, that there were virtually no cormorants alive in the Great Lakes region then.

By blaming the cormorants and lobbying for a multi-million dollar cormorant control strategy, governments could claim they were doing something worthwhile for the perch fishery. The fact that numerous studies concluded that cormorants are a trivial influence on perch was not important (Ludwig *et al.* 1989; Diana *et al.* 1997; Belyea *et al.* 1997). Nor was the fact that perch populations did not recover as cormorants were slaughtered. Moreover, some 'sportsmen' enjoy the annual slaughters of the large black birds as a demonic sort of recreation, a cultural cousin of annual crow hunts or the English running the fox to ground so that it can be torn to shreds by the hounds. The governments were doing something concrete, even if it was an expensive avian holocaust.

That this action will do nothing to resolve the fundamental problem of gyrating Great Lakes perch populations is not important, for the fisheries interest groups had changed the subject and were doing something visible, just as my son did by plunking dead crossed billed birds on the table in front of DNR commissioners. As this new cormorant control policy was implemented toward the end of the Clinton administration, one might suspect that it was really a political bone thrown to the catfish pond farmers from the south where a multi-million dollar industry suffered from cormorant depredation in the winter months, Mr. Clinton called home and a culture of 'rednecks' with shotguns seems to prosper. Much of the recent political history of the Great Lakes is really about similar actions, many being thinly disguised attempts to change the subject. When you cannot find the cause of a problem or produce an answer, then just change the subject so that you can provide a plausible answer—even if you know the answer is a *de facto* lie or a speculative invention.

A variation on this pattern is to refuse to recognize new information when it makes a hidden failure of government obvious. A perfect example is the widespread refusal to recognize that the toxicity of residual PCBs is far greater than the PCBs originally discharged into the lakes; that would require a huge revision to the way fish advisories are implemented. The political cultures of the United States and Canada often ignore responsibilities if it is deemed necessary to protect conventional thinking or consistent with inaction to repair damages to the Great Lakes. This pattern has roots in neoliberal political philosophies of small government, least possible regulation of industries, decreased attention to public health and welfare driven by a market economy based on inexorable economic growth at the expense of public resources like the lakes.

Alexander (2009) showed how the narrow focus on economic growth and the hubris of post WW II contributed to the decision to build the St. Lawrence Seaway that laid open the Great Lakes to many horrid exotic species' invasions. The least possible government intervention and oversight becomes the over-riding goal for all decisions (Gilbertson 2008). The political history of Great Lakes management consists of many attempts to change the subject, especially when damages by toxicant substances were implicated as causes of damage to property, wildlife or health. The *modus operandi* is clear for the Great Lakes: If a problem cannot be fixed cheaply, then deny it is important, just ignore it, blame someone else or another species. Just change the subject and default to an exceptionally broad and unfocused ecosystem approach! Politicians and agencies love the ecosystem approach, for it has camouflaged genuine scrutiny of their failures to adhere to the specific mandates of the BWT and GLWQA.

Denial of significance is also a well-honed strategy to avoid doing what is right for the resources of the Great Lakes. However, it is disturbing how many scientists sign onto such attempts, apparently to curry favor with politicians rather than do careful reviews and analysis of all the available data. Part of this is owing to a penchant of some scientists to stray far beyond their fields of training, research or competence. Among the most egregious recent efforts was the attempt to discredit peer-reviewed research into toxic chemical effects on the lakes' biota through a forum on Great Lakes issues convened by the Ecological Society of America in 1995.

The lead paper for this forum titled "Risks of organochlorine contaminants to Great Lakes ecosystems are overstated." was written

JAMES P. LUDWIG, Ph.D

by Bill Cooper, a well-connected ecologist whose influence went far beyond this issue owing to his chairmanship of the Michigan Environmental Review Board and his role in education of a generation of Michigan's regulators. Bill never did ecotoxicological work and had published nothing of substance as peer-reviewed Great Lakes research. Worse, he was virtually ignorant of the recent literature and numerous advancements in the field by dozens of Great Lakes scientists between 1980 and 1995—even the landmark contributions by John Giesy, Don Tillitt, Paul Jones, Miguel Mora and others from his own university. Regardless, Cooper stated emphatically that toxic chemicals were no longer a threat to wildlife or human health in the Great Lakes in 1995 and probably never were (Cooper 1995). Many fisheries scientists accepted this conclusion because most in the field have held that effects on fish populations were always multi-causal and not related to toxic chemical exposures. And, it was a perfect fit for the proponents of the ecosystem approach. My response was a letter to the editor of Ecological Applications (appendix 2).

Interestingly, the impacts of toxicant chemicals on fish populations were the least well researched and understood for all Great Lakes taxons in 1995. I was criticized often for including fish as impacted species by several fisheries biologists. I relied on evidence of numerous toxicant-specific metabolic and developmental problems among the salmonids (IJC Salmonid Roundtable 1990; Mac and Edsall 1991; Borgmann and Whittle 1991). The definitive research linking dioxin-like chemical damage to fish reproduction was published by Cook *et al.* (2003); they showed that the extirpation of the native Lake Trout from Lake Ontario during the three decades after WWII was driven by the sum of toxic chemicals as TCDD-EQs *alone*. TCDD-EQs killed all embryos of the wild lake trout in Lake Ontario for over 20 years, extinguishing the stock. No other cause was needed to produce this extirpation. No amount of traditional habitat management or closure of harvests would have prevented this outcome once the dioxin-like chemicals were in the lake and above critical concentrations. TCDD-EQs behave exactly like any other limiting factor: when present above the critical concentration for any species reproduction, that population dies out. Period: end of story.

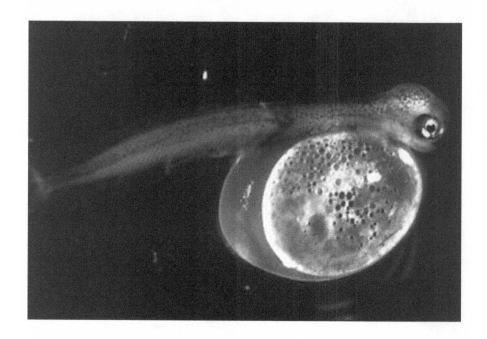

Lake trout larval fish at the swim-up stage from Lake Michigan in 1987 showing hemorrhages, incomplete upper jaw (homologous to crossed bill in birds) and blue-sac disease (homologous to chick edema disease in birds). Photo credit Michael Mac.

Cook's work explains why the lake trout did not recover self-sustaining populations in Lake Michigan and most of the main body of Lake Huron in spite of four decades of massive investments in fish hatcheries, many valiant efforts to conserve wild stocks and effective lamprey controls. TCDD-EQs were as effective a limiting factor to this top predator as a lack of oxygen, to little of any essential micronutrient or a superabundance of a toxic metal. If we wished to have lake trout in the TCDD-EQ-contaminated waters of Lakes Ontario, Huron and Michigan, the only option was to raise fish in protected hatcheries where the females were fed clean food and then plant those artificially-raised fish continuously—exactly the strategy followed for the last 50 years. But, this was not a message the parties wished to share with the public because the actual causes could not be addressed when budgets shrank under neoliberal political regimes. Even so, many fisheries managers still reject the Cook data, clinging to a belief that because lake trout produce thousands of eggs, only a few would have to survive to reach maturity in order to sustain the populations on the various Great Lakes. Some cite the theory that thiaminase acquired from eating alewives was the real cause of the salmonid failures to reproduce and maintain healthy populations. However, thiaminase would not behave as a limiting factor, but could only reduce competitiveness in sensitive populations.

Fisheries scientists, like any interest group, share biases, assumptions and beliefs and form networks that reinforce their beliefs based on the paradigms currently held by most in their field. It is long overdue for fisheries scientists to re-examine the multicausal paradigm that has so dominated their view of the Great Lakes. Moreover, this example illustrates precisely why the ecosystem approach is bankrupt. Whenever a change occurs in the Great Lake ecosystem that drives a population toward extinction because one limiting factor is exceeded for that species, those embracing the ecosystem approach will deny the impact automatically. In essence, the ecosystem approach and multicausalism in fisheries are clear-cut violations of the time-honored scientific principle of 'Occam's Razor', to wit: *One should not increase, beyond what is necessary, the number of entities required to explain anything*. By doing so, attention is diverted from addressing the true cause of a problem towards processes and factors that are irrelevant to the outcome, just like shooting a dead horse or (in this case) spearing a dead fish.

It should not surprise anyone that different interest groups interpret the available data in different ways for their own purposes. Scientists searching for funding emphasize what they can do as new specialized research in their narrow academic fields. Scientific peer review practices demand that narrow, disciplined focus. One tactic practiced often by scientists seeking funding is to link their proposals for funding to the vague language of the ecosystem approach, rather than to focus on the numerical and virtual elimination criteria for restoration and remediation of the GLWQA. However, clear thinking and parsimony demand that scientists test null hypotheses. Testing hypotheses requires numerical criteria with measurements taken and verified by independent research. Those that focus on the numerical criteria, especially on human and wildlife health effects, are often attacked by proponents of the ecosystem approach, precisely because they work to confirm singular causes of damage.

True interdisciplinary work is rare among scientists except as long-term collaborations. Industrialists and sewage plant managers discount the effects of their discharges and always point to other causes for the problems to which they contribute. Fisheries biologists are hampered by the difficulties of researching species that live in a liquid medium. Those of us who can study 'our species' on land or in the air can manipulate potential causal factors more easily; this allows us to accept unicausal explanations more readily. We can experiment and control variables in surrogate populations used to test cause-effects hypotheses far more easily than those doing fisheries work. In truth, my perspectives are highly colored by my studies of more than 40 years on reproductive damage to water bird species by contaminants. For the public, it is a huge challenge to sort through the plethora of data, the varied views of interest groups and the lack of agreement within the scientific community on the root causes for the dismal state of the lakes. Many reduce their confusion to the simplistic questions—"Well then, who *is* right? And, *what* did it?"

The correct answer is no one is completely right and everyone is partly right in the scientific game. All scientists have the obligation to puzzle through the data sets in search of the truth as it can be known from the data available. And, we must be willing to set aside the hubris that our interpretation is right and everyone else wrong, or at the least 'less right' than we are. It may be that each scientist has only one small piece of the puzzle. A major contributor to uncertainty is applying the scientific method to a system where large new variables appear quickly, as happened with the Newcastle Disease Virus during my work on cormorants in 1992.

However, one infallible guide to judge what research and published opinion is the more accurate and relevant is whether it tests actual hypotheses formally, or merely expresses undocumented opinion. Scientists must also wrestle constantly with their paradigms informing theory that generates hypotheses they test. New information has overturned the major paradigms of science before and certainly will again. For example, Wegener in 1912 believed the (then revolutionary) idea that continents move over the earth's surface (the continental drift hypothesis). But almost all geologists of his time rejected his theory and most ridiculed the man. However, by the 1950s, especially after the data from the International Geophysical Year in 1957 were analyzed,

Tuzo Wilson and other geologists reformed the paradigm of continental stability through convincing evidence for plate tectonics. In essence, a very large part of the science of geology and beliefs of geologists were deconstructed, and then reconstructed on the new plate tectonics paradigm.

More than ever, a commitment to scientific parsimony requires that each network of Great Lakes scientists examine the paradigms of their specialties continuously. Unfortunately, an unfocused ecosystem approach and multi-causalism are substantial *de facto* barriers to this essential aspect of sound science. For example, when I finished my 37 years of field studies on the Great Lakes in 1995 I thought I had a good grasp on where these systems were headed biologically. I saw contaminants as the principal driver of biological damage and expected this variable would be the principal problem of the lakes for the next three decades, my expected life span. I failed to anticipate the subsequent explosive impacts of the zebra and quagga mussel invasions overlain on the arrival of gobies with the wholesale distortion of traditional food webs. Nor did I expect the vastly improved water clarity and increased nutrition that has stimulated a huge shift in phytoplankton communities from green algae towards blue-green species (Becker *et al.* 2006; Boyer 2006). Barely one decade after I finished my research, the conditions for all Great Lakes taxa and contaminant dynamics were hugely different. I predicted none of it.

I have been forced to reexamine my belief that contaminants would be the primary force acting on Great Lakes biota at least for the rest of my life. The new variables coincident with alien species invasions have effected immense changes on in the lakes, put new processes in place and even determined which species are important. The effects of these immense new populations of aliens threaten to change limiting factors for many other species. For example, the phytoplankton shifts of populations now include dominance by many of the primitive blue-greens (also known as cyanobacteria) that often liberate a different and new set of toxins into waters of the lower four lakes that can cause direct damage to human health. The World Health Organization warns against drinking water with concentrations of the blue-green toxin microcystin over one ppb. But, this was exceeded regularly in western Lake Erie and southeastern Lake Ontario after 1998 as blue-greens dominated these areas in late summer of most recent years.

This change threatens many domestic water supplies (Boyer 2006). Furthermore, type E botulism in fish and wildlife is on the rise in all four lower Great Lakes (USEPA 2008). What relationship this botulism has to the highly altered algal species composition remains to be described. But, I believe it is a safe bet that the coincidence of the two toxin types are related and probably initiated by the mussels. Murphy *et al.* (2001) posited a relationship of blue-greens to type C botulism outbreaks in waterfowl, a supposition I believe is also correct for water birds that eat fish and acquire type E botulism as well.

Diversionary reframing is a fancy term for a combination of the two strategies of changing the subject and reframing the problem in a less threatening manner. Mike Gilbertson documented how the IJC lost its way after the 1993 Windsor public biennial meeting (Gilbertson and Watterson 2007; Gilbertson, 2008). The Windsor biennial meeting occurred just after the new appointments of neoliberal commissioners to the IJC were in place. Gordon Durnil who had championed the concept of virtual elimination and clean-ups to numerical criteria was replaced (Durnil 1995). Certain IJC advisors promoted the vague ecosystem approach relentlessly (Allen *et al.* 1993), and most NGOs bought into the attractive rhetoric.

Very few NGO members understood the subtle changes of attitude held by the new commissioners. One aspect was the wholesale politicization of the agency and its retreat from the treaty-mandated requirement to review the progress of the parties, partly owing to the lack of focus of the ecosystem approach (Allen *op.cit.* 1993). But the public and NGO activists smelled the blood of corporate polluters in the political waters and disrupted the 1993 biennial meeting continuously, demanding action in a none-too-polite manner (Visser 2007). The public did not know it, but this would be the last of the biennial meetings they would be encouraged openly to attend. The new IJC commissioners considered the open conflict over contaminants and clean-ups dangerous, and a threat to economic stability. They listened politely, but did not act on public demands. By this indifference, the public lost whatever traction had been won in the three decades-long battle to control contaminants.

Strategies were already in motion to choke off public input from the new administrations in both countries. In truth, the governments feared the open disgust, contempt and potential violence of protestors, similar to what did occur later at the Vancouver World Trade Organization meeting in 1994. Things were threatening to 'get out of hand'; the parties had to devise clever means to suppress public involvement without seeming to do so. Moreover, the fuzzy concept of the 'ecosystem approach' had been given credence through the IJC report on the concept (Allen *et al.* 1993). The stage was set to move from actual remediation tied to specific numerical criteria of the GLWQA, especially regarding toxic substances, to the ecosystem approach and do it very deftly.

One prominent casualty of this moment was the USEPA decision to *de facto* abandon the Great Lakes Water Quality Initiative that was premised on new water quality criteria derived from actual damage to wildlife and humans by toxicants. Even though a great deal of careful analysis confirmed the accuracy of the initiative (e.g. Ludwig *et al.* 1993b), it was emasculated. The political regimes of both nations were terrified of the cost to accomplish remediation when tax cuts and deregulation were being implemented by neoliberal politicians.

The new State of the Lakes Environmental Conferences (SOLECs) were designed to substitute for widespread public involvement of biennial IJC reviews and to allow the diversionary part of the strategy to be implemented. By having SOLECs on each lake, the size of the public group demanding change was reduced to those interested in that lake and the critical mass was lost. Content and public relations control of the SOLEC agendas would complete reframing of traditional GLWQA criteria to be just one small part of the new 'ecosystem approach'. The very expensive toxicant chemical and nutrient damage issues could be finessed out of the agenda neatly. It was exceptionally clever diversionary reframing.

Further, the recent spate of serious new alien invasive species was seen to be a greater and imminent threat by most people. The centerpiece of the treaty and GLWQA to redress damages from toxins and nutrients were gutted from the real Great Lakes agenda as neatly as a competent surgeon removes a diseased appendix: Only an ugly scar and crippled lakes remain. The cryptic strategies of the parties were simple. First, divert attention from specific water quality goals and criteria to 'ecosystem management'. Then, geld the IJC advisory boards by appointing persons who would not insist on accurate reviews of agencies' performance in relation to water quality goals of the GLWQA, and thereby reframe the issues so as to appear to be less threatening.

The coincidental and rapidly emerging damage from the mussel and goby invasions materially aided the reframing. Once reframed successfully, agitation for clean-ups would evaporate and the parties could proceed quietly without having to spend billions to clean-up the worst of the AOCs. It is also instructive to consider the ambiguities of meaning inherent to 'state of the lakes environmental conferences.' The governments could comment endlessly on the complex *state* of each lake without obligation to fund actual remedies. The fundamental charge of the IJC to evaluate programs in order to find and publicize their deficiencies had no role in the SOLECs and was never on their agendas, a neat trick indeed. In truth, the SOLECs have been little more than self-congratulatory parties of the neoliberal governments and are no more than forums for limited information exchanges on the 'politically acceptable topics' for each lake. Worst of all, SOLECs have accomplished absolutely nothing substantial for two decades, other than offering people a chance to talk and 'schmooz' with old friends over Great Lakes issues.

The diversionary reframing strategy went far beyond the natural resource management agencies. From 1987 to 1995 staff of Health Canada had worked industriously to assemble all the human health statistics for disease morbidity, mortality, congenital anomalies and cancers that might be related to pollution in the 17 Canadian Great Lakes AOCs and the people living in the communities of these areas. The original intent was to ask epidemiological questions of this immense database to enable Health Canada to determine definitively if people had adverse health outcomes from their greater exposures to contaminants in the AOCs.

This database was complete in 1995, but it was suppressed by the Canadian government until 1999. Moreover, very little government funding was applied to analyze any of it under either the liberal or conservative regimes, for neither political party would allow bad news to be publicized on its watch. Several investigators did analyze parts of the database (See Environmental Health Perspectives **109**, Supplement 6.) using their own funds. Mike Gilbertson analyzed one small piece

JAMES P. LUDWIG, Ph.D

of this database related to mercury exposures. He found a statistically significant relationship of mercury exposure to an increase in congenital cerebral palsy in male children (Gilbertson 2009). Gilbertson and Brophy (2001) used the database to produce a community health profile for Windsor, Ontario, arguably the most contaminated of the Canadian AOCs. They found mortality, morbidity and congenital anomalies elevated significantly compared to Canadian cities of similar sizes and lower exposures. One is driven to ask just how many other significant relationships to toxicants lie hidden—*and officially ignored*—in this massive database Health Canada assembled, then suppressed and declined to analyze?

In retrospect, it is quite remarkable how successful the diversionary reframing process was. Many activists, myself included, were just bone tired from two decades of work, protest of government inaction and the tacit refusal of the parties to do what was right for the lakes. Many activists refocused on other pressing environmental issues, particularly climate change. Given the recalcitrance of North American neoliberal governments, some international and national NGOs refocused their efforts on Europe where there was a more responsive political climate. Others faced budget shortfalls that restricted their capability to continue. Activists had to make a living in the free market economy of North America too: but, activism does not pay well. Most NGOs simply have withered.

Only a very few activists and scientists recognized the hidden effects of governments and agencies shifting away from water quality and specific clean-up criteria to the nebulous ecosystem approach. In essence, all responsibilities for Great Lakes clean-ups were defaulted to the professional resource management agency staffs. Those agencies were constrained by the increasingly limited budgets of the federal parties, states and provinces. This was inevitable when the prevailing philosophy was that the markets would 'take care of things' while governments promised and delivered tax cuts, and did minimal regulation of just about everything. After the 1994 congressional election in the US, the WTO debacle in Vancouver and the strong desire to 'keep the lid on' public agitation in both nations, steadily reducing funding for the natural resource agencies of both countries was normal (Gore 2007).

Many representatives of the very same industries and corporations that had discharged so many of the legacy pollutants were appointed to advisory boards or given a seat at the table in regulatory agencies that were supposed to protect the public interest (Chopra 2009), even in the IJC (Ludwig 1995). For the next decade, there were endless meetings between agency staffs and potentially responsible parties of contaminated areas, considerable site-specific research (much of it useful), but precious little actual clean-up except by natural dilution and attenuation. The clean-up ship was becalmed, then run aground deliberately. Agency staffs were comfortable once again. The pressure was off. The neoliberal politicians were safe. But, the inexorable deterioration of the Great Lakes continued, virtually ignored. In the interim, invasions of exotic mussels and gobies may well have delivered the *coup de gras*—a perfect Great Lakes' ecological storm. In truth, alien species were given lip service by the governments that have grossly mismanaged virtually every aspect of prevention of exotic species invasions (Alexander 2009).

The September 11, 2001 attacks added yet another physical layer of distance between agency staff and the public. By mid-2002 if you wished to visit an agency staff member in almost all jurisdictions there were new physical barriers and often armed guards between you and staff. Staff you could simply drop in to see and 'talk shop with' in 2001 were behind armed guards by 2002 where they remain sequestered today. Visits to discuss issues or data became formal appointments with sign-ins and vetting required, all of which made it far easier for agency staff to avoid anyone who might ask tough questions, provide unwelcome data, or demand changes.

Surprisingly, the publics of both countries have accepted these changes passively. Al Gore (2007) noted *"It is the public's lack of participation that empowers its abusers."* The terrorism of 911 played into the hands of the neoliberal parties, making it far easier for agency staff to hide from those they were hired to serve. One of the hidden victories of Osama bin Laden was the loss of effective access to agencies, but you will never hear any politician or agency administrator admit that. One net effect of 911 was *de facto* support for the complete implementation of the Republican neoliberal agenda from 2000 through 2008 in the US and a complementary agenda in Canada under Stephen Harper's leadership. It is human nature to avoid conflict when there is no ready solution.

JAMES P. LUDWIG, Ph.D

Avoidance has become a veritable art form among Great Lakes politicians and agencies.

Two quotes from Mike Gilbertson's doctoral thesis (2008) help shed light on the true manifestations of the pernicious nature of the unholy alliance of the neoliberal policies of governments for the Great Lakes that came together in the late 1980s. The ideology of the Reagan administration in the US and Mulroney government in Canada were dominant completely by the mid-1990s.

> *"Since the 1980s the economic politics of the two nations has been profoundly influenced by neoliberalism, and one of the consequences has been the removal of environmental health as a priority from respective political agenda. Advisory bodies seem to have been captured not only by the prevailing neoliberalism, but also by corporate interests and these factors seem to underlie the reluctance to report the injury to health from exposures to persistent toxic substances."*; and,

> *"The inclusion of social, economic and political considerations in the forensic audit* (the subject of the Gilbertson thesis, 2008) *has revealed the dangers inherent in any renegotiation to the Great Lakes Water Quality Agreement."*

The limits of Great Lakes science should be understood. Sound science operates as a formal system to generate knowledge by repeated testing of null hypotheses generated from theory. Scientists formulate null hypotheses that are accepted or rejected by experimentation and observations. Importantly, a null hypothesis is always phrased as H_o: 'There is no relationship between the phenomenon X and the outcome Y'. Data are collected to accept or reject this type of formal statement through observations and research. *However, because these are tests of null (i.e. negative) hypotheses, these are never an unequivocal statement of a proven (positive) causal connection.* At best, one can infer the opposite conclusion as a positive statement of causality.

Because sound science advances by accepting or rejecting null hypotheses only, science never actually proves anything to an absolute certainty. Further, there is a large debate among scientists themselves about the use of scientific knowledge about risk. Some prefer to wait for unambiguous evidence of a cause-effect relationship and will act only when there is no reasonable question of multicausality—even if this means there will be damage and even deaths before policies are changed. Others adopt the precautionary principle that shifts the burden of proof to a suspected cause without waiting for nearly absolute proof of substantial damage (Kreibel *et al.* 2001). In layman's terms, one group waits for the corpses to appear; the other acts if risks and damages are likely. Generally, those associated with the producing or regulating toxicant chemicals and invasive species insist on waiting for unequivocal evidence of repeated damage before they will act.

The key to creating knowledge by the scientific method is keeping the variables to a minimum so that the only variance between independent tests of the same hypothesis is the observer and the way the observing scientist records data. For example, of ten drug trials testing the same cause-effects hypothesis for efficacy and side effects of a new drug, perhaps seven reach substantially the same conclusions, two are equivocal and one reaches an opposite conclusion. It is reasonable to ask 'How can this happen?' There are many reasons why the same study provides inconsistent results. Subtle differences in design, different test populations of humans, surrogate animals or cell lines, investigator techniques, purity of test reagents, etc. all can influence results. The list of important technical criteria to be controlled among all tests of any hypothesis is very long and rarely identical among studies.

Further, in any test of probabilities, if one repeats exactly the same test enough times, there will be one or more repetitions with a contrarian result. This is no more than a manifestation of statistics and probability. This means most scientific 'conclusions' are not conclusions of absolute certainty at all, but rather are based on the balance of probabilities and sum of all the evidence. The primary constraint of sound science is that it cannot prove anything to absolute certainty because only null hypotheses are tested.

One prominent source of controversy in Great Lakes science appears when individual scientists forgo the testing of null hypotheses that must relate to specific criteria for a philosophical approach to questions of causality. The ecosystem approach and its noisy adherents are all too often splendid examples of this departure from the proven methods of sound

JAMES P. LUDWIG, Ph.D

science. And, they almost always reject the precautionary principle as a management philosophy for the Great Lakes with the notable exception of strong opposition to alien species introductions (Allen *et al.* 1993, Cooper, 1995).

It is also important to understand the different paradigms of the scientists doing the research when the data were collected. For example, very few fisheries scientists during the 1980s were comfortable working on contaminant effects when almost all their peers believed contaminants were insignificant influences on fish health. Conversely, at the same time my bird and mammal colleagues were far more comfortable testing hypotheses of cause-effects relationships of contaminant exposures to effects on their taxa (Fox 1990). As others have pointed out, just because there are no data on contaminant effects that does not mean the effects are not there. Often, the lack of information means only that no one qualified has tested null hypotheses. The lack of information may well be a reflection of the varied social networks of scientists themselves and how they and their peers view values like the precautionary principle (Kreibel et al. 2001). In truth, science is a social process performed in a social construct. Scientists reflect the assumptions, beliefs and paradigms of themselves and their colleagues. It is these values that influence what they and their managers decide to fund and study, how they design their research, and how they chose to interpret and disseminate their findings. Furthermore, scientists must always be cognizant of the priorities of those wielding power over their funding or else they may not be awarded the resources to complete their research.

Many variables have been added to, or lost from, these lakes over time. Substantially, there is no way to repeat most of the important historic studies, especially those related to toxic substances. *By the time one could set up an identical confirmatory field study, the conditions already have altered so radically that the experiment cannot be the same—regardless of design, care of the experimenter or intent of the research.* For example, suppose a bird biologist wished to return to the question of the acute impacts to eggs and embryos of water birds from exposures to the dioxin-like chemicals today. One could ask the same questions about embryo viability and frequency of deformities related to dioxin-like chemicals today that John Giesy, Don Tillitt, Paul Jones, Tim Kubiak, Nobu Yamashita and I pursued from 1986 to 1995 with Caspian tern and cormorant eggs. Those experiments could be replicated with precisely the same laboratory methods and field techniques we used. But, in the last two decades there were immense changes in bioenergetics, weathering mixtures of contaminants, new contaminants like the PBDEs, new food webs contaminated by novel algal toxins, bird colonies in different locations and habitats altered fundamentally by mussels and gobies. The conditions in the lakes are so altered that any new study would be different—even if the experimental design, controls used and execution were absolutely identical to those we used.

In short, we are stuck with interpreting the data and history we have. The scientific community cannot restudy most historic Great Lakes phenomena to confirm conclusions by the usual repetitions of studies and null hypotheses that careful laboratory scientists use to achieve consensus. The Great Lakes are simply too unstable for the proven method of repetitions of studies by independent scientists to create sound science. Field scientists are always trailing the changes inflicted on these lakes. We have to trust that scientists who made observations reported both their methods and data honestly. This requirement for trust plays into the neoliberal philosophy of some critics, because time-sensitive findings cannot be verified by the traditional methods of science. However, it is obvious their criticisms cannot be validated at all because their approach does not rely on the accepted methods of science. In my view, this is a very strong justification for application of the precautionary principle to Great Lakes' issues.

The alternative would seem to devolve to how you choose an expert to listen to, and whose judgment do you trust? From my perspective, that means paying attention to history and all of the existing data sets on all taxa and limnological conditions. I will express my bias here by trusting data sets and scientists who have actually done field research on the Great Lakes. I do not trust those who have done Great Lakes work only from a desk, reading scientific papers, through a model or by reinterpreting the basic work of others. Remember, precious little basic science and fieldwork is actually done by persons employed in regulatory agencies any longer.

The agencies effect change through the policies of their organizations and almost always default to, and rely on, models alone. Scientists who

JAMES P. LUDWIG, Ph.D

default to models and promote untestable theories, or those merely politically connected, I regard with profound suspicion. I am prone to trust the work and reports of those who have worked in teams that correct individual biases by bringing many perspectives to their collaborative research efforts. Sweat equity delivers accurate results in the practice of science just as it does on farms or in factories. Blisters and wet feet acquired testing hypotheses count for a hell of a lot more in my book than using theories or the latest model for guidance.

I recall the change in attitude expressed by Randy Croyle from Dow Chemical vividly after I inveigled him to visit a Saginaw Bay Caspian tern colony with me when his employer was funding our Saginaw Bay Caspian tern research in 1988. Randy watched us open eggs that had died, band chicks and saw victims of the wasting syndrome he knew of only from reading about the effects of the dioxin-like chemicals and review of our research proposals and annual reports. Randy began to appreciate the gravity of our work only when he experienced it first-hand. Until those moments of real fieldwork he actually took part in for a day, our research was just a paper exercise of conjecture and hypotheses in a proposal.

Eighteen years later I dropped in to his office unannounced; there was the feces-bespattered baseball hat he wore on that day hanging on the wall behind his desk. It was his reminder of Dow's obligation to protect our Sweetwater Seas even though he had moved from environmental affairs to a completely different corporate assignment more than a decade earlier. Perhaps, this was also evidence of the large impact a few very contaminated birds had on one man. Indeed, bird shit does happen to land on your head from time to time when you visit a bird colony. The only real question is how does that kind of experience, and the knowledge that rains down with it, influence what you believe or think you know?

IV.

Navigating the uncertain future of Great Lakes instability.

EXPLORERS WHO FOUND the Great Lakes in the 16th century called them the "Sweetwater Seas". No European or Asian had ever seen such an abundance of fresh water—five immense lakes and connecting channels that extended into the very heart of North America, well over a thousand water miles from the early French settlements at Quebec City and Montreal along the St. Lawrence River. The lakes seemed to be an inexhaustible treasury of fish and wildlife, and possibly a passageway to the orient.

In the next 200 years many wars were fought worldwide between the French and English. The intense desire to control Great Lakes resources contributed to these chronic disputes. Ownership was not settled until the English victory on the Plains of Abraham in Quebec in 1759, followed by the treaty of 1763 that substantially ended French aspirations for a North American empire. However, within a generation the English lost control over the southern and western parts of the lakes by the American Revolution and War of 1812. England would retain the northern and eastern part as Canada until the Crown allowed confederation in 1867. The modern nations of Canada and the United States have shared the Great Lakes since, although not always without distrust and disputes.

The history of the Great Lakes is dominated by rampant over-harvesting of resources, pollution and collateral damage to natural systems. The earliest French voyageurs and priests sought to extend Catholicism and the French empire through the fur trade. Beaver, marten, fisher, mink and muskrat pelts were harvested for export to European fashion houses. Each of these furs had their time of large demand for the fashion trades. Voyageurs penetrated to the heart of the continent in search of furs throughout the seventeenth and eighteenth centuries when France was the dominant political power. French firms then gave way to English fur companies, particularly the Hudson Bay Company, near the end of the eighteenth century after the English won political control.

American interests in the fur trade developed after the War of 1812 had largely settled the boundary. During the early nineteenth century beaver, marten and fisher were harvested with great intensity. Overharvest of each, induced trappers ever further west in search for new sources of pelts. In the decade of 1820 to 1830 an average of over three million pelts passed through the Great Lakes warehouses of the Hudson Bay Companies alone every year, and more through French Canadian companies in Quebec. The fur harvest shipped to Europe in the first three decades of the nineteenth century probably approached an average of five million pelts annually, with more used in North America. By the 1880s, the largess of furs in the Great Lakes region was gone and the trapping business had pushed ever deeper into the continent all the way to the Rocky Mountains, Peace River and Great Slave Lake. But, the Great Lakes were the only reliable export route to European markets until almost the middle of the 19th century.

During the first two centuries of European occupation, the Great Lakes region was a difficult place to survive. Displaced native North Americans resisted the European invasion and expropriation of their lands, contributing to the risks. As territories around the lakes were settled, stable local governments were usually organized about two generations after the first European settlements appeared. Statehood was granted to Ohio in 1804, Indiana in 1816, Michigan in 1837, Illinois in 1839, Wisconsin in 1858 and Minnesota in 1868 reflecting the settlement patterns from the east and south to the west and north.

The same pattern of slow settlement from east to west proceeded in Canada, but with roughly one-fifteenth of the American population. In general, Canada was a generation behind the United States in developing settlements, infrastructure and industry, largely owing to the smaller population base and the geology of the Canadian Great Lakes. The best agricultural soils of the region were in the United States along the lakes' southern shores. The great Canadian Shield of ancient Precambrian rocks, poorer soils and the harsher Canadian climate propelled most immigrants into the United States until late in the 19th century.

There was a profound cultural difference between the US and Canada that resonates today. Canadians remained loyal to the British Crown, taking pride in British citizenship right up to 1967 and the subsequent repatriation of the Canadian Constitution in 1982. Americans, steeped in the lore of the American Revolution, hold fierce values of personal independence, minimal taxation, the right to bear arms and other aggressive symbols dear to their hearts. Perhaps the 1775 flag of Continental Congress bearing the inscription 'Don't tred on me' and a national anthem about 'bombs bursting in air' are the more accurate reflections of fundamental American attitudes than 'America the Beautiful'. The taproots of the two nations were cut from the British tree in fundamentally different ways that resonate in policies and attitudes today (Adams 2003).

Transportation of commodities was largely on the water between 1700 and about 1850. Most roads were little more than deeply rutted trails, more suited to horseback riders dragging sledges or pedestrians carrying packs than wheeled wagons, especially during spring break-up. Sails were the motive force for most travel. Even by ship, only small quantities of goods could be moved. Most commercial vessels were in the 40-100 ton range with six to eight foot drafts throughout the lakes prior to 1850. Groundings and shipwrecks (often from collisions) were commonplace hazards. Sandbars, shoals, and unpredictable weather threatened ships, but there was no large system of lighthouses and life-saving stations, just the experience, knowledge and luck of the captain to save sailors and ships. Only natural harbors could be used because dredging technology and steam power were decades away. Industrial processes were restricted largely to potteries, brickworks and tanneries for local or regional markets. Industries before 1850 were powered by local stream flows or wood burned for steam; the widespread use of coal and transportion by self-powered ships was still over a generation in the future.

Rails penetrated the region about 1850 and steam powered ships appeared more frequently after the American Civil War and the landscape changed rapidly. Large quantities of raw materials and finished goods could be moved reliably over long distances. Mined or harvested resources could be shipped over the lakes' surfaces and by rails. Modern infrastructure such as centralized water supplies, sewers, docks, harbors and warehouses emerged in cities in the last half of the 19th century. Steel-making, hundreds of new manufactured products and large-scale timber harvesting were feasible when reliable means to ship value-added products to markets and Great Lakes cities developed. The vast white pine and hemlock forests of Michigan and Wisconsin were harvested to build Chicago, Detroit and Milwaukee; central Ontario forests were cut to build Toronto and the 'Golden Horseshoe' in Canada. The vast majority of that lumber was shipped on sail-driven schooners or by rail to eastern states and provinces replacing their local timber. Steam-power penetrated the fishing industry, allowing men to exploit fish anywhere instead of those near-shore areas that could be reached by sail reliably.

The near simultaneous discoveries of large deposits of iron ore, limestone and native copper in northern Michigan, Wisconsin and Minnesota in the mid-1800s provided the minerals on which two national economies would be built when brought together with the vast coal reserves of Pennsylvania, Ohio, Illinois and the Appalachian states. Great Lakes waters provided the cheap pathway, and coal-fired steamers the means to bring the coal and mineral resources together to make the steel on which the two nations were built. Lakeshores provided the waters and harbors for steel mills. Many refineries, metal and machinery manufacturing businesses sprang-up on lakeshores. The Great Lakes became the industrial heartland of both nations. But, rampant local pollution, much of it with novel impacts, was a large price of this completely unregulated economic growth.

As these industrial processes descended on the Sweetwater Seas, so did a flood of immigrants. In the latter half of the nineteenth century, the human population burgeoned fourteen-fold. Pollution control was essentially non-existent. Raw sewage was dumped into the lakes, connecting channels and wetlands. Shorelines were filled and bulk-headed to provide stable docks. Harbors were dredged to accommodate ships of ever-larger dimensions and greater drafts. Many harbors used coal ash, clinker—even sawdust, bark and mine tailings— to back-fill bulkheads in harbors or wetlands. These were cheap fill and their polluting chemistries and instabilities were not understood or appreciated.

Industries and mines simply piped their wastes back into harbors leaving a legacy of metals, coal dusts, especially PAHs, other combustion by-products and metals in harbor sediments. Mine tailings, trees, sawdust and bark all were dumped into harbors and tributary rivers as North America developed. Pollutants were simply externalized into the lakes that were taken for granted as a convenient and free means to dispose of almost anything. For a long time, wastes just seemed to go away by natural assimilation, reinforcing the belief that waste management was unnecessary for several generations.

The last half of the nineteenth century was an era of frequent epidemics, especially water-borne typhoid fever, typhus, cholera and polio transmitted by human sewage discharged to surface water. Sewage discharged into the lakes that provided drinking water caused rampant epidemics, especially in summer months. Many developing cities on the Canada US border were forced to confront cross-border pollution, leading to the Boundary Waters Treaty of 1909 (BWT). Article 4 of the BWT was based on the simple idea that those who caused damage were responsible to stop and repair the damage to the shared resource. The BWT is the bedrock of all subsequent agreements to remediate damage, but it has never been enforced comprehensively by either nation.

The stage was set for multiple invasions by alien species when a shallow version of the Welland Canal was constructed to bring small ships and barges into Lake Erie from Lake Ontario in the early-1800s. The larger modern version of the Welland Canal was not completed until 1920, but a biologically-viable connection that could have allowed invasions of the upper four lakes from Lake Ontario was present quite early, at least eighty years before the invasions of key alien species began. The Erie Canal also made a connection via the Hudson River to the Atlantic Ocean. But, these early connections were shallow with strong currents; few oceanic species reached the lakes until the 1920s.

Lake Michigan was connected to the Mississippi drainage through the Chicago Sanitary Canal and other small streams in the early 1900s. Metropolitan Chicago sought a cheap way to get rid of its sewage and developed the canal to compete with the railroads by barging goods on the Mississippi River and its tributaries. Among the alien species arriving from the south were several North American native warm-water fish and crayfish species that had not entered Lake Michigan on their own.

Interestingly, up to about 1920 there were few irreversible changes from pollutants or damages by alien species, although the native lake sturgeon was almost extirpated and replaced by the common European Carp after their release in Wisconsin about 1875. Each lake continued to produce good commercial catches of native fish, although the landlocked Atlantic Salmon was extirpated from Lake Ontario early in the 20th century. Some harbors became hostile habitats as early as 1870, but most polluted harbors were localized. The human population was small enough that natural assimilation still worked to control discharged sewage. Some fisheries, especially in Lakes Ontario and Erie, were over-harvested. Sedimentation of soils, domestic sewage, tree bark and sawdust from sawmills were important local pollutants. The high natural alkalinity of the lakes waters precipitated metal pollutants into their sediments, removing them from biological cycles. Soils eroded from rapidly developing farms and cities tended to form natural caps, trapping many pollutants deep in sediments where benthic organisms could not access them. Poor forest-harvesting practices contributed soils, bark and sawdust from many lumber mills. Some fisheries, particularly in Green Bay of Lake Michigan and Saginaw Bay of Lake Huron, were damaged severely by sawdust and bark from the many mills built to saw the great coniferous forests of the region into lumber after the Civil War.

Even so, nutrient pollution and biological oxygen demand were still modest. Artificial fertilizers were used seldom in farming until petroleum-fuelled tractors and cheap mineral fertilizers were introduced near the start of the 20th century. Little nitrogen and phosphorus was discharged by the earliest industries; nutrients increased modestly up to World War I, except immediately downstream of emerging cities from human sewage. Although many bays and harbors suffered egregious sewage pollution, relatively little lake-wide eutrophication developed in any of the five lakes until after WW II.

Up to the end of the First World War the lakes functioned pretty much as they always had, providing cheap transportation, drinking water, sewage disposal and sustained native fish harvests. Some fish stocks in Lakes Ontario, Erie and Michigan were damaged by over-harvesting in the late 1800s, but most were maintained by natural reproduction well into the 20th century. Some changes accompanied development, but the assimilative capacity of the lakes had largely accommodated conventional pollutants. Synthetic industrial chemicals had not yet appeared. Significant damages were seen only near larger cities or mines that discharged tailings to the lakes. Other than introduced carp and depletion of sturgeon, the native fishery was largely intact and healthy.

Human populations in the Great Lakes watersheds were still relatively modest at the end of the Great War, although growing rapidly. The demand for fish products moved beyond the Great Lakes to markets in the eastern and southern states that developed as rail and truck transport improved. Chronic over-harvesting of walleyed (blue) pike from Lake Erie, whitefish from Lakes Huron and Michigan, and lake trout from Lakes Ontario, Huron and Michigan appeared between the two world wars. Planted hatchery-raised fish made up for some of the deficit, especially in Lakes Ontario and Michigan. Fish communities were stressed, but still intact.

The biotic changes that would overwhelm the assimilative capacity of the Great Lakes really began in the interval between the two world wars. The human population of the whole Great Lakes' watershed increased by close to 80%, approaching 26 million (22 in the US, 4 in Canada in 1940) at the start of World War II. Most municipalities built primary sewage treatment plants and chlorinated effluents. The frequency of water borne human diseases dropped rapidly with drinking water chlorination and filtration. Drinking water supplied by central water treatment plants provided clean and healthful fresh water to most urban households.

Horses and cattle disappeared from cities as cars and streetcars replaced animal-powered transportation. This was a huge net public health improvement, although novel air pollutants, industrial and automotive toxicants appeared. The acute risks of bacteria, parasites and viruses from animal wastes on city streets disappeared when streetcars, trucks and cars replaced horses and wagons. However, very little attention was given to nutrient pollution from sewage, mechanized agriculture, developing industrial processes and new phosphate detergents between

JAMES P. LUDWIG, Ph.D

the world wars. These high intensity stressors would fester to culminate in widespread eutrophication in the 1960s and 1970s, especially in Lakes Erie, Ontario, and southern Lake Michigan. Bays that received large flows from agricultural watersheds or heavy loads of human sewage from cities like Green Bay in Lake Michigan, Saginaw Bay in Lake Huron and western Lake Erie were stressed severely.

Some pundits called Lake Erie 'dead' in 1968, which was the biological oxymoron of the day. The problem was precisely the opposite. The waters were far too alive and productive, creating excesses of algae and far too much biological oxygen demand (BOD) for natural replenishment to sustain fish in these hyper-eutrophic waters during annual summer stratification. Many fish populations were stressed, some extinguished. The magnificent blue (walleyed) pike fishery of Lake Erie that had provided over ten million pounds per year for decades was extinguished in the 1960s. But, plantings of a different, more pollution tolerant, subspecies revived the Lake Erie walleye fishery in the late 1970s as nutrient pollution was brought under control by actions taken subsequent to the first Great Lakes Water Quality Agreement.

The intensity of industrial production, especially automobile and farm-machinery manufacturing, electric power generation by coal, and steel-making accelerated rapidly. During the fifty years of 1890-1940, chemical, pharmaceutical, electrical generation, machinery manufacture, cement production and petroleum refining all entered the basin. New synthetic pollutants, including chlorinated dioxins, furans, polychlorinated biphenyls and many others were discharged with no regulation. Often, these novel toxicants were made inadvertently and the unique damages they cause were unknown. Petrochemical plants and moderate-temperature fires made dioxins and furans.

At the time, dilution and natural attenuation were trusted to eliminate pollutants because this strategy of benign neglect had worked for metals, pathogenic bacteria and nutrient pollutants for generations. During the immense mobilization of industrial production of the war years 1939-1953, the huge growth of Great Lakes industries led to immense increases of loadings by these novel toxicants and nutrients. Synthetic agricultural pesticides, the chlorinated phenolic herbicides, DDT, methoxychlor, dieldrin, aldrin, endrin, toxaphene, mirex, PCBs, dioxins and furans—the persistent organochlorine pollutants (POPs)—all entered the lakes in large quantities after 1947. Some would break down reasonably quickly, but most would persist to pollute the Sweetwater Seas insidiously and grossly contaminate their sediments.

Other than aesthetics, there was no strident alarm given to confront the effects of these pollutants because they were silent and cryptic. In retrospect, the degree of human naiveté about the significance of these synthetic pollutants—especially how long the ignorance persisted—is quite astonishing. For example, a thorough review of the Green Bay ecosystem assembled by the scientific experts of the day in 1975 failed to mention dioxins or furans as pollutants even though these were present for the previous 40 years, and had damaged many species for at least 20 years! Arguably, this kind of convenient ignorance of the inconvenient truth persists in many quarters today: it is part of the bedrock for inaction by governments and agencies of governments that choose to ignore contaminated areas or try to pass on the responsibility for exotic species invasions to others (Alexander 2009). Barry Commoner showed the incredible bioconcentration of radioactive cesium and iodine isotopes from nuclear fallout in 1963, and issued a clairvoyant warning that pesticides and industrial chemicals would act the same way (Commoner 1968). Society failed to act on his analysis and the lakes became another victim of this convenient avoidance of the inconvenient truth. The social movements of the day—peace, health, feminism, environmentalism, and racial equality—coalesced into outraged activist publics. Political responses included the passage of many new laws including those directed toward remediating water and air pollution, the formation of new agencies like the USEPA and many new agreements like the GLWQA.

The major damages to fish populations of the lakes actually have roots in the second half of the 19th century. In 1850 a major part of the total fish biomass of the lakes, particularly Lakes Erie, Huron and Michigan and their connecting channels was in lake sturgeon, a very large species that occupied the bottom scavenger niche. Sturgeon were so abundant that fisheries were virtually impossible in many bay areas. A few hundred pound sturgeon with spiny bone plates in their skin wrought havoc on nets set for the valued whitefish and lake trout. Fishermen set out to destroy the 'useless sturgeon' to enhance their catches. In Green Bay alone, several million mature sturgeon were harvested and killed annually in the decade of the 1860s; many were dried, cut up and burned for heat in the winter, just like cordwood. In fact, during the 1860s, the twin cities of Marinette, Wisconsin and Menomonee, Michigan held an annual January festival where millions of sturgeon carcasses were incinerated—a great sturgeon holocaust.

In the1880s, the value of the sturgeon for roe (caviar) and byproducts such as isinglass derived from their swim bladders was recognized, stimulating a second harvest episode nearly extinguishing them, leaving the bottom scavenger niche wide open. The European carp was introduced to waters connected to Lake Michigan by British immigrants to Wisconsin about 1875. Soon, they spread throughout the lower four lakes filling this niche by the onset of WW I. The carp established a pattern to be repeated many times in the next thirteen decades—intentional or accidental removal of native species that opened a niche for an aggressive invader brought in by immigrants. This pattern of squandering native Great Lakes' resources provides many vivid illustrations of the law of unintended consequences.

A second very significant introduction was the anadromous smelt planted into Silver Lake at Frankfort, Michigan only to escape into Lake Michigan about 1923. The smelt population exploded. By the late 1930s, annual spring runs were common all over the middle three Great Lakes. The dip-net harvesting of smelt became a popular regional ritual, a cultural successor to the January incineration parties that nearly extirpated Green Bay's sturgeon seventy years earlier. Although interactions with other species were not documented fully, smelt must have preyed on larval fish of many game and commercial species and did provide a significant forage base for lake trout for at least three decades. It is likely the smelt was ten to twenty percent of the fish biomass in the middle Great Lakes by 1940. Large annual harvests of carp, whitefish, chubs, lake trout and smelt were made in the decades between the world wars. Even though most commercial fish stocks were not overly depleted, some population gyrations occurred, an ominous prelude to many species crashing after WW II.

In this period three significant new connections were made to the upper four Great Lakes. The modern Welland Canal for deep draft sea-going vessels was built between Lakes Ontario and Erie in 1920, the Lake Nipigon diversion was completed into Lake Superior, and the Chicago

Sanitary Canal providing a deep-water connection of Lake Michigan to the Mississippi River drainage was opened. The Lake Nipigon diversion brought into the upper lakes water to replace the 32,000 cubic feet per second permitted to pass down the Chicago sanitary canal from Lake Michigan into the Mississippi River drainage. The sanitary canal opened southern Lake Michigan to invasions via the Mississippi drainage. Several crayfish, the gizzard shad, possibly the redhorse and some small centrarchids (bass family) probably entered the lakes through this route (Hubbs and Lagler 1958). Now the lakes are threatened by Asian carp species via this route.

The modern Welland Canal was (as it is today) the most important connection to salt waters and became the principal route of alien species invasions. The most significant destabilizing invasions of the last eighty years have followed this route into the Great Lakes. Six—five accidental, one intentional—had the greatest significance: the sea lamprey, alewife, the intentionally introduced salmonids, the spiny water flea, zebra and quagga mussels and the gobies. Only the introductions of the salmonids intended to replace the lamprey-decimated lake trout were intentional.

The species blamed almost universally by fishery managers for major destabilization of the upper four Great Lakes' fisheries is the sea lamprey, the parasitic anadromous jawless fish that parasitized trout, walleye and the larger whitefish species relentlessly after 1945. During the 25 years between 1936 and 1960 the lamprey invasion engulfed the upper four Great Lakes. It established spawning runs in virtually every small stream tributary. Undoubtedly, the lamprey invasion benefited by the coincidence with the Second World War and its aftermath when attention was focused on industrial production for war efforts. By the early 1950's the lamprey population had exploded and large predators in all five lakes were at risk. Huge in comparison to the seven very small native brook lamprey species, the sea lamprey exploited an open niche. Parasitism is common among the more complex marine fish communities, but less frequent among fresh water fish. Commercial and sport fishermen watched helplessly as the native large fish stocks crashed in the early 1950s and 1960s.

One political response was to establish the binational Great Lakes Fishery Commission in 1955. Another was to capture adult fish breeding stocks made safe from lamprey predation in hatcheries in order to restock the

JAMES P. LUDWIG, Ph.D

lakes. A third response was to search for marine salmonid fish species that could resist lampreys, since these species had co-evolved with lampreys in marine habitats. Led by Howard Tanner of the Michigan DNR, a suite of salmonids, most from west coast Pacific Ocean stocks, were introduced to Michigan waters of the upper Great Lakes in the 1960s and early 1970s. Wisconsin, Indiana and Ontario later joined these stocking efforts. A fourth major management response was to develop a large system of electrified wiers on breeding streams to capture spawning lampreys, and later a selective larvicide, 3-trifluoromethyl-4-nitrophenol (TFM), was employed to kill only sea lamprey larvae the streams. Both strategies were developed to interrupt the lamprey's life cycle. Once in-place these programs spent hundreds of millions annually, created new government agencies, and stimulated numerous interest groups of sportsmen and other conservationists to support the noble missions to restore sport fisheries.

Almost coincident with the arrival of the lamprey was the appearance of the alewife. Alewives established dense populations in Lake Ontario in the 1920s, apparently finding passage through the St. Lawrence River. It appeared in Lake Erie about 1930, and was found in Lake Michigan in 1949. By 1960, the biomass of the species in Lakes Huron and Michigan was about equal to the smelt. Late spring alewife dieoffs were seen in Lake Ontario in 1953, Lake Erie in 1958, Lake Huron in 1961 and Lake Michigan in 1962. Alewife mortalities escalated rapidly, becoming a dominant feature of spring. In Lake Michigan alone, the 1967 dieoff was estimated at 0.75 and 1.5 billion alewives; their biomass was estimated to be well over half the biomass of all fish in the lake!

Two bird species, the ring-billed gull and Caspian tern, responded by rapid population growth. The tern population nearly doubled, and the gull population grew more than eight fold in eight nesting seasons 1960-1967 (Ludwig 1968); most other fish-eating birds did not. Botulism mortalities in birds that scavenged dead alewives followed, particularly outbreaks of type E in ring-billed gulls and common loons. Cormorants were nearly extinguished by DDT pollution while year-round resident herring gulls suffered from continuous exposures to many POPs compounds.

In the 1980s and 90s many more alien species followed, especially the spiny waterfleas, gobies, zebra and quagga mussels. Like the previous alewife invasion, these invaders produced huge changes to the ecology of the lakes. Food sources that had sustained many native species were decimated; the reduction of sculpins and darters and their replacement by gobies is an example. Some species that were rare or declining exploited these changes. For example, beach-fouling *Cladophora* algae has benefited from the rain of mussel pseudofeces, rapid recycling of nutrients and improved water clarity that followed the explosive growth of invasive mussel populations. Worse, a suite of blue-green algal species that produce toxins have exploded in all the lakes except Superior and may have initiated the new botulism outbreaks in wildlife since 1998. These changes are symptoms of a grossly imbalanced unpredictable Great Lakes ecosystem roiling in turmoil, beset with chronic instability. Ironically, all these horrid changes were predictable once the natural Great Lakes ecosystem barriers were breeched by alien species and synthetic pollutants.

The immense good-faith effort to restore the Great Lakes over three generations has not produced sustainable ecological systems. These lake systems are not self-replicating with reliable annual crops of fish for sportsmen or healthy wildlife populations. The subtle effects of introductions like the spiny water flea on larval fish foraging, or the displacement of obscure native species assemblages by the gobies are difficult to see. Some species benefit, even as others are harmed. Most recently, the zebra and quagga mussel clarified waters led some to conclude that healthy ecological systems are emerging, but this is a cruel illusion. Clear water is not always clean water. The mussels have revolutionized the entire food web by effecting two important changes. Light now penetrates a far deeper water column than before, promoting new algal and benthic (lake bottom) communities. These mussels filter over half of the phytoplankton and suspended sediment starving native food webs based on pelagic green algae and zooplankton.

Before the mussels arrived, zooplankton ate green algae, and were food for the small fishes that were the forage for valued sport and commercial fishes. After mussel invasions, most energy now goes either to produce more mussels or passes to the bottom as pseudofeces, forming a new dominant benthic food web. Species that depended on mid-water and surface water food webs are suffering, including the introduced salmonids. Many bird species are starving; some like the Caspian tern have abandoned historic nesting areas where they once thrived, but can no longer find enough food to raise young. Others, including many top predator fish species, have reduced growth rates. Sport fisheries once managed through plantings no longer produce fish with good growth rates because these predator fish simply starve or cannibalize each other.

Where these systems will end up, and if they will stabilize within a few decades, is anybody's guess. The lakes are in the throes of a perfect storm of massive ecological change. Only a fool would predict the final outcome. But, it is clear the Great Lakes are less stable than at anytime in the 400 years they have been observed. Ruptured food webs, crippled native assemblages of fish and wildlife and even common human uses like swimming and drinking water supplies all are hostage to these changes. So long as new alien species invasions are allowed to occur and bioaccumulative toxicants are present in toxic concentrations, ecological stability with reliably productive fisheries and healthy wildlife will not develop. The socioeconomic effects of these biological changes are sure to reverberate through the lives of all Great Lakes residents (Braden *et al.* 2008a, 2008b). Just as the North American automobile industry was crippled by global competition, so are biotic resources of the lakes: our human economy is damaged by foreign product invasions, the Great Lakes biota by invasive alien species and synthetic chemicals.

However, the damage to human interests in the Great Lakes is far greater than what is obvious. On the surface, the history of the lakes appears to be relatively simple: Settlement followed by overharvesting of resources, attendant pollution and alien species have led to the current poor state of the lakes. But, is there more than the obvious to this story? What are the cryptic factors that were, and will be, important to a competent strategy to restore these waters to at least a semblance of ecological stability and high value to humans, fish and wildlife? How has government policy and politics affected these outcomes? Most importantly, how do we decide on what to do and where to devote limited funds for restoration and begin to get effective Great Lakes management? A review of past decisions and problems to understand their effects is the only reasonable means we have to build a secure base on which to build competent future management. It is exactly the famous dictum so often ignored by our leaders that we must pursue first: for, *"Those that refuse to study history are condemned to repeat it."*

Introductions of alien species from commerce through the St. Lawrence Seaway and arrivals via the connection to the Mississippi drainage are not fully under control. Nor is it likely they can be fully controlled because those who may make introductions would have to know how to prevent releases, understand the potential for drastic consequences if they do and be committed not to. Unfortunately, invasive species are a lot like pregnancy: Once started, the result is inevitable. The immense changes that will follow in the wake of climate changes are just now beginning. And, just how these stressors will interact with the chaotic ecological communities already present is a complete mystery. Too many variable conditions are now present to support firm predictions of outcomes, or even the direction of changes with great confidence.

When a niche is open or abandoned and a fecund invasive species arrives capable of exploiting the niche, it will fill that niche very quickly. If a second species capable of occupying that niche arrives, then competition will determine which species dominates and one of the invaders, or the local native species that was in that niche, will become rare, possibly extinct. Moreover, these events can occur quickly in a few generations of the invader species if there is no effective predator or parasite to control it.

The alewife invasion deserves analysis because of its huge impacts on the rest of the native biota. This species became so abundant so rapidly, that it was more than half of the fish biomass in Lakes Michigan and Huron by 1968. The coincidence of the lamprey damage was a major factor favoring the immense population explosion that elevated alewives from a rare fish in Lake Michigan in 1949 to the most abundant fish in just nineteen years. Alewives, in turn, had major impacts on other fish species like the emerald shiner. But, alewives had great difficulty adjusting to the osmotic pressure of fresh water compared to saline waters, and were poor feeders at temperatures colder than 3°C (37°F), often starving in late winter. Their abundance and osmotic vulnerability exacerbated by the low iodine concentrations in the lakes (necessary to make thyroid hormone that is the primary hormone for osmoregulation in fish) combined to cause massive spring die-offs.

By 1967 Chicago was paying for front-end loaders and dump trucks each spring to remove the massive numbers of dead alewives from city beaches. One popular report on the 1967 die-off near Navy Pier in

Chicago estimated 2-3 tons of dead fish for every 100 feet of beach at Chicago, roughly 1,220 dead fish per foot of beach! These mortalities continued through the mid-1970s as the alewives adjusted by selection for a more fit stock. The capacity to osmoregulate is directly related to gill area where excess water is excreted. Small-headed alewives with less gill area died more frequently than larger-headed fish. Soon fish biologists found the mean head size of alewives had increased by about 11% in the population of the 1984 year-class in Lake Huron compared to the 1965-1967 year-classes. Annual alewife die-offs diminished after this genetic adaptation spread through the population.

The sudden abundance of a small forage fish easily caught by colonial water birds was reflected by rapid growth of some of their populations. The growth of the ring-billed gull population was unprecedented for a large gull species. Chick fledging rates were more almost three fold greater than required to replace deaths. In the eight years of 1959-1967 required for three gull generation times, their population quadrupled in Lakes Huron and Michigan (Ludwig 1974). By 1971, the Great Lakes population that had been roughly 100,000 nesting pairs in 1959 approached a million pairs. Ring-bills were nesting even on mainland sites like the limestone mine dock at Rogers City MI, power plant waste piles at Monroe, MI and building roofs in Milwaukee, WI, Port Clinton and Cleveland, OH by the 1970s and 1980s.

Spring farm work, especially plowing and hay cutting, always attracted massive flights of ring-bills that ate worms, beetles and insect larvae. Studies of ring-bill diets during nesting between 1963 and 1967 in Lakes Huron and Michigan found half their food was alewives (Ludwig 1974). Birds in some colonies provided 70% of food fed to chicks as alewives until the early 1970s when most ring-billed gulls shifted to agricultural sources, leaving alewives to herring gulls, terns and cormorants. However, exploitation of the alewife was not without risk. Some areas, especially Saginaw Bay and northern Lake Michigan had gull die-offs from scavenging dead alewives in which type E botulism bacteria flourished (Ludwig and Bromley 1988). In the Grand Traverse Bay region, ring-bills even took to eating sweet and sour cherries in the mid-1980s until many birds were culled.

The Caspian tern population also grew in the period of alewife abundance, essentially tripling between 1959 and 1992. They mostly ate alewives from 1960 into the 1980s, then added other species to their diets, especially perch in Canadian waters of Lake Huron and planted salmonid smolts in the northern Lake Michigan colonies. In 1994 and 1995, the MDNR raised, tagged and released 7,000 Atlantic salmon smolts each year between the Straits of Mackinac and Les Cheneaux Islands as part of cormorant-perch study. Cheryl Summer and I found 168 of those salmon tags in Caspian tern nests 30 and 38 miles from the Carp River planting site on Hat and Ile aux Galets islands in the Beaver Islands when we banded tern chicks. No tags were found in cormorant nests on the large St. Martin's Shoal colony in the study area of northern Lake Huron, just nine miles from the river's mouth, hardly what the fisheries biologists had expected. The irony was profound—a threatened bird species feeding on the smolts the fish biologists expected the cormorants to be taking. But, the 'pest' cormorants ate alewives and sticklebacks, but no perch or salmon smolts when nesting! Our observations that terns ate the salmon were omitted from the final report issued by the MDNR on cormorants and perch in the Les Cheneaux.

However, the three small terns—common, Forsters and black—all declined rapidly after 1960. Historically, these elegant small tern species fed on emerald shiner populations, and could capture only small fish near the water surface by plunge-diving. Alewife competition and predation on many minnow species probably reduced the food for these birds while dioxin-like contaminants most certainly played a major role in their lack of success after 1965 (Kubiak *et al.* 1989).

The sea lamprey history is especially interesting both for the lamprey's responses to the vigorous campaigns of five decades to control their populations with electric weirs and TFM in spawning streams. Lampreys devastated all large fish stocks of the upper four lakes in the 1950s. Biologists were convinced that lamprey control was the highest priority if any native stocks were to be saved. Under the leadership of the Great Lakes Fishery Commission, thousands of electric weirs were constructed on tributary streams to capture the spawning lampreys and TFM was used widely after the late 1960s. In the next fifteen years the lamprey population yielded to these measures. Relatively few were able to reproduce, reducing damage greatly. However, a few lamprey spawned in the connecting channels between lakes (e.g. the St. Marys River between Lakes Superior and Huron) and even in open lake habitats, places unaffected by either electric wiers or TFM. In the last two decades the lamprey population has rebounded, killing or injuring many large fish again, especially in Lakes Superior, Huron and Michigan. Similar to the appearance of larger-headed alewives, the lamprey had adapted by selection. If damage continues to escalate, some new means of lamprey control will be called for. Recent studies of lake trout in Lake Superior reported serious damage by the resurgent lamprey population at all depths (Harvey *et al.* 2008; Sitar *et al.* 2008).

These examples of how these invasive species were altered by selection and adapt to exploit resources—whether from natural (osmotic pressure) or human-causes (fish plantings, wiers, TFM)—are instructive when evaluating the effects of invasive species. Essentially, whenever the gene frequency in a population is altered by mortalities, the species will change as the survivors reproduce: then the species evolves new capabilities. Their adaptations may not be beneficial to the health of the larger biological community and human interests as the lamprey resurgence shows. This property of life and the capacity of species to change their diets should warn us that an apparently-effective lake wide management strategy of the type contemplated by 'ecosystem management' is fraught with dangers unless thought through from many more perspectives than simple culling of one species. It gives credence to that marvelous line of the biologist in the first '*Jurassic Park*' movie when he observed that the supposedly reproductively incapable genetically-engineered female dinosaurs had reverted to parthenogenic reproduction that does not require males. Indeed, Nature and invasive species find a way to prosper.

Adaptation of invasive populations is inevitable. It will be especially dramatic for species native to salt water or saline habitats like the alewife, lamprey and mussels. Many invaders appear in the Great Lakes habitat free of the parasites and pathogens that afflicted them where they are native because intermediate hosts are absent. Invasive species' populations often explode when their natural controls are absent (Kvach and Stepian 2008). Among the more interesting aspects of the responses of Great Lakes scientists and agency administrators is the myopic approach to understanding of the dynamics of invasives. The focus has been relentlessly on what these species are doing in the Great Lakes. Initially, this was warranted to assess their gross impacts: but, this strategy is unlikely to lead to effective controls. When there was successful control of widespread invasive species, it has usually come from persons with a worldview.

Substantially, *all effective natural sustainable population control strategies* come in one of three guises, a predator, a competitor, or a disease/parasite. Usually, all three of these natural control agents coexist with the invader *only* where that alien species evolved. There can be high-tech solutions for some species if their breeding cycle has a 'weak link', such as females that mate only once. or an exploitable response to pheromones. If males can be bred in large numbers, sterilized and released, then sometimes this is a way to control an alien or pest species. However, large investments in research, requiring time and money, are always required.

There are instructive examples of invasive species control to consider. The invasive plant purple loosestrife staged a huge invasion of Great Lakes watersheds in the 1970s and 1980s. Many native emergent wetland plants used by coastal wetland wildlife were damaged. Wetland plant community simplification was the result; in turn, many resident native animal populations were stressed. A solution emerged when entomologists found a specific plant consumer, the *Galerucella calmariensis* beetle that feeds only on the loosestrife in central Europe. Where imported and released in North America, the resulting control of the loosestrife was astonishing. Many coastal wetlands of the Great Lakes are recovering lost diversity and complexity as the long-suppressed native species seed banks restore native plant communities.

A similar example for an invasive animal was provided after the introduction of the European rabbit to Australia. The rabbit population exploded, practically denuding the landscape of food, threatening to extinguish native marsupials. The solution was to go back to Europe for the rabbit disease *myxomatosis* and release it in Australia. Presently, a modest number rabbits survive in Australia just as in Europe. The two alien species coexist and the native marsupials are recovering even though the Australian rabbits are developing inherited resistance to this disease slowly by selection.

A second example of selection, adaptation and population explosions in the Great Lakes occurred with the cormorants. After WWII the synthetic pesticides and dioxin-like chemicals flooded into the Great

JAMES P. LUDWIG, Ph.D

Lakes. Previously, I related the story of the collapse of the most successful herring gull colony in Lake Michigan at Bellows Island in Grand Traverse Bay in the 1960s and the cause-effect relationship to DDT group chemicals (DDT_r). However, all species in this community of water birds were exposed to DDT_r through consumption of Great Lakes fish. One species was virtually extinguished—the double-crested cormorant.

Herring gull embryos could tolerate up to 60 ppm to DDT_r in their eggs; eggshell thinning was insufficient to lead to broken gull eggs until the >60-120 ppm range was reached. But, cormorant eggs broke at concentrations above 6 ppm. At 20 ppm, roughly a third of the low effect concentration for herring gulls and the concentration (60 ppm) Carl Tomoff and I found in eggs from the unaffected Pismire Island herring gull colony in 1965 (Ludwig and Tomoff 1966), over 95% of cormorant eggs have an incompetent shell and those embryos die (Weseloh *et al.* 1983, 1995; Ludwig *et al.* 1995). At the end of WW II cormorants were nesting on at least eleven Michigan and Wisconsin Great Lakes islands, at probably fifteen or more islands in the Canadian North Channel and Georgian Bay and on half-dozen islands in western Lake Erie. The total population was probably near 5,000 pairs in spite of routine persecution by fishermen. The last unsuccessful nesting outside of the North Channel and Georgian Bay of Lake Huron in the upper three lakes was on the Huron Islands of Lake Superior in 1958. Only on inland impoundments in northern Wisconsin protected by dams did the cormorant survive the onslaught of DDTr.

The nadir of the Great Lakes nesting population was reached in 1972, the year DDT was banned in the US; only 117 nests were present in the North Channel and Georgian Bay of Lake Huron and eight nests in Lake Erie. The total Great Lakes population had been reduced to 125 pairs and the average concentration of the DDT_r compounds in eggs was 22 ppm. Only 3% of those eggs hatched (Weseloh *et al.* 1983; 1995). Cormorants were extinguished from the Great Lakes waters of Michigan, Wisconsin and Minnesota; they were listed as threatened in Wisconsin and extirpated in Michigan. In the early 1970s Wisconsin actually had a significant program of erecting artificial nesting platforms for cormorants, first in their inland impoundments, and by 1976 on Green Bay. The goal was to restore the species. This time, it worked because DDTr concentrations fell rapidly (Ludwig et al. 1995). By 1995 the whole Great Lakes population was probably between 80,000 and 105,000 nesting pairs with birds firmly established nesting in each of the lakes (Ludwig and Summer in Diana *et al.* 1997). The recovery was achieved in spite of the presence of dioxin-like contaminants for two reasons. The cormorant was the only foot-propelled fish-eating diver in the system other than loons; only these divers could capture fish denied to all other colonial water birds. In fact, two-thirds of banded cormorants recovered between 1932 and 1944 on the Great Lakes were killed in deep-set gill nets for lake trout and whitefish, some at depths greater than 120 feet (36 meters).

Second, the cormorant lays up to five eggs per nesting attempt and was able to replace lost clutches more rapidly than other water birds. Fledging 3 to 4 chicks per year was normal in the less contaminated areas and 2 to 3 in the more contaminated regions. Adult death rates were similar to gulls and Caspian Terns, hovering just above 11% per year (Seamans *et al.* 2012). But, cormorants mature in just two years where ring-billed gulls average 2.7, Caspian terns 3.8 and herring gulls 4.0 years to reach maturity (Ludwig 1968). In short, cormorants had tremendous advantages over other colonial water birds, provided food and nesting space were available when they regained capacity to reproduce in the late 1970s. Once their eggshells remained intact, the cormorant was poised to exploit the Great Lakes as never before. Alewives were superabundant, smelt still numerous, there were few traditional predators (e.g. eagles) left to prey upon them and fisherman had forgotten about them. Their population exploded. In Michigan Great Lakes waters alone, starting from the 22 nests Mark and I found at Gravelly Island in 1978, the population grew almost a thousand fold to near 20,000 nests by 1995 (Ludwig *et al.* 1989, Diana *et al.* 1997).

For ten years from 1979-1988 I recorded the fish eaten by cormorants during nesting and over 80% by weight and 88% by number were alewife. Our team correlated the frequency of alewives in the cormorant diet with the Lake Michigan trawling data collected by federal scientists that had characterized alewife abundance for many years. We found that cormorant diets matched the trawling data for five years between 1979 and 1988—obtained at an annual cost of more than a quarter million dollars twenty five years ago—with an r^2 value of 0.88 (Ludwig *et al.* 1989). This meant that simply walking around cormorant colonies and picking up the fish vomited by the birds gave as accurate a picture of the lake wide alewife population as did an expensive piece of fishery research! When these data were shared with fishery scientists, it was received with a grunt, not boundless enthusiasm.

The cormorant recovery was interesting in other ways. When a species passes through a period of low population, it also passes through a 'genetic bottleneck' because the birds carrying genes forward in time are few and genetic diversity is much reduced compared to a large population. In this case, the agent driving adaptation was eggshell thinning. The only birds that reproduced laid eggs with the thickest shells, and their offspring inherited that tendency. North American cormorants today lay eggs on average with shells that are 8-9% heavier than the mean eggshell weight of the ancestral population before 1947 and the flood of DDT, meaning the North American cormorant population evolved some resistance to eggshell thinning.

However, the rest of the cormorant genome appears to be largely unaffected by whatever selection is proceeding in North America. One aspect of cormorant biology deserving careful scrutiny is the propensity of all cormorant species to die in periodic episodic disease outbreaks. Ornithologists monitoring cormorants and shags worldwide have reported severe episodes of diseases whenever their populations become dense or food sources fail. *Pasturella sp.* bacteria, and viruses are the common pathogens (Blaxland 1951). For example, cape cormorants in South Africa and great cormorants of northern Europe each have experienced three episodes of severe mortalities since WW I (MacPherson 1956; Crawford *et al.* 1992).

Each epidemic followed a sharp rise of the local populations. These same populations required one to three decades to restore numbers after each disease outbreak. This phenomenon is well known to population ecologists. When a population is rare but growing, it is unaffected by intraspecific competition, parasites or diseases; it is a density-independent population. However, as population density increases, intraspecific competition for food, nesting space and other resources intensifies until disease, parasites and lack of food limit population size. Then, it becomes a density-dependent population. Pandemic diseases, often triggered by food shortage, starvation, parasites or viral disease are common mechanisms of density-dependent population control (Lack 1954).

A good case can be made that the USDA animal control program for North American cormorant populations actually has the effect of continuously reducing intraspecific competition and disease transmission among Great Lakes cormorants, allowing the cormorant population to stay in the density-independent fast growth phase rather than reaching a density that would cause them self-regulate. Thus, a permanent program of expensive artificial control will be required unless the cormorant population is allowed to behave normally. It is interesting to compare the Great Lakes cormorant history with the ring-billed gull experience. Once the ring-bill population reached its maximum density of about 1.1 million pairs between 1972 and 1980, it stopped growing and then shrank by itself to a total present Great Lakes population of about 650,000 pairs.

The interaction of cormorants with their Newcastle Disease Virus (NDV) in North America is especially interesting. It is likely that all cormorants are exposed to the benign forms of NDV during their lifetimes, quite similar to the way humans are exposed to the HN flu viruses that include the much feared '1918 Spanish [H_1N_1] flu', the 'bird [H_5N_1] flu' and many other non-pathogenic HN viruses. The vast majority of the 117 known HN viruses are only mildly pathogenic and infective. However, occasionally HN viruses mutate to become exceedingly pathogenic and infective, especially in periods of high stress for their hosts and or when host populations are dense. For humans, the coincidence of trench warfare concentrating troops in stress-filled environments and civilians in war zones set the stage for the great human H_1N_1 flu pandemic of 1918-1919 that killed at least 40 million people.

For cormorants, the triggers of episodic diseases have been high populations and sometimes food shortages, especially for the cape cormorants in South Africa. Twice in North America as the cormorant population grew rapidly, NDV broke out in a classic disease pandemic. In 1990, an intestinal form of the disease killed many birds in the colonies of Saskatchewan (Wobeser *et al.* 1993). In 1992, a neurologic form of the disease broke out all across North America, killed between 7 and 40 percent of all hatched chicks and probably disrupted at least half of the total normal reproduction of the species from the Rocky Mountains to Nova Scotia (Glaser *et al.* 1998).

JAMES P. LUDWIG, Ph.D

However, since these outbreaks, cormorant control programs have kept the population low enough so that disease episodes no longer occur. Epidemiologists know that the transmission of parasites and diseases depends on a dynamic interaction of four factors—the pathogenicity of the disease, host susceptibility, the frequency of contact of infected and uninfected individuals and host food supplies. To halt or prevent an epidemic, the trick is to influence one or more of these factors. For example, we influence the susceptibility of our human population to the HN flu viruses with vaccinations, control transmission by isolation of infected individuals and changing the ways we could be exposed such as donning face masks and washing hands. These strategies cannot be applied to wildlife, but their exploding populations will sow the seeds of pandemics by their own rampant population growth, just as the North American cormorants did by the early 1990s. Yet, our response was to spend several millions annually for 'control', when—if we just left the species be—history and population ecology tell us bluntly that their natural pathogens will do that job for us at no cost.

All of this suggests that what we ought to be doing to control the invasive species and the irruptive natives is to study what ails them and promote those natural factors instead of using expensive artificial controls. This means that agencies working to protect the Great Lakes should support research on mussels, gobies, lampreys and similar deleterious invasive species to find their predators, parasites and pathogens in their native marine habitats and then import these agents as control measures if it is safe to do so, just as was done with purple loosestrife and its beetle. It is far more likely we can find effective low-cost natural controls where these species evolved than by searching the Great Lakes for answers. In the long-term, artificial means like TFM, egg oiling or shotguns are expensive fools' gambits. However, agencies cannot pursue this type of research under neoliberal governments if politicians cut research and monitoring budgets consistently. The alien species prosper, supported by a pathogenic political philosophy.

This observation on cormorant adaptations and diseases also puts an unusual observation on herring gulls into perspective. From the late 1970s into the early 1990s it was very common to find herring gull nests with five to six eggs in Lake Michigan colonies. These are produced by female:female pairings (Fry *et al.* 1987). Herring gulls have a natural genetic resistance to eggshell thinning and were affected much less than cormorants. In essence, it takes about 10-20 times more DDT_r to thin herring gulls eggshells than cormorant eggshells. However, this natural resistance to eggshell thinning was not necessarily advantageous to the gulls in the long term.

This greater tolerance to DDT_r exposed the year-round resident gulls' embryos and immature birds to continuous exposures to the potent estrogenic and antiandrogenic properties of DDT_r. Recent research on the pathway of sexual differentiation in birds found that normal aromatase enzyme concentrations in the brain that converts estrogen into testosterone are required for sexual differentiation of males during development (Elbrecht and Smith 1992). DDT_r interfere with this mechanism. Male gulls were feminized, creating hermaphrodites that could not breed successfully. Super-females that would mate with other females appeared; any adult (lesbian) pairings of these damaged birds produces infertile eggs and twice the normal clutch of three eggs are laid in these nests (Fry *et al.* 1987). For example, I found 2.3% of the nests at Hat Island in the Beaver Islands archipelago of northern Lake Michigan with these doubled clutches in 1986, fourteen years *after* DDT was banned. For a species like the herring gull that generally matures at age four and has an average lifespan of 11.5 breeding seasons with some individuals breeding for over 30 years, the population-level damage from DDT was projected far into the future, *decades after* DDT was banned. In fact, I found one of the doubled clutch nests in 2005 during my last trip into the Beaver Islands—33 years after DDT was banned. This delayed effect has caused many years of recruitment losses. It is especially pernicious when two reproductively-capable females are lost in a lesbian pairing and too few capable males are available. It may help explain why the herring gull population failed to keep pace with ring-billed gulls, cormorants and Caspian terns during the period of alewife superabundance. It is critical to understand that the same chemical stressor and exposure concentrations can have very different impacts on different species and lead to very different outcomes by different mechanisms. Sensitivities and responses to pollutants differ widely among species in every ecological community.

The recent history of the small terns—commons, Forsters and blacks—on the Great Lakes has been especially stark. When I began field studies in

1959 it was a rare day when individuals of all three small terns were not seen and heard almost anywhere on the bays of Lakes Huron, Michigan and the connecting channels to and from Lake Huron. By 1995 it was a rare day to see these species in these places. Before WW II, the two gulls, Caspian terns and cormorants all were less abundant than the common tern.

In 1933 my father and grandfather banded 6,122 common tern chicks in Saginaw Bay and Thunder Bay at just two Lake Huron colonies with two days of effort. From 1986 through 1995 the family banded 2,407 common tern chicks in all of US Lakes Huron and Michigan by visiting every known colony (excepting three colonies studied by others) at least once every year. The reduction of several minnow species owing to alewife competition and increased competition from ring-billed gulls did damage common terns (Ludwig 1962). However, there were many islands, bars and shoals with excellent common tern habitat that were not used for 30 years or longer. In 1963, about 1,700 pairs nested in the Beaver Islands archipelago at five sites and our family banded 1,836 chicks there. In 1995 there were none nesting there and just one of these historic common tern sites had ring-billed gulls nesting. The Forsters and blacks both seek out floating mats of vegetation, especially cattail mats, in coastal wetlands to nest on. The mat habitats are still there, the small terns mostly are not. Gulls and cormorants do not use this habitat.

The stressor in common for all these small species is exposure to the dioxin-like chemicals. Owing to their small size (80-150 grams) compared to other colonial water birds (475-2,400 grams), the small terns have much higher standard metabolic rates than their competitors. They must eat far more per gram of body weight to survive, predisposing them to accumulate toxicants from their lake-derived foods far more rapidly than their larger competitors (Ludwig 1996a). Tim Kubiak's landmark work on the Forsters tern from Green Bay and inland Lake Poygan, WI showed how sensitive this species is to the dioxin-like PCBs (Kubiak et al. 1989). Embryo death was greater, incubation behavior was disrupted and fledging rates were half of the Lake Poygan rate in Green Bay. Tim's egg-switching experiment also showed a behavioral component to these outcomes. I saw similar failures to hatch among common tern nests in Saginaw Bay colonies in the 1980s, but no one observed them carefully to verify the subtle effects of dioxin-like contaminants on fledging and survival.

But, for me it was the virtual extirpation of black terns from Lake Michigan and Lake Huron bay areas that is the most troubling of all. These tiny swallow-like black sprites of the coastal wetlands lent sheer elegance to the Les Cheneaux Islands in northern Lake Huron, the marshes of Green and Saginaw Bays and the St. Marys River; now they are virtually extinguished from these areas. From 1986 through 1995 I spent 106 days in the field in Saginaw Bay and saw one black tern in 1987 and one in 1990, none afterwards. In the early 1960s they were dirt common. Their loss was a grievous wound. The dioxin-like contaminants must be the prime suspect for their absence because black terns continue to thrive and reproduce at the inland sites like the Houghton Lake, Michigan marshes, protected from Great Lakes contaminants behind three dams on the Muskegon River. They thrive in this low contaminant habitat in spite of being far more exposed to their traditional predators—hawks, owls and raccoons—than they were in their once prime Great Lakes shoreline habitats.

For the reptile taxon, the disappearance or the reduction of several snakes from abundance to very rare or absent bears an eerie similarity to the small terns. The black water snake (*Natrix sipedon*) is a predator on small fish, especially sculpins and darters, from the shallow water zones around islands; chicks of some ground-nesting birds were eaten too. It virtually disappeared from the coastal zones of almost all islands of Lakes Erie and Michigan between 1967 and 1986 as well as the North Channel of Lake Huron. A similar fate overtook large common garter snakes (*Thamnophis sirtalis*) at many sites.

Between 1960 and 1966 Dad and I recorded 19 instances of common tern or ring-billed gull nesting attempts on snake infested islands that were damaged severely or destroyed by these two snakes in Lakes Michigan and Huron. In the Beaver archipelago large water snakes were so abundant in 1960 they ruined completely an attempted nesting of 400 common tern pairs at Timm's Island. We saw intense snake predation on ring-billed gulls at Batture Island and Egg Island in 1963-1966, and at Middle Grant Island in 1962-1967 in the North Channel of Lake Huron. Similar predation on terns was seen at Thunder Bay Island near Alpena, MI up to 1979.

But, from 1986-1995 our field teams did not record an instance of snake predation on bird chicks while we revisited these historic sites of large snake infestations repeatedly. Neither did we did find a single large snake on any of the historically snake-infested sites we visited. Large snake predators were just absent from many islands we visited that once had many. Large black water snakes on Lake Erie limestone islands in Ohio and Ontario were infamous before WW II, but exceptionally rare after 1970, although they seem to be staging a comeback through predation on the introduced gobies as contaminants decrease (Alexander, 2009).

We must ask what could have caused this pattern of lost diversity? The most likely common stressor was the presence of the dioxin-like contaminants in the bird chicks and fish the snakes were eating that led to adult snake mortality and reproductive failure. Christine Bishop (Bishop *et al.* 1991) found the same suite of developmental deformities in contaminated snapping turtle populations of coastal wetlands on Lakes Erie and Ontario during the 1980s that our team and Gilbertson *et al.* (1991) reported from birds. It is ironic that these snakes are now returning to Lake Erie islands where they eat a new, relatively clean food—the gobies—after the mussel and goby invasions. It provides another excellent example of the chaotic nature of the modern Great Lakes.

Extirpations of coastal mink and otter populations of the middle Great Lakes have been reported by a number of investigators. Chris Wren looked at the trapping records for mink on the tributaries to Lake Erie in the 1980s and found no reproduction among mink in the townships bordering on the lake (Wren 1991). In the rivers flowing to Lake Huron from Michigan's lower peninsula between 1988 and 1993 our team, John Giesy and Don Tillitt found no reproduction of mink or otter below barrier dams that prevented Great Lakes fish from inward spawning migrations (Giesy *et al.* 1994b). Only above the dams were there reproducing animals even though these mammals were eating the same fish species in both locations. Tillitt and Giesy analyzed carp from the Saginaw River and calculated that if just 3-8 % by weight of carp sampled in 1992 from that polluted river were eaten by mink, the PCBs alone in those fish would provide enough TCDD-EQs to destroy their reproduction.

The lessons of these complicated population explosions, extirpations and patterns of selection are many and can help unravel complex cause-effect relationships. Foremost is the nearly ubiquitous damage to the reproduction and survival of all top predators from every vertebrate taxon from synthetic contaminants. Serious damage began to virtually all populations of every taxon simultaneously after the mid-1960s. It was coincident with, but has persisted long after, the massive point-source discharges of PCBs, other diaromatic dioxin-like chemicals and DDTr were banned or regulated.

Effects on the long-lived predators were masked at first by their long generation times. It took many years for adults in these populations to age and die once contamination was serious. Cook *et al.* (2003) found it took over 20 years of continuous reproductive failure to extinguish the Lake Ontario native lake trout stock. Very similar time spans for virtually all other large vertebrate predator populations to suffer extirpations or serious population declines were observed, except migratory ring-billed gulls that fed primarily on relatively clean earthworms and insects from agricultural areas (Ludwig 1974, 1996a). Some species, like the cormorant, were exceptionally sensitive to one of the synthetic toxins (DDT$_r$) and disappeared first, only to reappear when that substance dropped below critical concentrations. A few species, like the herring gull, were generally somewhat resistant to all of these pernicious chemicals and managed to keep reproducing modestly through multiple waves of different toxic substances. But, herring gulls suffered significant chronic, but subtle and easily overlooked, damage. Others, such as the snakes and small terns, probably suffered continuously depleted reproduction over four decades. Now these species are reduced to rare or extirpated status in many places where they were once abundant.

The most important consequence was community simplification. One of the fundamental tenets of ecology is that species diversity, especially among predators, promotes community stability and the capacity of an ecological community to self-regulate. Synthetic chemicals and invasive alien species have reduced that diversity massively, and thereby led to ecological destabilization that makes invasions far easier for newly arrived alien species. For example, the gobies of today did not have to contend with predation by a high population of the voracious black water snakes when they arrived, unlike the native sculpins and darters that evolved with these predators.

JAMES P. LUDWIG, Ph.D

Given the residual contamination still present, recycling from contaminated sediments, new contaminants and the slow rate of contaminant evaporation and new depositions from the air, a fair question is 'Can the lakes recover their diversity and stability in a reasonable time span?' Let us set that span to be the average North American male human lifetime of 78 years. For the coastal wetland plant species the answer is likely yes, simply because these plant species largely survive in a seed bank where seeds remain quiescent until germination conditions are right. Most coastal wetland plants germinate and reestablish only in the driest years of water cycles, roughly every 22 years. If we can control their invasive competitors, then we reestablish conditions for their restoration. Seed banks, cyclic lake levels and time will do the rest.

My opinion for the animal denizens is that *only* if no new source of pernicious chemicals are added to the system, *and* the toxins now emerging from blue-green algae prove to be insignificant, is this possible. Even if a pipe dream of instantaneous contamination clean-up were accomplished, the legacy chemicals are not likely to disappear fast enough to meet this criterion. In 1993 a team of us looked at the presence of dissolved total PCBs in the waters of the lakes measured in 1986-1988 and related these data to the real uptake pattern and effects on six resident wildlife species and humans. We concluded reductions >90% in Lake Superior and >99% in Lakes Michigan, Huron, Erie and Ontario of the total PCB concentrations were required to reach a 'no-effects' criterion for all predaceous wildlife and humans that eat fish from these waters (Ludwig *et al.* 1993a).

Researchers monitoring chemical deposition from the air have shown PCB inputs from the airshed and watershed just about match the PCB export through evaporation and water outflow for Lake Michigan. This means meaning the lakes are approaching a steady state for total PCBs. Because air circles the earth in about three weeks, PCB dynamics are now mostly under control of the global atmospheric reservoir. We cannot make reductions to this aerial source by any regulatory actions taken in the Great Lakes basin, the US or Canada alone. Only international political acts to ban production and use can accomplish worldwide reductions (Visser 2007); these are not under control of the US or Canadian governments.

The only bright spot to this picture is that the PCBs entering the lakes are probably deficient in the worst dioxin-like congeners compared to the weathered PCBs stored in the sediments from historic point sources (Burkhard *et al.* 1985; Oliver *et al.* 1989). Even so, the probability that these lakes will reach no-effect concentrations protecting all wildlife and human health in the next 78 years is nil unless we address *both* sediment and atmospheric sources simultaneously.

These substances must be thought of as a fact of life, notwithstanding the many good-faith efforts of those working on remedial action plans (RAPs). They are present. They cause damage. They will not be gone soon. There will be slow improvement for the predators as contaminated sediments with the worst congeners are buried slowly. But, it is not likely to come fast enough for humans living today to be alive when there are no effects. The more sensitive species like mink and otter, and the smaller species with higher metabolic rates, will suffer longest. These will have slower recoveries, provided their populations persist. If not, they will be extinguished. Sadly, we must accept it, for those are the most likely outcomes. For example, Keith Grasman led a team to assess whether there were substantial improvements in the immune competence of Herring Gulls and Caspian terns from two of the AOCs between 2010 and 2012. They found these birds immune suppressed between 51 and 57% compared to reference area birds in a cleaner northern Lake Huron region (Grasman *et al.* 2013). In the 20 years since his original work there was negligible improvement of immune competence in these species.

The Great Lakes will not regain either its predator diversity or its historic stability until these substances are virtually gone. Perhaps this will happen in a century if we continue to ignore the problem of highly contaminated sediments and there is worldwide action to control the existing uses in the third world as well as the developed nations. If we want to achieve recovery sooner, then we have to clean up the worst sources of contaminated sediments in the AOCs and we must negotiate a worldwide ban on these substances. It is that simple. The environmentalist mantra has been to *'Think globally, but act locally.'* We must change that to *'Think and act globally and locally.'* if we are ever to get control of synthetic POPs contaminants and their substitutes.

JAMES P. LUDWIG, Ph.D

It would be wonderful to be able to report that the governments of developing nations have assimilated the clear lessons provided by the Great Lakes experience, Barry Commoner and Rachael Carson, but they have not. Progress has been inconsistent in North America and absolutely abysmal in developing nations. Essentially, the horrid toxicological picture for the Great Lakes was completely known to the federal, provincial and state parties based on sound, peer-reviewed science well over twenty years ago (McKinney *et al.* 1985; Peterson *et al.* 1989; McFarland and Clarke 1989; Safe 1990; IJC 1991a; Birnbaum 1993). We knew the fundamental truths about bioconcentration and bioaccumulation five decades ago (Commoner 1968). We knew that all dioxin-like substances used the same intracellular and metabolic mechanisms and processes to elicit damage to individuals and populations 25 years ago (McKinney et al. 1985, Safe, 1990). Yet, even with all those data and verified knowledge, governments still refused to consider and address the horrid implications.

While there are very large differences in the sensitivities of exposed vertebrate species, ultimately all vertebrates react the same way (Peterson *et al.* 1991, Birnbaum 1993). Only the threshold concentration where effects begin is different for different species (Schecter 1994; Giesy *et al.* 1994d, Karcher *et al.* 2006). This has been common verified knowledge in the scientific community for more than two decades, fully understood by every regulatory agency in North America and the European Union. One might expect the rational response was to ban the manufacture and use all substances that are dioxin-like (MacKay and Gilbertson 1990). Did that happen? No. Instead, governments have allowed industries to play the game of substitution of different chemical families with the same toxicological properties for those banned only because the public was once aroused. Some industries have even encouraged resurrection of the use of banned toxic substances, like DDT for malarial mosquito control, under those neoliberal governments that have dominated politics recently (Gilbertson and Watterson 2007).

Consider the problem plastics manufacturers face. Most plastic polymers are naturally brittle at ambient temperatures. Polymers of many plastics are mixed with diaromatic chemicals to give them impact-resistance and flexibility. For four decades that was one large use of PCBs. If you are my age and kissed your first date when seated on the plastic seat covers of your dad's 1957 Chevy, regardless what else you were doing, your butts were caressed by plastic seat covers kept flexible with PCBs until those additives evaporated and the seats cracked. Hundreds of products incorporated PCBs. When PCBs were banned in 1978, plastics and other synthetic petrochemical product makers faced a huge problem. Many simply turned to other halogenated diaromatic compounds that had the same desired material properties and dioxin-like effects. These included the halogenated diphenyl toluenes, diphenyl ethers and other non-diaromatic compounds such as pthalates with endocrine disruption properties (Murk *et al.* 1991; Thomas and Colborn 1993). When the diphenyl toluenes were exposed as dioxin-like with effects identical to dioxins and PCBs in the late 1980s, the diphenyl ethers entered the picture—first as the chlorinated congeners, then as the brominated congeners.

In 1986 the polybrominated diphenyl ethers (PBDEs) in herring gull eggs from the Beaver Islands archipelago were present at trace levels of <0.014 ppm. In 2005 they were present at 2.1 ppm. Over the same two-decade period the total PCBs in gull eggs from the same site dropped from about 8.3 to 5.6 ppm as Lake Michigan approached the steady state of lake waters in equilibrium with the air. *In essence, in 20 years all that happened was to replace one legacy toxicant class with a new toxicant class with the same effects on wildlife and people.* In fact, the PBDEs might even be worse than PCBs because they seem to have even greater thyroid-toxic effects on vertebrates.

Most products imported by Canada and the United States are not tested dioxin-like or endocrine-disrupting substances. In fact, WTO regulations discourage vetting of value-added manufactured products for toxicants as a hindrance to commerce. The average cellphone imported to the US in 2006 from Asia had 3% by weight of PBDEs in its plastic and electronic parts! If you have dropped your cellphone, inadvertently stepped on it or thrown the damn thing at the wall you already know how hard it is to break those plastic parts. It is the PBDE or other halogenated additives to the plastic that accounts for the great impact resistance.

The problem of substitutions is huge, impacting aquatic communities far beyond the Great Lakes. Recently, PBDE contamination in bottlenose

JAMES P. LUDWIG, Ph.D

dolphins from the Charleston, South Carolina harbor and open waters of the Florida coast were compared. Massive quantities of PBDEs were found, exceeding even the legacy total PCB concentrations, in dolphins from Charleston. Pat Fair correlated PBDE concentrations to very poor health status of the Charleston harbor dolphins that carried three to six times more PBDEs than coastal Florida animals (Fair *et al.* 2007). Recently, I reviewed data on bald eagle eggs and fostered chicks from the Delaware River in western New Jersey in 2004 and found similar increases of PBDEs in that predator (Unpublished New Jersey DEP data).

Finally, we must consider the most recent layer of instability layered onto the lakes in the form of the near simultaneous invasion of the mussels and gobies. Gobies are interesting fish. Gobies lack a swim bladder and are essentially confined to the bottom-feeding niche, sharing this habitat with the carp, native suckers, and the elegant darters and sculpins. The native sculpins and darters once transferred benthic energy to upper level predators like trout, walleye, small-mouthed bass. The gobies compete with these native species and replaced them in most Great Lakes waters, especially where cobbles and rocks provide cover (Reid and Mandrak 2008). Only the (abyssal) deepwater sculpins may be relatively safe from goby competition, but even that is far from certain.

Gobies have become most of the fish biomass in this niche, relegating sculpins, darters and many native fishes to insignificance in most coastal areas. Some fisheries biologists wonder if predators can eat gobies fast enough to control their populations. One reason for their exceptional success is in the ability to utilize resources and energy associated with the pseudofeces of the invasive zebra and quagga mussels that native species are ill-adapted to use. Both the gobies and mussels came to the Great Lakes in ballast waters taken in by ships in the Black and Caspian Seas; obviously, they coevolved in Eurasia.

These mussels are quite amazing filter-feeding creatures. The Saginaw Bay population has been estimated to filter half of the water volume of the bay every day. In 1988 before the arrival of the mussels, outer Saginaw Bay water clarity measured by secchi disc was generally about 1-2 meters. By 1998 water clarity had increased the readings to 7-9 meters. Increased water clarity allows the penetration of light to the bottom. Where the water is shallow enough this has led to the explosive growth of surface-attached algae like *Cladophora*. The clams also produce a partially digested waste called pseudofeces as they discriminate between green and blue-green algae. They divert the less digestible, potentially toxic, blue-green algae into their fecal waste without digestion. The undigested blue-greens are excreted as a semisolid that drops to the bottom. This provides an immense rain of food and nutrients (and blue-green toxins) to the upper layers of the benthos. This also deprives the mid-water zooplankton of access to their traditional food of green algae. There is much evidence emerging that type E botulism toxin develops in live gobies, but I believe a link to the toxins of the blue-greens dropped into their habitat in pseudofeces will be found soon (Murphy 2001). Gobies appear to develop the botulism toxin while still alive (USEPA 2008). That could be owing to paralysis of their digestive tracts by blue-green toxins that allows the *Clostridium botulinum* Type E bacteria to grow in anaerobic conditions inside the dying fish. A similar condition often develops in the intestines of elderly humans infected with *Clostridium difficle,* a closely-related bacterium, that grows in damaged human intestines poorly supplied by oxygenated blood.

Moribund gobies are captured by loons, cormorants and other water birds and acquire a fatal dose of the botulism toxin. Since 1998 there have bird mortalities in most years linked to type E botulism in eastern and northern Lake Michigan, Georgian Bay, Saginaw Bay, central and western Lake Erie and eastern Lake Ontario. These botulism outbreaks were preceded or coincident with blue-green algal blooms (Becker *et al.* 2006). Often *Cladophora* was present as well in the substrate, encouraged by the rain of pseudofeces and improved water clarity. In the decade of 1998-2007, an estimated 70,000 birds, including 20,000 common loons and even federally-endangered piping plovers, were killed on the Great Lakes (USEPA, 2008).

Blue-greens produce many toxins of two basic types (Boyer 2006). There are bioaccumulative hepatotoxins, including microcystin, that cause organ failure. Sublethal doses may be acquired over several weeks of moderate exposure until a lethal dose is accumulated. Then, liver failure follows. Microcystin is dangerous to humans above one part per billion in drinking water. Concentrations above 1 ppb have been detected in the open waters of western Lake Erie and eastern Lake Ontario in August and September at the end of blue-green blooms since 1999. Some of this water is drawn for municipal water supplies. Keith Grasman (*pers. comm.*) detected microcystin in freshly killed Caspian tern chicks in a Saginaw Bay colony in 2011.

Neurotoxins are produced by some blue greens (e.g. *Anabena* sp.), dangerous at the part per trillion (ppt) concentrations in drinking water (Boyer 2006). Fortunately, these 'super-toxins' are broken quickly, probably by exposure to ultraviolet light. Although there are no known human deaths from these neurotoxins in the Great Lakes, large dogs (>35 kg) were killed by a blue-green algal neurotoxin in Lake Champlain in 2001 (Watzin *et al.* 2006). One of a dozen children sickened by direct exposure during swimming in an inland Wisconsin lake with a blue-green bloom in 2005 died. Humans in many African and Asian third world nations only have access to blue-green infested drinking water. The World Health Organization reports thousands are sickened and many die every year.

Although blue-greens have been present in the Great Lakes for decades (probably centuries), their previous emergence as toxic threats was only briefly during the period of hyper-eutrophication of the 1960s and 1970s in harbors, river mouths and bays. But, since 1998 the invasive mussels and climate change (warming) have created the right conditions for regular annual blooms. The most interesting change is the shift towards a general threat to all Great Lakes wildlife from an historic problem that was once associated specifically with the hyper-eutrophication of a few vulnerable bay areas (Boyer 2006). Historically, these blooms were common only in hyper-productive shallow bays where a major river (e.g. the Saginaw or Maumee Rivers) supplied water rich in available phosphorus and nitrogen; today, whole lakes are threatened.

It is likely these regular blue-green blooms and the invasions of typically southern blue-green species will add new species to the toxic algae already here, even new toxins never before seen in Great Lakes biota. For example, eagles and coots are killed by a blue-green toxin developed by a novel algal species that grows on the underside leaves of an alien floating water plant species in reservoirs of southern states that never freeze over. Mortalities became common in South Carolina, Arkansas and Georgia in the last two decades (Birrenkott *et al.* 2004) from avian vacoular myelinopathy (AVM). This neurotoxin causes degeneration of substantial parts of the cerebral cortex of afflicted birds leading to their death. We ought not be surprised if AVM or some other blue-green toxin initiates new fish and wildlife mortalities soon in the Great Lakes.

What these toxins mean for humans remains to be seen, but they will not be beneficial. It is even possible the blue-green toxins will emerge as a chronic threat to domestic water supplies pumped from the lakes. Worse, they could appear in fish, rendering them dangerous for human consumption. As climate change warms the lakes, penetration into the Great Lakes watershed of southerly-distributed toxic algae seems inevitable. Because these species produce fast-killing toxins, they could become more acute threats than the dioxin-like chemicals that have caused chronic problems for decades.

The pattern of global climate change with continental warming will also allow a host of household and agricultural pests to survive that annual freezing to sub-zero F (<-18° C) has killed previously. Historic winter climates prevented disease outbreaks in animals and humans and the penetration of the region by many non-native plants and animals. Among the alien pests that should be expected to arrive are the vine kudzu, at least three more mosquito species capable of transmitting both malaria and eastern equine encephalitis virus and other human and domestic animal disease agents. Some species, like the dreaded southern chiggers, are likely to be only profound aggravations. Others will transmit human, domestic animal and wildlife diseases readily.

Finally, warmer waters, especially lakes without ice cover in winter, have much greater evaporation than iced-over or cold lakes. This means much greater water losses than have been occurred since settlement. It is far from clear that greater precipitation will make up for losses. Climate change models predict a slight decline in precipitation for the watershed, but greatly increased evaporative water losses. In 2012, Lakes Huron and Michigan have experienced their all-time lows of water levels and the region was very droughty, harbingers of things to come.

Hard choices on the consumption, export and discharge rates of Great lakes waters are on the horizon. The largesse of Great Lakes fresh waters in the midst of a hotter and drier continental climate will trigger regional political conflicts; to some extent, it already has. One response is the intergovernmental Compact agreement to restrict all water exports from the basin. Low lake levels could force the expenditure of large sums to dredge harbors and connecting channels, effectively removing options for clean-ups of contaminated sediments or other beneficial management strategies too.

Clearly, the stressors acting on these lakes have never been so severe, complex and as far out of our control as they are today. The governments dominated by their *lassiez-faire*, market-driven ideologies have failed to protect the resources and people of the Great Lakes region miserably. We are facing a time when a large number of very bad trends that aggravate the deleterious effects of each other are coming together—a sort of *perfect ecological storm* for the Great Lakes. We had best find the courage to face them now before the passage of time makes the condition of our Sweetwater Seas much worse, maybe even unmanageable. It is far from clear that our two governments are guided with intelligence policies or persons committed to do what must be done.

The lessons of this history should be crystal clear. If our neoliberal governments allow these dioxin-like compounds into manufactured products we import through 'free trade', regardless of what we do here, these chemicals will escape into our water resources, wildlife and us in North America. It is as simple as that. No amount of temporizing, prevarication or litigation under NAFTA, the WTO or any other body operating to promote international trade will change this fact. Sadly, this situation has been allowed to persist for many years under the political-economic philosophy of minimal government, *lassiez-faire* economics, free trade agreements, and the privatization of traditional government roles for private profit. It has been 'Just let the market take care of it. *Wink, wink*: technically they're not PCBs or another class of banned substances, so just go ahead and use them. We won't regulate against their use until we are forced to do that.' Al Gore put it this way *"The private foxes have been put in charge of the public henhouses."* (Gore 2007). If we want our hens to lay clean healthful eggs, then we have to evict the neoliberal foxes from our henhouses forever. And, we must never forget that the precautionary principle is utter anathema to North American neoliberal governments with their free trade, minimal regulation philosophies.

A good case can be made for the supposition that this pattern of deception grew a robust taproot in the promises of Newt Gingrich's 'Contract for America' initiated with the 1994 US elections with the *de facto* concurrence of the administrations of John Chretien in Canada and Bill Clinton in the US. Many of the US scientific community witnessed in helpless frustration the utter emasculation of the USEPA and Department of the Interior after 1994, delayed slightly in the Clinton years and completed viciously under George W. Bush (Gore *op. cit.*). Coincident reductions of funding and muzzling of government scientists in Canada occurred (Chopra 2009) and continues robustly under the 'Harper Government'. And, of course, the pattern of political control of scientific findings was abetted in the Great Lakes region by the muzzling of public participation in the International Joint Commission activities, the SOLEC diversions and a default to "the ecosystem approach". This is not new: but, rarely has it been so pervasive or damaging to the commonweal.

The two-decade long pattern of callous substitution of one family of the dioxin-like chemicals for another without regard to effects and impacts is one of the prominent and important legacies of those elections, bureaucratic decisions and what can only be called intellectual corruption. An identical pattern of avoidance and obfuscation has surrounded all attempts to control invasive species. The failure of the parties to address legacy contamination and invasive species is rooted in, and nourished by, neoliberalism, plain and simple. It is the exact outcome the TEA party in the US and Conservatives in Canada aspire to by demands for small government, poor regulation and minimal taxes.

At this time, one can only hope that the 2008 and 2012 repudiation of the Republicans in the US means a turn toward environmental sanity. It is remotely possible a more liberal president with the mindset of community organizations for the commonweal will mean genuine change. Unfortunately, Canada has also fallen into the neoliberal quagmire by the election of Conservative governments. Our politicians must be forced to understand the need to face these issues head-on, and to change policies that allowed chemical substitutions and alien species invasions to continue for so long, unregulated and obscured by the bureaucracies of governments themselves. Not the Great Lakes, nor the Arctic, our coastal marine habitats or even the immense oceans can tolerate more avoidance of BWT obligations. It is a form of ecological insanity that will complete the destruction of the lakes for the foreseeable future unless reversed. Reversal will require money, re-regulation of industry and commerce and extensive restructuring of the agencies that are supposed to protect the commonweal and these lakes. Politicians in both nations must be forced to support these changes or replaced. It is as simple as that.

V.

Are Great Lakes Water Quality Agreements Substantial or Illusions?

CLEARLY, THE GREAT Lakes now face the most uncertain and dangerous circumstances of their history. Wise and informed leaders with ecological knowledge, committed to change free-market policies of neglect, passivity and deception towards these resources are required if we are to reverse the damage. Sadly, this species of politician and agency administrator became as rare as the black tern in the last three decades as tax cuts and deftly avoided responsibilities were the usual strategies. But, today as we enter the last term of a liberal American president with commitments to community-based approaches to governance, I sense a tiny rekindling of hope for the Great Lakes last felt genuinely in 1972 with the signing of the first Great Lakes Water Quality Agreement. I want to give the man a chance to lead both nations toward better policy.

On the Canadian side, the current prospects for enlightened leadership are as dismal as the lakes' conditions with an ultra-conservative government in power led by western Canadians with no appreciation for the value of fresh water lakes. Canadians of the Great Lakes region suffer under a government abysmally ignorant of Great Lakes issues, disinclined to act to protect or spend public monies on natural resources, openly hostile to addressing climate change (as the 2012 withdrawal from the Kyoto Protocol showed), and fearful of any science and basic research on fresh water (as the defunding of the 30-year old experimental lakes program confirmed in 2013). Perhaps worst of all is their penchant to discredit their own scientists whenever new findings fail to conform to their doctrinaire neoliberalism or implicate unregulated businesses for ecological damage.

Modern neoliberal governments emerged from the Chicago School of Economics led by Milton Freidman over forty years ago. Substantially, these intellectuals espoused four central tenets of their vision for government. Government should be as small as possible (shared with libertarians); economic growth depends on tax cuts for the investing classes and businesses; regulation and interference of business and industry should be as small as possible; and, the path to prosperity lies with maximizing individual rights at the expense of collective rights which led to rampant privatization of public resources and destruction of labor unions. Moreover, free trade agreements under NAFTA and the WTO have exacerbated these changes by outsourcing manufacturing leading to fewer jobs and lower wages for many North Americans. These ideas gained credence in the late 1960s, largely as a reaction to Lyndon Johnson's Great Society, Pierre Trudeau's social policies and strong labor unions. Like an open wound, neoliberalism festered throughout the late 1970s, emerging full-blown in the culture of North American nations with vigorous endorsement from the Reagan and Mulroney administrations of the early 1980s, then continuing apace in all subsequent administrations of both countries.

These four principles of neoliberalism dominated political discourse as the decay of the Great Lakes accelerated rapidly. Neoliberalism reinforced the cult of individualism that soon impaired community organizations and NGOs with their sense of shared purpose. The vision of preserving healthy shared resources for the commonweal was relegated to a minor concern by most North Americans; many simply believed the lakes were not connected to them or relevant. Neoliberalism is consistent with American individualism, but much less so with the Canadian view of community and shared responsibility (Adams 2003). It is easy to see how these principles drove and supported the policies that led the world to the brink of economic disaster in 2008. But, this acute economic disaster has a quieter sibling in the ecological damage done to the Great Lakes, albeit far less dramatically, but with creeping insidious effects for the last four decades.

In the last decade there was considerable talk of renegotiation of the BWT or the GLWQA. The IJC, utilizing the resources of GLNPO, conducted a lengthy public review of the agreement in 2005; more than 4,100 people from the public participated. The resulting report revealed just how far the IJC and federal agencies have strayed from the specific numerical criteria and virtual elimination tenets of the GLWQA, even to ignoring their mandates under the law. The second and seventh bullet points of the executive summary illustrates the pernicious impacts of the ecosystem approach where good intentions and noble rhetoric displaced specific goals and criteria, to wit:

- *"Participants demanded good water quality and said it is essential to ensure a healthy future for the lakes and the socio-economic well-being of the basin's residents and their communities."*

- *"There was a great deal of comment on the lack of progress toward delisting and restoring beneficial uses in Areas of Concern, as well as the need to reinvigorate Remedial Action Plans."* (IJC 2006).

It is especially interesting to read this report and look for evidence of attempts to meet specific numerical criteria of the GLWQA that would move toward the larger goal of virtual elimination of toxicant substances or more stringent controls on nutrients. Instead, the report is replete with feel-good phrases like 'good water quality', 'lack of progress', 'hold governments accountable for achieving their Agreement commitments', etc., *ad nauseam*. Incredibly, the section on contaminated sediments failed explicitly to recognize the presence of dioxin-like substances and POPs as long-term problems! Clearly, the parties changed the subject so as not to pay the piper for the damage. It is that simple. One disillusioned participant commented:

> *'The underlying cause* (of lack of progress towards restoring AOCs) *is money. Governments cannot allocate the large sums needed for remediation over long enough periods to assign competent people to do the task at hand. . . . In our RAP it took forever to decide whether to dredge, then where to dredge to what* (clean-up) *concentration, and then how to dredge, only to decide not to dredge. . . . Public and political awareness of priorities for what needs to be done is lost.'*

In my experience, the frustration and bitter disappointment of this person is all too typical when the parties failed to meet their agreed commitments to move toward virtual elimination by adhering to specific cleanup criteria. The parties have failed to address contaminants and virtually every other important issue covered by the GLWQA, almost without exception. In societies dominated by the philosophy of cutting taxes and minimizing the size of government, programs that address pollutants externalized to the lakes simply are never well funded. The commonweal is damaged inexorably, until natural systems like the Great Lakes are threatened with collapse, just as they are today.

Perhaps the most amazing aspect of public concern is that anyone still participates in public review processes given the dismal record of failures and recalcitrance of agencies to implement the GLWQA. Regardless, NGOs continued to push for a renegotiation of the agreement believing that a revised agreement will solve the problem of the parties' failure to implement it. Most members of NGOs failed to connect the failures to implement existing agreements to the politics of neoliberalism and the vague feel-good nature of the ecosystem approach. The following letter was sent to both leaders under the signatures of representatives of 54 NGOs, just before the recent February 19, 2009 meeting of President Obama and Prime Minister Harper:

'Dear Prime Minister Harper and President Obama:

In a few days, the two of you will meet in Ottawa to discuss topics of deep concern to both the United States and Canada. Our two great democracies have a long-standing tradition of dialogue, respect and cooperation. This has sustained peace and prosperity and enhanced the security and quality of life for people from Canada and the U.S. alike. As you grapple with today's significant challenges, we look forward to a continued spirit of bi-national partnership—especially in the areas of economic recovery and environmental leadership.

Since 1972, the *Great Lakes Water Quality Agreement* has played an important role in shaping strategies of both our nations to protect and restore the freshwater wonder we hold in common: the Great Lakes. At your meeting on February 19th, we urge you to commit your leadership, and that of our nations, to renewed efforts to meet our shared commitments under the Agreement, and to forge a revitalized Agreement that will address the challenges of the 21st century.

As you discuss the economic challenges of our nations, the future of the Great Lakes is centrally important in this discussion. Protection and restoration of these waters benefits numerous economic drivers for both nations.

We need to reinvigorate efforts in both nations to safeguard this resource at a time when the Great Lakes are beleaguered by invasive species, old pollution languishing in harbor bottoms, new chemical pollution, habitat loss, the return of dead zones, impacts of climate change and other threats. Such threats limit the economic potential of the region, which is of fundamental importance to employment and wealth generation for both nations.

A thriving Great Lakes system nurtures our shared economy and enhances our nations' cooperative relationships. A revitalized *Great Lakes Water Quality Agreement* will provide a new framework and platform to help achieve our shared goals. We seek your commitments to move forward with Agreement deliberations through a serious and concerted effort that will address the challenge of Great Lakes protection and restoration in the 21st century.

In particular, we ask that the joint communiqué at the conclusion of your February 19, 2009 meeting include the following commitments:

- To formally state, beginning this year, a revitalization and revision of the *Great Lakes Water Quality Agreement* will be undertaken within the context of 21st century challenges; and,

- To involve the Great Lakes public in the decision-making process around revising the concepts and language in the Agreement, including purpose, scope and public involvement.

JAMES P. LUDWIG, Ph.D

Thank you for your consideration. We look forward to a successful meeting next week, and to working with your administrations to renew and strengthen our Agreement to protect and restore the Great Lakes.

A short background paper with additional information about the *Great Lakes Water Quality Agreement* is attached.

Sincerely,

Signatories from 54 Non-Governmental Organizations'

While there is not a single thing to disagree with in this heartfelt plea for responsible management of the Great Lakes, I am left with a great sense of sadness by the obvious naiveté of the many good people who contributed to this effort. The letter shows public support to do restoration to achieve Great Lakes renewal, and a competent grasp of the ecological issues. But, it links the deleterious changes to 21st century conditions as if the original GLWQA did not commit to remediate or prevent the deleterious changes that happened in the thirty-seven years after it was negotiated and signed by the parties in 1972! This plea overlooked the rotten core of the problem—neoliberal governments.

In truth, the original GLWQA did identify and commit to address almost everything in the letter that is requested in previous versions. The problem was delivery of the management required under the GLWQA by the many fractured agencies of governments that were chronically underfunded, and had their missions sabotaged or diverted from GLWQA commitments. By default to the ecosystem approach that shies away from delivering real change measurable against specific goals and criteria, very little was accomplished for the last three decades. After substantial phosphorus reductions were achieved in the 1970s, virtually nothing of real substance was accomplished. We must ask why was so little accomplished, how did these failures occur, and who were beneficiaries of the persistent unwillingness to enforce the GLWQA? Until, and unless, the public and NGOs make a connection to the pernicious nature of the political neoliberalism of the last 40 years and its starvation of the government agencies assigned to deliver the GLWQA, the recent renegotiation will accomplish absolutely nothing but rhetorical flourishes and 'photo-ops' for politicians. The GLWQA was never deficient; rather, it was the abject failure of the governments to deliver consistent effort toward improvements committed to in the 1972, 1978 and 1987 versions of the GLWQA that led to the inexorable decay of the lakes.

Further, the laws of ecology will not change in deference to the neoliberal politics or the nebulous ecosystem approach. Limiting factors are limiting factors. Bioconcentration, evaporation and sediment sequestration are real processes and will be forever. Increased nutrient budgets will contribute to eutrophication. Invasive species and legacy contamination will continue to cause incredible damage to native species and food webs. And critically, if neoliberalism in its most dangerous current manifestations— called the Tea Party Movement in the US and the Conservative Party in Canada—continue to emasculate public agency budgets and dominate the politics of the parties, then a renegotiation of the GLWQA could only be utterly useless. This exercise only wasted limited resources of agencies and will leave the public even more frustrated. Agencies will not deliver improved management until there are fundamental changes of political attitudes, the structure of agencies in both nations and re-regulation by enforcing standards.

There are profound dangers in reopening either the BWT or GLWQA agreement if the intent is only to sign a vague ecosystem agreement in lieu of a commitment to address and remediate damages to real and measurable standards (Gilbertson 2007). *At least we had in place an unfulfilled treaty commitment in article 4 of the BWT to address damages.* That commitment to be responsible for damage caused to the shared resources of the Great Lakes must persist forever between the two nations, even it takes a very long time to be implemented.

What is needed is a genuine commitment with a plan, a timetable for implementation and funds to do exactly what the Boundary Waters Treaty required i.e. to remediate damages already allowed, or caused by, the parties to the shared resources, especially when these have led to injuries to health and property. That can be accomplished only by clean-ups to measurable criteria and strict controls on invasive species. Sympathetic language does not address criteria. When assigned to

JAMES P. LUDWIG, Ph.D

governments with fragmented structures and unclear objectives, those agencies with noble names avoided the hard work and large expense of addressing long-standing problems. Worse, when these factors coincided with agency leaders striving to be consistent with neoliberalism that favors corporations outsourcing of externalized costs to the environment rather than addressing their mandates, failure to protect the Great Lakes was one inevitable outcome (Gore, 2007; Chopra, 2009).

Over the last four decades, some agency attempts to avoid responsibilities have been plainly illegal. For example, Alexander (2009) has documented the egregious decision of the USEPA to transfer control of ballast waters to the US Coast Guard in 1973, a decision that resonates forcefully today. Had the EPA done its assigned duty under the Clean Water Act forty years ago, it is very likely the spiny water flea, gobies and the mussels would not have arrived as biological pollution to the lakes.

However, there could have been advantages to reopening the GLWQA provided the subjects open for renegotiation were identified explicitly in advance. Substantially, there were three aspects that could have been renegotiated to the advantage of both nations including: 1.) The institutional arrangements within each nation and those shared in common (e.g. the IJC and GLFC), with a commitment to encourage and restore open and transparent public participation; 2.) The means and formulae for funding rehabilitation programs and a shared court with the authority to adjudicate disputes; and, 3.) Developing a new science agency to select long-term monitoring, research and targeted programs that address Great Lakes issues through sound science. Sadly, these critical steps were never considered, either by agencies of the parties or the NGOs.

The failed institutions of the present include the Great Lakes Fishery Commission unable to cope with the combination of contaminants, new invasive species and a resurgent lamprey population; an emasculated International Joint Commission with only advisory authority bent on support for the fuzzy-headed ecosystem approach in lieu of numerical criteria for clean-ups; and, ineffective, haphazardly operated and chronically under funded regulatory and science agencies in both nations. The institutions of governments supposed to protect the Great Lakes are an accurate reflection of forty years of recurrent conflict between political parties in both nations racing one another to embrace neoliberal philosophies since the GLWQA of 1972 was signed, the 1978 and 1987 codicils were negotiated, and the agreement renegotiated in 2012.

Smaller government and starvation of agency budgets really began under the auspices of the Reagan and Mulroney Administrations and have continued apace for the last three decades. Most agencies responded to their political masters, operating to minimize public input to programs because public criticisms translate to votes for the other guys in the next election. From my perspective, the primary blame for inaction can be tracked right back to three nefarious tactics. First, restricting public involvement was a keystone in a larger strategy of doing as little as the governments in power can get away with and still get reelected. Second was the vague ecosystem approach allowing agencies to avoid enforcing criteria through effective regulations. Third, was the appointment of persons to head agencies that would force the missions of their agencies to be consistent with the principles of neoliberalism instead of acting to adhere to the GLWQA and BWT.

When challenged, the usual reaction of agencies and politicians alike is to claim the public purse is too depleted to pay for what should be done. However, given the hidden costs of delay addressing chronic problems, many inadequate maintenance or avoided restoration programs end up depressing property values in the AOCs. Ultimately, this strategy costs the public far more than clean-ups (Braden *et al.* 2008a, 2008b). For example, when contaminated sediment clean-ups are avoided for harbors and rivers, the governments have to spend huge sums to contain the relatively dilute, but still contaminated, dredged materials inside of confined disposal facilities (CDFs). Usually, CDFs were sited in adjacent wetlands, on artificial islands or fill areas on the shore of harbors and rivers. Then, vast quantities of modestly contaminated sediments are treated as hazardous wastes, held in an aquatic hazardous waste dump.

These CDFs are kept off-limits to all future beneficial uses. *The consumption of land, wetlands or lake bottom for these purposes has a very large and essentially hidden cost never recognized by the parties. One prominent aspect of these legacy externalized costs is depressed private property values in the AOC; a second are the impacts on human health (Gilbertson and Brophy 2001) or wildlife health Grasman et al. 2013).* In this example, there are often year-to-year costs in wildlife deaths or lost habitat for fisheries that are never quantified or recognized, such as the recurrent type C botulism kills of 500 or more ducks and migratory shorebirds every fall at the CDF in Cleveland for a decade (Simmers *et al.* 1990). Furthermore, Cleveland's CDF was by no means the only dredge disposal site with this problem. Alternatively, dredged sediments could be size-sorted and the sand fraction (typically the greatest fraction of river, harbor and connecting channel sediments requiring dredging) sold for reuse while only the hyper-contaminated fine fraction is treated as concentrated hazardous waste.

I suspect if all the hidden costs of refusals to clean-up persistent contaminated sediment problems were identified explicitly and tallied, those costs would exceed by far the outlay required to fix these problems at the root cause. Muir and Zegarac (2001) looked at the cumulative costs of four disease conditions with confirmed correlations to contaminants (diabetes, Parkinsonism, neurodevelopmental effects and hypothyroidism). *They estimated these morbidities cost the two nations between 568 and 793 billion dollars (USD 1999) of health care in the US and Canada annually.* These costs are transferred to the medical care systems of the parties and contribute to the health care crises of both nations, but especially in the US that treats medical care as a personal responsibility in a neoliberal free market for medical services. Many agencies have a vested interest in never addressing root causes because they were established to treat only the symptoms of these externalized problems, not the root causes. This is rather like the old medical school joke explaining why students should go into dermatology. By treating the only symptoms of skin diseases with salves and unguents, their patients never die, and they will never get cured; they become a perfect source of steady income! One must ask is that the same *modus operandi* for full time equivalents in an agency?

The entire US dredging industry as overseen by the US Army Corps of Engineers is very close to this. For, if USACE treats only the symptoms of contaminated sediments, the problem must be 'remediated' again and again. And that is precisely what the Corps does. If one wishes to dispose of huge volumes of unsorted moderately-contaminated sediments, the engineered CDF is the way it has been done. To no one's surprise, the Corps does that very well—again and again and again *ad nauseum* as rivers transport more sediments from upstream contaminated sites to harbors.

A comparison with how the Dutch handle their problem of contaminated sediments in the Rhine River reveals how bankrupt the USACE strategy is. Their Rhine River was even more severely contaminated than the Fox River entering Green Bay, the Saginaw River entering Lake Huron, the Detroit River above Lake Erie or Canada's Hamilton Harbor. Metal residues of thousands of years of human occupancy, ravages of two world wars and rapid reindustrialization after WWII with rampant use of PCBs, PCDTs, PBDEs and many other dioxin-like chemicals provide a steady supply of highly contaminated sediments to the Dutch-controlled lower reach of the Rhine. But, the Dutch have no place to put huge quantities of contaminated sediments. Instead of building a set of immense CDFs, the Dutch adapted the mining technology of water pressure-driven centrifugation called the hydrocyclone. Using this technology, they size sort the grossly contaminated fine organic silt and clay fraction from the clean sand reducing the volume of highly contaminated material to the minimum (~9% by volume). They create a cleaned coarse fraction (~91% by volume) reused safely in construction, road and dike building and only have to contain about $1/10^{th}$ of the gross volume of contaminated dredgings they handle.

Most interesting is that the USACE actually experimented with this technology at the Saginaw Bay CDF in 1990-1991; they concentrated the contaminated sediment fraction into about 10% of the volume and recovered a clean sand fraction using a relatively unsophisticated 1970s era mining hydrocyclone. However, they never pursued the technology after an internal audit concluded it would be uneconomic for the private contractors they hire for dredging to reengineer their vessels and equipment to hydrocyclone sort the contaminated Great Lakes sediments. The hydrocyclone project had a quiet burial because the Corps was unwilling to insist on it and get the extra funding from Congress because that would have increased private sector costs.

Of course, the fact the long-term use of this technology would mean far fewer CDFs, less design work and fewer positions for the USACE obviously played no role whatsoever in their decision not to adopt this effective solution for handling the contaminated sediments in US Great

Lakes AOCs. Now, if you believe that, please contact me immediately: I would like to offer you title to a large bridge between Mackinaw City and St. Ignace for pennies on the dollar! The truth is much simpler. Many natural resource agency decisions are not based on logic, science or accurate cost-benefit analyses if the agency's employees have a vested interest. If a correct decision to protect resources will reduce agency jobs, lessen their authority, or bring critical public review to the agency, then that agency is most unlikely to do what is right for the resources they ostensibly protect. For an agency leader to follow this path, that leader must be willing to risk their career. I watched that happen to Howard Tanner of the Michigan DNR in 1983 when he made decisions for the publicly-owned resources of Michigan ahead of his career. He was 'replaced' within six months. Sadly for the resources of the Great Lakes, that deleterious aspect of human nature flourishes in virtually all government-funded agencies on both sides of the border.

The USACE dredging example applies to a polluted habitat. Does this occur with those charged to protect and enhance the resources themselves? Here the record is far more mixed and fraught with genuine disputes over resource values. For example, the various incarnations of fisheries agencies in the federal, state and provincial governments over the last five decades have seen their role to promote the interests of commercial and sport fisherman as the highest, and sometimes the only, priority. Fishery agencies have planted various fish species, conserved many native fish stocks in hatcheries, attempting valiantly to restore those stocks, especially lake trout, introduced salmonids and walleye. They deserve great credit for those diligent efforts. At the state and provincial level, their roles were compromised by license sales that generated huge revenues for those same fishery resource agencies. And, if there is one thing the public using the sweetwater seas loves to do, it is to fish. If they can catch fish, especially big fish that taste good, licenses are the least costly item members of the public will buy to support their fishing habits. Sport fishing is very big business.

On the surface, the legendary work of Howard Tanner, Wayne Tody and others in the Michigan DNR to establish the Great Lakes salmon planting programs would appear to be a smashing success—equivalent to a new rock and roll band selling a million copies of their first album. But, rather like Jim Morrison and The Doors, there was a very dark side to this economic miracle. Certainly, the initial exceptional growth of the planted Coho, king and Chinook salmon and the wild elation of successful fishermen were wonderful to behold. Many acted like their team had won a sports championship when they landed record catches after decades of dismal sport fishing.

In the mid-1970s when the planted salmon took off and a different pollution-tolerant subspecies of walleye recovered in Lake Erie, the positive effect on economies of Great Lakes states and Ontario was immense. Boat manufacturers, marina operators, hotels, motels and any business supplying or servicing sport fishers thrived, even through the severe economic downturn of 1978-1982. A whole industry developed of guides, retired and near-retired persons taking people fishing. But, the planted species and stocks, especially lake trout and introduced salmonids, were very slow to build successful reproducing populations that replaced themselves. But, annual plantings produced in a large fish hatchery infrastructure at all levels of government supplied the fish, ensuring a high level of public support.

In most states and provinces, the revenue of license sales and taxes paid on fishing equipment balanced or exceeded hatchery costs. In the mid-1980s, although there were chronic problems, especially an aging and inadequate hatchery system and inexplicable metabolic problems with the fish themselves (possibly related to thiaminase in alewives), virtually no one questioned the wisdom and success of the salmon introductions. I took no issue with the decision to plant the salmon in the late 1960s because I thought it could reestablish an effective predator-prey system. Lampreys were yielding to control by TFM and electric weirs, and the totals of most known contaminants were falling. And, like everyone else, the effects of the dioxin-like contaminants on lake trout and other salmonid fishes, were unknown to me.

The dark side emerged inexorably. First, scientists like Mike Mac of USFWS, Richard Peterson with Mary Walker at the University of Wisconsin and John Giesy at Michigan State found the extreme sensitivity of many salmonids to the dioxin-like contaminants. The Lake Michigan Lake trout sampled in 1987-1988 laid eggs that either failed to hatch, produced larval fish with severe deformities or the fatal 'swim-up fry' mortality syndrome as the tiny fish reabsorbed their heavily-contaminated yolk sacs to become free swimming small fish (Mac and Edsall 1991; photo 14). All of these deformity conditions in the fish were homologous to the chick edema disease symptoms reported in birds by Gilbertson *et al.* (1991) and found in cormorants and Caspian terns from 1986-1995 (Fox *et al.* 1991 a,b; Yamashita *et al.* 1991; Ludwig *et al.* 1993a, 1996b).

Cook *et al.* (2003) showed that complete reproductive failure of lake trout in Lake Ontario for more than 20 years was caused by TCDD-EQ concentrations. The critical concentration in lake trout eggs causing deformities and swim up fry mortalities was near an astonishingly low 50 parts per trillion TCDD-EQ, about half the concentration in free living Lake Michigan lake trout eggs in the late 1980s and more than eleven times *below* the peak of TCDD-EQs in Lake Ontario trout eggs in the early 1970s. Finally, there was a plausible explanation for the inability of lake trout to recover in Lakes Huron and Michigan when the lamprey was controlled. And, there was a plausible cause for reproductive failures of the introduced salmon species (Ankley *et al.* 1989; IJC 1990b). Lake Superior lake trout reproduced naturally, because their eggs never exceeded 25 TCDD-EQs (IJC *op. cit.*).

Second, unlike the native lake trout that is an open lake breeder, typically over deep rocky shoals, the introduced salmonids migrate into streams to breed. Most rivers entering the Great Lakes are dammed at one or more sites (often by hydroelectric dams), preventing the ingress of spawning species. Although access to inland areas is quite easily addressed by fish ladders, the inward migrating salmon were found to be highly contaminated with TCDD-EQs and exceedingly dangerous to healthy populations of inland wildlife (Giesy *et al.* 1994 a,b,c; Freeman 2003). The threats to mink and otter from eating contaminated fish were mentioned previously, but the best example of the threat represented by these 'toxic fish' is the history of the bald eagle from Great Lakes and inland territories. During the period of DDT_r abundance, substantially the twenty-five years between 1955-1979, nesting eagles were damaged severely by eggshell thinning everywhere in North America. However, when DDT_r presence subsided to low effect concentrations for eggshell thinning in the early 1980s, lakeshore eagles did not resume a normal reproductive pattern in Great Lakes territories.

Eagles are mostly fish-eating scavengers, but they do take a significant number of waterfowl and gulls, especially in winter. Of these foods in Great Lakes territories, only the puddle ducks were generally low in bioaccumulated TCDD-EQs, but gulls and fish-eating ducks were very high. Many individuals of inward migrating salmon stocks brought exceedingly high concentrations of PCBs and some residual DDT$_r$ into eagle shoreline territories and Great Lakes accessible streams. Bill Bowerman and Tim Kubiak showed that addled eagle eggs in Great Lakes shoreline territories and along rivers where the salmon had access were three to ten times more contaminated than eagles on territories more than five miles behind dams or that distance inland from Great Lakes shorelines (Bowerman 1993, Bowerman *et al.* 1995).

Ultimately, this contamination would be carried to the headwaters of Michigan's rivers if passage of fish around dams was required by the Federal Energy Regulatory Commission (FERC). Fish above the dams were measured at 10 to 100 fold less TCDD-EQ by John Giesy's team in the above dam impoundments as the same species of fish attempting inward passage. Through five years of blood sample work on eagle nestlings and nest productivity, Bill Bowerman showed that shoreline eagles produced about half of the fledglings of eagles on inland territories, and inland eaglets were 4 to 12 times less contaminated than eaglets in shoreline nests. The same bill deformities rampant in cormorants on the lakes appeared in eaglets from shoreline nests. Eagles nesting on and near the lakeshores replaced a mate twice as frequently as occurred on inland territories (Bowerman *et al.* 1995).

In the late 1980s, the low head hydroelectric dams of Consumers Power Co. in Michigan came up for their 50-year evaluation to be relicensed by FERC. After a complete review of all biological data, including the expected wildlife impacts if the contaminated fish were allow to pass by dams, FERC relicensed the Michigan dams with the proviso that no fish passage was acceptable until the fish were toxicologically clean enough not to damage inland wildlife. Personally, I was pleased with the decision, but astonished by the reaction of some fish biologists who fought passionately to have fish passage restored. Several told me point blank that they did not 'give a tinker's damn' that inland birds and mammals would be injured and killed because their job was to promote fish and fishing—period. The birds, mink, otters, snakes and turtles

JAMES P. LUDWIG, Ph.D

could go straight to hell as far as they cared! Other fisheries personnel saw the contaminants and public health warnings on fish consumption for fisherman as a profound nuisance, hindering the sale of fishing licenses. That drumbeat of consistent publicity about threats from dioxin-like chemicals in fish threatened their budgets when license sales began to lag. With that, so did their capacity to deliver fish to fishermen, using the Lakes Michigan and Huron as the world's largest ponds to produce fish for the public to catch, and the 'hook' for fishing license sales.

The third and most pernicious element of this darkside, were the impacts on human health from eating these very contaminated introduced salmonids. In the late 1970s, a series of studies were emerging on two Asian industrial and farm-related accidents with the dioxin-like chemicals. These were studies of discrete human populations having babies after mothers ate a diet contaminated with PCBs or PCDFs leading to *in utero* exposures for the fetus. The investigators of those incidents reported virtually all the chronic effects that were being recorded in Great Lakes wildlife plus permanent damage to human cognition (Rogan *et al.* 1979).

Two Wayne State University investigators, the husband and wife team of Joe and Sandra Jacobson, thought it would be worthwhile to look at potential effects in children born to women who had eaten contaminated Lake Michigan fish. They established three cohorts of children born to women who had eaten 24 lbs or more of Lake Michigan salmon the year of their pregnancy, between 6 and 24 lbs, or less for a high-moderate-low dose comparison. By the early 1990s the Jacobsons reported twice on these children in their first and fourth years. The more exposed children had neurological and reflex deficits at birth, were born smaller and earlier, with smaller skulls. At age four, initial IQ testing suggested a deficit of mathematical skills, and lower overall IQ compared to the low dose children (Jacobson *et al.* 1990 a,b). When tested at age 11, the mental deficits had become fixed in the two higher dose groups. The neurological damage was permanent and dose-dependant to the amount of fish eaten and PCB contaminants ingested by their mothers (Jacobson and Jacobson 1996).

These were the identical findings to those reported by Walter Rogan's group studying the Taiwanese farming villagers inadvertently exposed to

PCDFs and PCBs in cooking oil. Rogan's team did exhaustive testing of 30 developmental parameters up to age 6 in those children and found statistically significant deficits in 29 of the 30 parameters. Most interesting were the impacts on cognitive skills, with the greatest deficits related to mathematics and memory and a five to seven point lower score on IQ tests of these skills that was not remediable: the damaged children were impaired for life (Rogan et al. 1979).

In the 1990s Helen Daly and her team of researchers from University of New York-Oswego and their successors would show similar permanent cognitive damage to rats, then to humans born to mothers who ate Lake Ontario salmon in an exceptionally well-designed study conducted from 1991-2005. Other research teams examining exposed human populations made similar findings to the Jacobsons on human children born to fish-eaters, but there had not been universal agreement between studies (Schwartz *et al.* 1983, Swain 1991, Koopman-Essenboom *et al.* 1996, Delzell *et al.* 1994).

The Oswego cohort was designed specifically to address all potential confounders of the earlier studies, and to replicate tests of a null hypothesis N_0: *In utero* PCB exposures from eating Lake Ontario Salmon have no relationship to human intelligence. They reported a significant reduction in capacity to adjust to repeated unpleasant stimuli at birth and later to impulse control at age 4 (Stewart *et al.* 2003). Worse, a loss of 3 IQ points per ng/g (ppb) of total PCB in the mother's placenta was measured (Stewart *et al.* 2008). At concentrations above 2.06 ppb, IQ reduction was up to nine points. With more specific congener-specific analytical data available in this research, the strongest relationships were found with the more chlorinated congeners having 6 to 8 chlorinations and a di- or tri-*ortho* substitution pattern. Seegal and Schantz (1994) found these *ortho*-chlorinated congeners caused the largest dopamine reductions in brains of experimental animals. Oliver *et al.* (1989) showed that sediments conserved the higher chlorinated PCB congeners (those having 5-10 chlorines) over time. Thus, the incredibly insidious pattern of environmental sorting that conserves the most damaging congeners of *ortho*-PCBs to human cognition in sediments was confirmed, just as it was for the developmental impacts of the dioxin-like *nonortho*-PCBs congeners in wildlife (Jones *et al.* 1993a).

One of the great joys of ecological fieldwork is meeting curious citizens as they see you at work. Over the years I chanced to meet dozens of fishermen during sampling. I recall vividly meeting one old charter boat captain on a late November day in 1988 as we electrofished the below-dam segment of the Manistee River for our Consumers Power studies of wildlife and contaminants in three Michigan rivers. We had just captured our fifth required brown trout for the research design in the river mouth when he passed us. As any good conservationist should do, when he saw us using fishing gear denied to the usual fisherman he asked what we were doing? Did we have permits from the DNR? And, could he see them to verify we were operating legally? We beached our boat and showed the permits. In the conversation that followed, I related the yet unpublished findings of the Jacobsons and some of our unpublished findings on deformities and egg viability in colonial water birds. He snorted derisively, pointed to the still moving trout in our coolers and shouted his opinion *"You're Goddamned fools! Any idiot can see from those live colors there ain't nothing wrong with these fish. I know. I eat 'em all the time. So do my kids and grandkids!"*

With that dubious blessing, we separated. Yet, he was absolutely correct in one way: no one can see this level of cryptic contamination in the fish, even as he was dead wrong about the effects. Attitudes like his become fixed because we all subscribe to the notion that 'seeing is believing': but, we cannot see all things that are important. Just as pathogenic bacteria, rickettsia, viruses and toxins often hide in visibly clean foods, so do POPs contaminants. I wonder these 25 years later—Is he still living? Was he damaged by the contaminants he acquired from those fish he loved so? Were his grandchildren damaged? If so, did he ever make the connection and change his mind on this issue? I suspect he did not, because those fish taste awfully good and old men (like him then, and me now) are rather slow to change anything we believe strongly.

Most interesting for him are newer data on the effects of the PCBs acquired from eating Great Lakes fish on adult humans. Schantz *et al.* (2001) reported on adults aged 49-86 tested in 1992; all subjects of this study were *in utero* well before (born 1906-1943) substantial PCB contamination was possible. They could not have effects of PCBs from *in utero* exposures, only adult exposures. Yet, these subjects had statistically significant reductions of several measures of memory and learning in a dose-dependant manner. The high dose group ate 24 pounds (median 36.9 lbs/year) or more of salmon per year.

Muir and Zegarac (2001) examined the externalized societal costs as economic and health costs of exposures to contaminants. One cost estimate was for a loss of five points of IQ, about the mean loss in children born to those women eating the Great Lakes salmonids reported in all studies and about half the deficit reported in adults that ate these fish (Schantz *et al.* 2001). They calculated the annual externalized cost of loss of intelligence to be between 305 and 356 billions of 1999 US dollars for both nations. Since about one-sixth of the total population of both nations live within the Great Lakes basin, this translates to about 55 billion of economic loss annually for the Great Lakes region alone. Moreover, owing to easy access to Great Lakes salmonids, the economic costs may well be much greater near the lakes than this crude estimate suggests.

If you take a moment to compare this number and the previously cited costs of four chronic diseases with the budgets allotted to the agencies charged with protection and management of the lakes, *it becomes immediately obvious that the externalized costs assessed to Great Lakes residents' health annually without their knowledge or consent exceed the funds allotted for clean-up and active management by at least a ten-fold margin.* These costs are the hidden poisonous fruits of restricted funding for regulation and clean-ups by the governments through our political processes now dominated by neoliberalism.

Of course, we cannot know with certainty just how many children and adults were (are) affected, but it is exactly these sorts of externalized costs that lead to injuries to health that the BWT and GLWQA were supposed to address ten to four decades ago when negotiated, respectively. Unfortunately, these critical analyses have been suppressed and ignored systematically by the agencies under neoliberal governments in both nations for decades. In truth, the externalized costs to health and welfare from environmental contamination and invasive species are never considered in the neoliberal agendas of the government parties. Alexander (2009) has shown similar massive externalized costs to the commonweal from invasive species.

JAMES P. LUDWIG, Ph.D

Simply put, these immense costs are ignored as an unrecognized cost of doing business as usual with minimal regulation and the smallest possible outlay for environmental management. Here are the mathematics of neoliberalism: Pay no externalized costs; Shift as many costs as possible to the environment and the public at large; and, conceal as many of these costs under the umbrella of other programs like health care where the private sector can make large profits dealing with the symptoms, but never the causes—for, that would eliminate privatized corporate profit centers. And, we all are less healthy for that, even as our medical and education systems suffer and threaten to buckle under the cumulative weight of covert policies to shift costs from actual 'internal' sources to the 'external' payers of the commonweal that include us all.

Thus, I see the contribution of salmon to these lakes by my deeply respected friend Howard Tanner to be a decidedly mixed blessing. Yes, the strategy to replace the ruined lake trout and other native predator populations with alien salmon stocks was a huge short-term economic success for all Great Lakes states and Ontario. Old jobs were saved. New jobs were created. Rural towns that had suffered population losses for years stabilized and prospered. Yes, for a time, the salmon did exert a major dampening effect on the runaway alewife population, converting an alien forage fish into a positive solution on the one hand, but a cryptic attractive nuisance on the other.

The dark sides of the salmonid strategy leading to wildlife damage and the permanent loss of potential in our human population are deeply troubling. The damages to human babies born to families of the Great Lakes basin and loss of cognition in adults that were exposed to far greater concentrations of the dioxin-like substances than they would have been if this direct and extremely attractive pathway for contaminants into people had never existed. It is not unreasonable to believe that Great Lakes salominids are a classic attractive nuisance. These are very large costs assessed to an unaware public and the wildlife resources of the lakes.

Even so, we should honor Howard Tanner and others in fisheries made took this decision in spite of controversy and effects. They showed the courage of their convictions and took decisive action *based on the best science of their day* to restore viable salmonid predators to the lakes at a moment when that was sorely needed. In fact, I cannot think of a single major decision of any of the governments taken since their action to plant the salmon that demonstrates Howard's life credo 'Do what is right for the resource' as well as this decision.

These conservationists did not know, *nor had they any way to know*, that contaminants would have the panoply of insidious effects from exposures acquired through the new salmon fishery when the decision was made in 1964. PCBs were not even discovered to be in the Great Lakes biota until 1968, dioxins and furans and many other synthetic toxins in the 1970s and early 1980s. The first appearance of chick edema disease in Lake Ontario colonial birds was not reported until 1974, and its cause verified with reasonable certainty until the mid-1980s (Gilbertson *et al.* 1991). The gross effects of DDTr and some pesticides like dieldrin on birds were emerging between 1957 and 1966. But, every set of data and published paper available when the first salmon plantings were made, including my own work (Ludwig and Tomoff 1966), suggested the pesticide contamination problems were localized near the places where these chemicals were heavily used. Aerial transport and their redistribution by air would not be found until 1978 in the Great Lakes, and environmental sorting leading to retention of the worst congeners would not be confirmed until the late 1980s. So, give these men credit for doing *something* important. Recognize how unique their attempt to restore an effective fish predator these waters actually was. It actually was the last time a serious attempt was made by any of the agencies of governments to restore the lakes to their former glory, possibly the last time bureaucrats showed any genuine backbone.

Still, as I write this I remember the intense frustrations of fourteen teachers' groups in Michigan, Indiana and Wisconsin I spoke to between 1988 and 1992. They related a consistent pattern of serious behavioral problems and lack of mental skills in generations of their students, many of whom they found to be virtually unteachable, especially those with attention deficit hyperactivity disorders that Rogan *et al.* (1979) found nearly doubled in his PCB-exposed human cohort studied in Taiwan. Indeed, think about 'no child left behind' and the relatively poor success of that initiative nationwide in the US. Think about the fact that Ritalin™ used for children with attention deficit hyperactivity disorder is prescribed more often in the Great Lakes basin states than any other region of the country; Michigan ranked number one among the 50 states in 1995 for Ritalin™ use. Is there a connection to eating fish from the Great Lakes? Is that important? Those are good questions that each of us must answer on our own.

In 2009 we saw the massive failures in the big three automakers to adopt innovative techniques as one root cause of their recent near-death experiences. Did those salmon fed to two generations of mothers whose offspring had become automobile engineers or were exposed as adults in Detroit affect their abilities to address the problems of the industry when those problems could have been fixed? One thing is now certain: The contaminants in these fish did not help to develop the reasoning capabilities of those exposed. The PCBs in them effected change of the worst sort as lifelong damage. Those with cognitive deficits will be a drain on society for many years until replaced by offspring and adults never exposed. In my darker moments I cannot help but wonder whether the angry recalcitrant responses of many Great Lakes fisherman and fishery biologists to contaminants data and careful studies of effects on human cognition does not have one root in their own exposures to the fish they work so hard to protect, catch and then eat with great relish. It may well be that those succulent fish will have the last hideous laugh through damage to their own health, and that of their children and grandchildren.

Returning to the question posed at the start of this chapter, do these experiences have any useful lessons for the question of whether to renegotiate the GLWQA and other international agreements? I believe they do. The planted salmon experiences would seem to be an example of the old wisdom to beware of what we wish for, for we may get much more than we expect. This is especially true when managing unstable ecological communities that have cryptic sources and levels of contaminants, beset with uncontrolled floods of invasive species. The decision to introduce the alien salmon stocks was essentially a joint proposal of the MDNR, USDI and GLFC and was not supported by everyone, particularly some in the US Bureau of Commercial Fisheries. In fact, it was a highly controversial action. The decision was made and implemented without consideration of probable system-wide effects other than on the fisheries and economies of the states and provinces.

Alexander (2009) has pointed out the same narrow focus on economics in the decisions to build the St. Lawrence Seaway that allowed many alien species invasions that now plague the lakes. There was no comprehensive review before these actions were taken by any responsible group like the IJC, nor by parties thinking about potential impacts of contaminants or invasive species on humans or other wildlife besides fish. Both the salmonid introductions and the seaway occurred before environmental impact statements were required, meaning they were never scrutinized fully for impacts. The salmon planting decision was driven forward by a great sense of urgency to something about those damned alewives rotting on the beaches in the 1960s before the voters threw out the politicians in power. Economic benefits were touted in the decision to open the lakes to international commerce through the St. Lawrence Seaway. Does it always have to come down to more money for commerce and politics?

I believe what these experiences tell us about any revision to the treaty or GLWQA is three fundamental things. First, no single interest group can be allowed to control management decisions for whole the system. Specifically, while fish and economics are important, these are not the 'be all and end all' of Great Lakes values. It is impossible to do just one thing in these lakes. Effects are always more wide-ranging than is obvious and, more often than not, only somewhat predictable even using the very best science of the day, as the introduced salmon experience should teach us. The potential for errors is especially great if only one of many interest groups is making decisions. The minority voices must be heard *before* major management decisions are made that could damage the whole system. Further, good policy must be decoupled from budgets. For example, can you have good fisheries policies when these policies are implemented largely through income from sport fishing licenses? Do these fees give fishermen a disproportionately greater influence on policies that influence outcomes as well as their own selfish interests because fish are really 'money in a finny disguise'?

Second, management from a single perspective often effects many unintended changes. Yet, with our current maturing knowledge of contaminants, nutrients, invasive species and ecological processes we should be approaching a time when many of the possible damages or undesirable outcomes can be identified before a management decision is made and implemented. However, under the IJC and GLFC, states, provinces and two federal parties in the treaty and GLWQA there is no formal means to conduct proper assessments *before* actions are taken unless the two federal governments impose requirements for environmental impact statements.

EIS decisions require an explicit declaration that the proposed action is a 'major decision' under NEPA and its Canadian equivalent. Those are complex declaratory actions made by political appointees who typically have little or no ecological knowledge of the Great Lakes. The only time I am aware of such a process for a Great Lakes-wide proposal was the proposed cormorant control program in the US. The USDI did conduct a formal environmental review and issued a draft statement for public comment and review well before the program was implemented. While I disagreed with the decision to cull birds strongly, I applauded the process to review a proposed action by a transparent assessment process. But, this was the rare exception in Great Lakes management since the passage of NEPA and its Canadian equivalent. The review function of IJC of GLWQA requirements assigned to the parties is retrospective under current practice, not prospective. One change that could be negotiated to great advantage would be to require the IJC or a successor body to review proposed major management actions prospectively without having to depend on the cumbersome politicly-influenced NEPA process.

The third lesson is that no existing political structure or agency involved in the governance of the lakes brings together all the necessary science and practical expertise to consider proposed management decisions comprehensively. The result is simple. Important management decisions, including inaction, can be forced through loopholes of the government structures themselves. Remember the USEPA decision to avoid its responsibilities to address ballast water from 1973!

As I write this in 2013 a huge volume of information is emerging on the environmental effects of endocrine disruptor chemicals that seem to be worse at lower exposures than the historic high exposures in the lakes. *Critically important new science emerges all the time, and most of it will not be coming from the traditional resource management agencies that are supposed to implement intelligent Great Lakes management.* In part, this is owing to compartmentalization within and between agencies (the silo effect), but mostly it is from budget cuts forced by neoliberal governments that effectively reduce agency staff to administrators only, no longer active research scientists.

In essence, no one is in charge either to implement beneficial changes or especially to review all the old decisions that had untoward or questionable impacts. On a practical basis this translates to a pattern of deferral of decisions to the 'sacred cows' of the Great Lakes, most of which now graze contentedly in the bureaucratic pastures of the GLFC, the USEPA (GLNPO), NOAA, IJC and various state and provincial DNRs. This situation suggests a GLWQA renegotiation must focus first on the responsibilities of agencies. It will require the negotiators to devise a new set of institutional structures to supplant the existing failed institutions of all parties. Interestingly, the recent official review (IJC 2006) and the recent plea by NGOs to renegotiate the GLWQA, failed to identify cumbersome agency structures as a cause of failures to implement the GLWQA. But, since that review was done under the auspices of the sacred cows of the Great Lakes, this convenient omission by commission should come as no surprise to anyone.

The second major thrust of renegotiation should focus on how to fund management initiatives and a means to adjudicate disputes between the parties. In this regard, I believe the parties should be construed to be the two federal governments, the eight states and *two* provinces. I see the most logical approach to be a Great Lakes Compact of these twelve parties defined by the geographic limits of the watershed plus the inclusion of the St. Lawrence River as far eastward as Quebec City; hence, the province of Quebec becomes a Great Lakes party. The practical reason for this expansion is simple. The vast majority of biological invaders enter through the St. Lawrence Seaway or the connection to the Mississippi River drainage via the Chicago Sanitary Canal. Attempting to exert bio-containment controls for invasive species hitch-hiking in ships' ballast water even at Montreal is a fool's game. The authority to do so must include Quebec to be effective for two reasons—the strong provincial-weak federal government structure of Canada, and the time required for quarantine and effective sterilization of ballast waters in marine ships passing inward through the seaway.

The only effective means to do so in a timely manner will be a bio-control program that starts ship inspection, decontamination and enforcement in Quebec City. Further, the St. Lawrence River is still fresh water until well past Montreal. I argue that this segment of the river is an ecological part of the Great Lakes even though it is considered to be outside the Great Lakes Basin. Inclusion of Quebec will be a major political change. Similarly, Canadian provinces and states besides Illinois should have an equal weight in any decisions to manage the threat of invasive species that may enter through the Illinois River and the sanitary canal connection to the Mississippi River. If Asian carp get into the lakes, Canadian and other states' interests will suffer too.

Another aspect is the assumption that existing agencies exist to protect the lakes. In each nation the fundamental regulatory structure is based on missions to protect, enhance and regulate specific media like water and air. For example, in the US we have the USEPA and its counterpart of Environment Canada charged to manage water quality. Each agency derives its powers from specific media or toxic substances focused laws such as the Clean Water Act (CWA), several Air Pollution Control Statutes (APCSs), the US Federal Insecticide, Fungicide and Rodenticide Act (FIFRA), the US Toxic Substances Control Act (TOSCA) and many other laws aimed either at specific substances or media. Further, each state and province also has laws focused on media.

Essentially the US Congress, the Canadian Parliament, states and provinces reacted to damaged ecologies as each was identified, establishing authorities to address the causes one medium (air, water, pesticides etc.) at a time. What we have achieved in these laws is a laser like focus on regulation by permits that end at the pipes discharging effluents to water, stacks discharging gases to air, or licenses to manufacture and use toxic chemicals. These are all based on numerical standards that set 'acceptable' concentrations for discharges or end-uses. A fundamental assumption of organizing government this way is that each medium—air, water and land—and each environmental problem like synthetic toxicants—should be regulated independently and a separate responsibility of an agency with its own programs. In essence, this assumption denies the reality that substances cross media boundaries (e.g. pesticides evaporate from the land to the air, and are returned in rain to the water). Worse, bioconcentration, bioaccumulation and chemical transformations are not recognized in these laws explicitly.

But, those assumptions are disproven every instant of every day and violate the bedrock principles of process-based ecosystems. As you are reading this, mercury and PCBs are falling or condensing from the air to the earth or entering the water. In turn, the water of the lakes is evaporating PCBs and many other substances back to the air. The land and soils are capturing and holding some of the air pollutants deposited in rain, dustfall, etc. but are giving up other substances to waters flowing from the land or air over the land. This is how a process-based ecosystem functions, but our legal systems spring directly from the false paradigm that media must be regulated independently.

This focus on the individual media is a prescription for agencies to narrow their programs to as small a mandate as they can get away with, just as the USEPA did when that agency carved the ballast water issue out of the Clean Water Act in 1973. The USEPA passed the issue to the U.S. Coast Guards, an agency that had absolutely no expertise or resources to deal with the threat of invasive species hitch-hiking entry into the great lakes in ballast waters. Worse, the Coast Guard had a very tight relationship with the shipping industry they were supposed to regulate (Alexander 2009). There the responsibility for ballast water controls of invasive species rested for 35 years while at least 48 new invasive species entered the lakes and the shippers saved a few million dollars a year.

The Coast Guards primary mandate was to protect the lives of seamen and the floating investments of ships entering the Great Lakes from international ports. In essence, the Coast Guards of both nations saw their primary mission to protect sailors and the interests of corporate shippers. Arguably, invasive species controls were the very last thing on their list of priorities. Indeed, why should it have been otherise when the *Environmental* Protection Agency thought the mandate was so unimportant that they foisted off the responsibility onto an unqualified sister agency! 'It could not be very important to environmental quality if they gave it to us, right?' That was the attitude toward invasive species in the Coast Guards for two decades, then utter confusion as to how to approach the problem for the subsequent fifteen years before the an American federal judge decided the 1973 EPA decision was illegal (Alexander 2009).

Within each media or taxon-focused agency or program responsible for some aspect of Great Lakes resource protection and management, the problem is the same. The Great Lakes Fishery Commission is focused narrowly on fish, the National Forests on timber production, the state, provincial and federal regulators on whatever media and permits they are responsible to address. *But, no one or no agency is responsible for management of the whole resource of the Great Lakes ecosystem, and few programs are interested genuinely in interactions between media. Moreover, even if administrators recognize process issues and the inter-relatedness of all the pieces of the ecosystem, the limits of their legal mandates do not allow them to address these issues effectively.* This creates a huge conundrum for the advocates of the ecosystem approach. For, if no agency is responsible for the whole system and each is confined to its own 'silo', is it even possible to deliver ecosystem management? I think not. Is it any wonder the public is frustrated with governments and their agencies over what has occurred in the Great Lakes?

At the level of the public, the non-governmental environmental organizations and many individual citizens there is a similar disconnect leading to irresponsible behavior. The many state and National Audubon Societies focus on birds, the Izzak Walton League on fish, the Sierra Club and Greenpeace on selected environmental issues of the day, etc. Each NGO selects what issues and actions it will address and pays little attention to the potential for collateral damage at the ecosystem level as they pursue their narrow focus while espousing faith in the ecosystem approach.

For all of the good and lofty goals held by environmentalists, some of their actions have had terrible effects. In 1991, the IJC proposed the idea of a chlorine ban, more precisely a ban on organo-chlorine substances and the use of chlorine in industrial processes like paper pulping in the Great Lakes Basin. Many environmental groups embraced the concept, but then some extended it utterly irresponsibly to all chlorine uses, far beyond the IJC proposal. Soon some activists were demanding that chlorination of drinking water and sewage be banned as well as the use of chlorinated compounds in pharmaceutical manufacturing. This utter foolishness culminated with some activists lobbying fiercely against the use of chlorine to disinfect ballast water tanks of ships on the seaway. Consider this: the addition of chlorine is the time-tested (since the 1920s) safe means to disinfect drinking water and remove pathogens from sewage effluent. Every swimming pool is chlorinated daily to prevent person-to-person transmission of human pathogens. We accept those chlorine uses as perfectly normal because they are proven to have many public health benefits and manageable risks.

Yet, some NGOs and environmental activists lobbied successfully against chlorination of ballast waters, confusing the threat of chlorinated organics with well-understood and safe uses of chlorine that have reduced risks for a century in the Great Lakes basin. For those of us who had worked diligently to raise public awareness of the immense threat of many chlorinated organic chemicals, it came as a bitter irony that some environmentalists misconstrued our message completely. That obstinacy helped keep open the way for invasive species for almost two decades after the virtual elimination debate on synthetic halogenated organic substances started. Clearly, there are those in the environmental community for who a small amount of knowledge is a very dangerous matter, especially if that knowledge can be perverted. Once again, the lakes were injured by those who focused only on their narrow goals, regardless of the nobility of their intent.

The second key change required revolves around money. How do the parties fund future Great Lakes Management? Presently there is a hodge-podge of funding in both countries that passes through many agencies, often going to support long-established programs that are not subject to critical external review. Previously, I have mentioned defects in the dredging programs of the USCOE and the fisheries management programs of many agencies. These are example programs that should be subject to external public review and updated to incorporate the latest knowledge, technology and science.

Within each branch of every US federal cabinet-level agency that addresses a Great Lakes issue there is a fiefdom of personnel in a hierarchy that incorporates a long and often disconnected reporting path to its parent agency. Worse, there is absolutely no interagency accountability, often there are interagency rivalries at the cabinet level and intra-agency rivalries among programs in the same agency that can be intense and do damage to the larger mission of effective Great Lakes management.

Consider the seven major federal cabinet-level players on the US side. The USEPA has three initiatives of high importance to the Great Lakes— The USEPA regulatory arm that handles various federal permit programs that have not be transferred to the eight states, audits various program authorities from specific statutes that have been transferred to the states, and the Great Lakes National Program Office which handles special initiatives for the lakes and performs a modest in-house research program. One may ask 'Do these programs interface routinely and coordinate well?' Unfortunately, they do not. Each tends to function as its own fiefdom within USEPA because their lines of reporting are to different subsections of the agency in Washington, far from the Great Lakes. One has only to discuss the subject with persons who work in one of the USEPA regulatory programs for specific media to realize how little actual coordination and exchange of information there is between regulatory programs in USEPA and GLNPO.

Similarly, the US Department of Interior (USDI) has Great Lakes related programs in more than a half-dozen sub-departments ranging from contaminants and endangered species to the Bureau of Indian Affairs, the National Wildlife Refuge System, Mining, Bureau of Land Management, National Parks etc. Coordination on Great Lakes issues is haphazard at best, partly because the lines of accountability within the agency do not conform to one another.

The USACE reports to the Department of Defense. It controls wetlands with some advice from USDI and state DNRs, plans, implements and contracts for dredging, channel maintenance and regulates the Sault Ste. Marie locks, supposedly with the help of the US and Canadian Coast Guards. The US Coast Guard has been part of the Treasury Department and most recently Homeland Security since 911. It protects shipping in the lakes and supposedly regulated ballast water issues for 35 years until the courts ordered that responsibility back into the jurisdiction of the USEPA.

The US Department of Agriculture controls a major part of the US portion of the watershed through the management of the National Forest system, is responsible for animal control programs like the 'cormorant holocaust' and influences virtually everything to do with agriculture in the basin through many programs. The National Oceanic and Atmospheric Administration has a major hand in air monitoring programs, operates several quasi-independent aquatic laboratories and programs and is part of the Department of Commerce. Finally, the International Joint Commission reports to the US State Department and the Canadian Department of Foreign Affairs.

Just considering the United States federal presence, there are seven different cabinet level divisions of the federal government involved with many independent programs—each with its own line item budget, each reporting to a different bureauracy! All have their hands in Great Lakes management. Only a fool could believe these programs coordinate well or that funds are well spent with that degree of fragmentation. The reality is that between these cabinet-level divisions of the US federal government there are many barriers to effective communication, incredible redundancy, very poor accountability and no clear place for the public to go to redress grievances. Again, no agency is responsible for management of the lakes, but all agencies' staff get to talk about it, express lofty intentions and develop plans to implement whatever narrowly focused, media-based legal mandate they happen to operate under. It is an incredibly complex system of agencies that just does not work.

Any one of the subagencies from these seven major cabinet-level divisions can point to someone else as the responsible party of the federal government whenever a contentious issue around non-delivery of the GLWQA or protection of the lakes arises. It is a fertile ground, nourishing coordinating committees and delays to any action. Jeff Alexander has reported on the federal response to the discovery of the ruffe in Duluth harbor and the St. Louis River. In essence, three federal and two state agencies wrangled for months among themselves about what to do to contain this invader and ended up doing absolutely nothing but monitoring the spread of the invader after spending several million dollars in talking and coordination (Alexander 2009). That is an example of what counts now for a 'coordinated response' to a crisis— lots of talk, a serious dose of public relations angst, many interagency meetings, but no substantive action. Meanwhile, every bureaucratic meeting bled money from actual management activities.

Now, multiply that US federal haphazard organization that features overlapping roles and jurisdictions, redundancies, inter and intra agency conflicts and avoidance of mandated responsibilities by eleven other parties and some sense of the excessively complicated, rickety structure for Great Lakes resource management emerges. When I took ancient history, one of my professors introduced us to the utterly ineffective government of the ancient city state of Byzantium. From that history we have inherited the wonderful word *Byzantine* to describe any government filled with redundancies, foolish organization, obfuscation, graft and politics. Intelligent management of the Great Lakes as a shared resource is not possible with these semi-competitive, often antagonistic, Byzantine fiefdoms in control of their own destiny, a destiny often far more important to each agency than is the mission to prevent damage and restore the Great Lakes.

Rather than management by this chaotic group of agencies, the Great Lakes deserve a streamlined body for governance that replaces the very inefficient, obviously ineffective mess now in place. Most especially, the lakes need a focus not on the individual media through laws like the Clean Water Act or the individual interests of the agencies, but on the entire resource that is the Great Lakes, including the ecosystem level processes that are given lip service by everyone, but no genuine attention by anyone. The current regulatory system can never succeed at the ecosystem level precisely because ecological processes do not fit into the legal mandates and agency organization of each jurisdiction.

We must replace programs derived from individual laws of Congress and Parliament with a management scheme that has but one concern—the health of these magnificent lakes and the people that are affected. Hence, my proposal for a Compact for Great Lakes Governance that is developed in the next chapter. For the moment I will leave that concept with a final assertion that merely combining the monies each cabinet-level department now spends into one budget and administrative agency would provide far more money to manage than is now misspent for the poor administration of many ineffective programs!

At the state level, the innovative Great Lakes Protection Fund (GLPF) was established in 1990. In essence, the eight states formed their own compact to do research based on the notion that each contributed funds based on the miles of Great Lakes shoreline in that state. The fund had total assets of about $100 million USD and essentially spent the interest earned on this endowment annually. However, the fund was damaged by the withdrawal of Michigan's interest share in 2006 to balance their state budget. I believe that was a reasonable way to assess research costs and the endowment structure was a brilliant feature. But, I would modify that formula to include the area of the watershed in each state or province. Further, I suggest including as full partners Ontario and Quebec in those calculations of a revised GLPF formula. Obviously, there would be a one-time charge to the two provinces to join a GLPF.

Under the Canadian system, that could be properly paid as a one-time grant from the federal government under the established Canadian pattern of revenue sharing. Further, I suggest that both federal governments simply grant research funds to a joint research directorate comprised of representatives of the states and provinces through a GLPF-like entity with the two federal governments acting in concert. More research and management funds can be generated if all fines for permit violations in the watershed were added and those funds generated by the USDI federal program for remediation of contaminated AOCs where the responsible parties are known already. I will even suggest that there already is sufficient money misspent through existing agencies—much of it squandered on attempts to communicate between and within agencies from different cabinet level divisions—to accomplish intelligent management. However, it must be combined with a sensible plan for one joint American-Canadian agency to govern Great Lakes programs in order to succeed. We already know the fragmented mess we have simply does not, and cannot be tweaked enough, to work.

On the subject of finances, the problems of maintenance of infrastructures like the Sault Ste. Marie locks system, Welland Canal and many others could be centralized into one directorate. A large part of maintenance in the Great Lakes is really dredging and hardscape management, i.e. maintaining public docks, locks, harbors etc. Maintenance and repair of these infrastructure elements has long been a fiefdom of the U.S. Congress or the party in power in Canada. Traditionally, proposed projects were in competition with one another for funds. As often as not, in the US decisions on what projects were built depended on the seniority of elected members on powerful congressional committees and what political jurisdiction those politicians just happened to represent.

From a resource conservation and management perspective, that is no way to 'run the railroad'. Political seniority has no correlation to management of resources. Especially in a system like the Great Lakes, ecological instabilities develop quickly, often after the most recent alien species invasion. These deleterious impacts have no relationship whatsoever to political jurisdictions, and have no relationship to federal, provincial or state boundaries. Again, by centralization of the two nations' federal funds intended for these projects under one agency focused broadly on the whole system and not congressional districts or ridings, the potential to get priorities right with impact assessments based on the most recent sound science will improve greatly. Critically, the response time to address fast arising, inevitable changes should decrease markedly. This would be consistent with the movement in the US to eliminate congressional earmarks.

The idea of using the most recent sound science as a guide to management is hardly new, but few have thought through what that actually means, and how to deliver the advice to those in the parties who can make a difference. The present Science Advisory Board of the IJC has been one means to examine scientific issues, emerging management needs and recent research findings. But, the SAB is advisory only, and then only to the IJC commissioners that control an agency that itself is advisory only to agencies that are free to ignore the advice. Far too often, that is exactly what happens. I liken this system of scientific review to attempts by a naive pastor who wants to save the soul of a rebellious teen-aged boy, but can do that only through advising a controlling stepfather the son disrespects. The probability of the advice getting where it could be effective is tiny. Worse, the IJC messengers often are seen to be foolish irrelevancies by those in agencies.

What is required is a science directorate, similar to that in, and between, the many nations cooperating to manage the CERN high-energy hadron collider facility in Switzerland. Such a directorate should have the responsibility to review the existing and emerging science, recommend new research, and those practical projects that should be implemented on a realistic timetable. Presently, service on the SAB is essentially an honor, for it has no practical effect or relevance to which research is funded, nor what practical projects should be implemented or reengineered and reconstructed. That must be changed if the Great Lakes are to be managed in an intelligent and effective manner.

We simply must use the most recent and best available peer-reviewed science if we are to have any chance of effective lakes management under an ecosystem approach for we need a far more ecologically based management than now prevails. We should be giving attention to the processes of change—including genetic adaptation by invasive species, substitutions of new chemicals for old legacy pollutants and climate change. We must acknowledge and face this irrefutable fact: The current ramshackle system of multiple agencies with divided responsibilities focused on media, spread over many levels of each governmental party has no chance whatsoever of delivering effective management in a timely manner at a reasonable cost—regardless of how often the GLWQA is altered.

The political systems charged with responsibilities to protect these resources are broken into many ineffective fragments. Like Humpty-Dumpty, these cannot be glued together in an effective manner. It is time to discard these failures and search for a new way forward. The very structure of Great Lakes management is fatally flawed. And, all of us in the basin—even the most dedicated agency staff, activists and environmentalists—have been parties to this mess. We have been seduced to the neoliberal notion that we can pay less taxes, have less government and somehow the lakes will take care of themselves no matter what we allow to get into them and how horribly fractured our management is. That is wrong. The lakes and the commonweal have paid an immense price for these failures by covert damage to education, healthcare and their other essential attributes. We all are part of the problem in this neoliberal world we have accepted for economic reasons. It is time we fixed this mess.

JAMES P. LUDWIG, Ph.D

VI

A proposal to implement the Boundary Waters Treaty by a Great Lakes Governance Compact.

2 009 AND 2013 had great political significance with the inaugurations of Barack Obama in the United States. That political change came after a decade of intense frustration for thoughtful Americans. 2009 was also the 100th anniversary of the Boundary Waters Treaty when I hoped fervently the long history of gross insults to the Sweetwater Seas, exacerbated with ineffective management, would finally revive a passive public to demand action that protects the Great Lakes. But, that did not happen with the many impacts of the worse recession since the Great Depression. Most of all, we must get beyond the neoliberal economic arguments for less government and lower taxes with convincing analyses that show allowing the *status quo* to continue for the lakes will ultimately cost us far more than the neoliberal policies of benign neglect.

The change most needed is to governance structures. This does not mean tweaking the existing GLWQA and continuing to flounder about like fishes out of water with our fractured agencies. Instead, it means a complete restructuring of those agencies that contribute to Great Lakes management in both nations. Moreover, this means that money must be invested to deliver the research and programs that sound management requires. These fundamental changes will not happen under our present neoliberal governments where taxes are cut and government is reduced consistently. It is time for neoliberals, libertarians and the TEA party activists to admit to the horrific damage their political philosophies have inflicted on the lakes, and the collateral damage to other aspects of human life in North America, such as public health.

I will also opine that the Boundary Waters Treaty should not be reopened for two reasons. First, it was negotiated between the US and Great Britain acting on behalf of the commonwealth of Canada in 1909, long before the 1931 Statute of Westminster. Therewith, the BWT has the full force of international law. A new bilateral treaty between the US and Canada that would provide effective commitments would not. Further, a revised treaty might well never pass the scrutiny of Congress or Parliament in these days of the 'Tea Party' politicians in the US and staunch conservatives in Canada whose principal political tactic is not to cooperate when the commonweal is threatened.

Second, the present treaty covers all of the boundary waters from New Brunswick/Maine to British Colombia/Washington. For the most part, the IJC has adjudicated boundary disputes and problems of water quality and quantity over most of this immense length of shared border competently. There is no compelling reason to tamper with an aspect of a treaty that works. The failures of IJC to critique the governments and cajole them into implementation of the treaty are largely in the Great Lakes region. What follows is my proposal for new structures of government shared between the two sovereign nations, two provinces and eight states. The basic vehicle proposed for this effort is a **Great Lakes Resource Governance Compact.** Such a compact can be negotiated under the existing BWT as a replacement for Great Lakes Water Quality Agreement that will only perpetuate the mess as long as it is driven by an ecosystem approach that avoids actions to enforce criteria and depends on dozens of fractured agencies and programs for results.

The Compact I envision will consist of three program directorates, jointly funded by the twelve parties to staff and control one comprehensive management agency for the Great Lakes. Importantly, this will require existing agencies in all parties to cede regulatory authority and part of their budgets. For example, in the US that would mean that all the authorities now managed by the USEPA and six other cabinet level federal agencies, the states under existing laws are assigned to the Compact.

However, first a note of warning about the negotiating posture of the twelve parties is called for, especially between the two federal governments. The US is an imperial superpower; Canada is not. The countries are very different culturally on some fundamental issues. Michael Adams has recently studied the attitudes of American and Canadians and made the following observations:

"From distinct roots Canada and the US have grown up with substantially different characters: group rights, public institutions and deference to authorities have abided north of the border while individualism, private interests and mistrust of authority have abided south of the border." (Adams 2003).

In particular, Adams found an increasing emphasis on exclusion, status and security in the US between 1992 and 2002 that did not cross the border. Of course, this is precisely consistent with the rampant neoliberalism that has dominated American politics for the last three decades. Even though Canadians have elected similar neoliberal governments, their core values have not changed, perhaps hinting that Canadians will soon reject the doctrinaire neoliberal Conservative 'Harper Government' once they figure out just how dangerous it really is.

The United States is used to being the top dog in negotiations and has a long history of 'throwing its weight around', whether justified or not. The hegemonic posture the US has maintained on NAFTA must be discarded. None of the parties need a bully at the table, whether it is a federal, state or provincial government. As a dual citizen, born in the US who has lived in Minnesota, Michigan, British Colombia, Ontario, Nova Scotia, Saskatchewan and Alberta, I am most sensitive to the unethical tactics applied to Canada in the recent softwood lumber dispute by the United States under NAFTA. There is simply no room for such acts around Great Lakes resource issues that are increasingly time-sensitive.

We are losing the battle to preserve the qualities of the Great Lakes we all care about. Time is of the essence. If any of the parties approach the negotiation table with the old ways of doing business in control of their mindset, effective management will never emerge. And, if the existing structural mess of the parties persists, then the "NAFTA attitude' and the 'ecosystem approach'—two bitter fruits of ethically-compromised neoliberalism—will dominate and continue to degrade the Great Lakes. If we continue on that path, then real progress toward Great Lakes renewal will be abysmally slow, perhaps impossible, trapped in the miasma of permanent bureaucratic gridlock, reduced budgets and piecemeal management.

Second, each party must bring to the table the perspective that individual agencies within their jurisdiction must be made to bend to the requirements of a new compact requiring them to surrender significant pieces of their funding and authority. This means there will be many agency oxen circling the negotiating table fearing they will be gored. Unfortunately, that administrative carnage is necessary. It is undeniable that the existing agencies have failed to do the job. These were not small failures. Rather, many plainly illegal actions were taken, often with many untoward consequences. These changes will require congressional and parliamentary changes to many existing laws.

We are left to embrace the errors of our governments in a public search for new means to do the job (Michael 1967, Ludwig 1982). Sadly, it is no more likely to be accomplished with the current institutions than hell is to freeze over. To quote Mr. Obama's 2009 campaign, 'We need change we can believe in.'. And, with the hubris only a native-born American can muster, I call on Mr. Obama to give clear instructions to the US State Department first to propose a new GLWQA on which a compact can be based, then to instruct American negotiators to act in good faith, with the respect and consideration due to Canadian and Quebecois sensibilities.

In the following paragraphs, those fundamental aspects of a Compact structure I believe makes the most sense are outlined, leaving the parties to negotiate the details. I emphasize this is a starting point, and remain certain there are many others who will have better ideas to improve on the proposal. In some places I have used the mandatory 'shall' where I believe there is an important principle to be implemented or protected.

The Compact's dimensions should include three directorates under which some parts of existing agencies may survive. I suggest a **Knowledge, Science, Research and Planning Directorate, an Intergovernmental Management Directorate, and a Programs and Projects Directorate**. While each directorate will have specific duties, they will all have equal status and will report to a Commission of Compact Governors that shall establish priorities and approve programs. The federal parties will appoint one governor; governors will rotate the chairpersonship of the Commission to the other federal party every four years. When a chair is serving, the chair shall vote twice to break tie votes; otherwise each party shall have one vote. Majority votes shall be required to implement policies, authorize actions and spend funds.

Each state and province shall *elect* one governor for terms concurrent with the government leadership in each of these ten jurisdictions. Candidates shall not run for election as a member of a political party. The Commission shall have the powers to fund research, management, maintenance and new infrastructure projects from the funds under the control of the Commission. Duties of the Commission shall include: Review of extant social and ecological conditions, monitoring programs and data especially emerging science, and technology appropriate to address and prevent problems, and human and wildlife health in the entire basin, regardless of which political jurisdiction the condition(s) exist within; Taking those actions consistent with funds and budgets to address needs including long-term monitoring, targeted research and projects at specific locations; Working with the parties on projects outside the basin in so far as such efforts are likely to promote improved environmental quality and economic progress within the basin; and, Liaison with all government agencies of the parties and other nations that request assistance, consistent with the availability of funds.

All meetings of the Commission and within directorates, and all records thereof, shall be open to the public at all times. The three directorates are established to implement the will and consensus of the Compact Commission and the parties.

The existing hodge-podge of agencies must be folded into a new treaty-mandated Compact for the lakes. However, a fundamental question for each of the parties remains: To which cabinet-level department of the twelve parties will the Compact be attached? At the US federal government there are presently seven cabinet level departments with substantial duties and presence in the Great Lakes. Each department will want this plum as it will increase their influence over the region and budget very substantially. It will be the same for each state and province.

For example, in Ontario there are two logical choices, the Ministries of Environment or Natural Resources, and there would be good arguments mustered for either choice. These decisions shall be up to each party.

One of the obvious benefits of a Compact approach is elimination of redundancies and large cost savings. The Great Lakes are the largest shared freshwater resource in the world; only Lake Baikal in Russia has a larger water volume than the Great Lakes. In resource and biotic terms, they are without boundaries except at the limits of their watersheds. The swimming fish and flying terns neither know nor care if they are in Ontario, Canada or Michigan, United States. Political boundaries and jurisdictions are largely the result of historic accidents that date to European settlement, three wars between 1755 and 1814 and innumerable boundary disputes between the federal parties, states and provinces, some of which were not resolved until the late 1800s. Many have colorful histories. For example, Michigan and Ohio actually fought a brief 'war' over the narrow strip of land that runs along their present border from the center of Michigan's lower peninsula eastward to Lake Erie, the infamous "Toledo Strip", in 1835-1836. Michigan lost the war, but received the Upper Peninsula in compensation when the logical step from a geographic perspective would have been to keep the Upper Peninsula part of the Wisconsin territory.

The biota, water and air pay no attention whatsoever to these modern, often illogical, political jurisdictions. The biota use high quality habitats while the air and water respond only to heat energy, pressure gradients and gravity. These realities are outside human control, although man can exert some influence on water flows, air and water quality through management. But, to be effective for the whole system, a management scheme must be comprehensive and well thought out for all potential impacts. More than any other factor, it is the political fragmentation into a dozen jurisdictions each with its multiple agencies and panoply of programs that prevents intelligent management. A compact structure bringing all existing jurisdictions (plus Quebec) into one agency with one comprehensive political process under a structure designed specifically for the Great Lakes is the only intelligent solution, regardless of the divisive politics that often prevail among twelve jurisdictions.

Assuming a Compact as envisioned were agreed upon amongst the parties, what might be included in the three directorates from existing

JAMES P. LUDWIG, Ph.D

programs? Personally, I view the **Knowledge, Science, Research and Planning Directorate** (KSRPD) as the most important element of the Compact, probably owing to my career choice first as a field research ecologist and then ecotoxicologist. It is crucial that accumulated knowledge, the latest science and peer-reviewed research be used as the basis for decisions and planning. We simply can no longer afford not to use all of the latest information and resources available for these efforts. However, to do so we need one place to assemble all of it for scientific peer review and evaluation. That implies a Science Advisory Board to advise all political jurisdictions equally and without concern for how advice and reviews may stimulate negative political fallout or consternation within the parties. It must be understood that some evaluation and advice will run contrary to the immediate goals of particular interest groups, especially when the advice is prepared from critical reviews of the effectiveness of agencies that have contributed to management. This is key: Embracing errors and successes dispassionately and equally is essential (Michael 1967; Ludwig 1982). Some persons and groups will have their 'oxen gored' in this process. Others will be the 'winners'. This is the nature of a fair review process.

With respect to historic records and process, the KSRPD should act to assemble (reassemble) a comprehensive library of all records related to the Great Lakes, especially previous management activities, research and programs. It is an unqualified disgrace that both the IJC and USEPA GLNPO agencies eliminated their library holdings in a foolish attempt to save money. This implies a connection to (a) university system(s) with demonstrated skills and expertise to manage documents and information. A clear goal should be the preservation of institutional memory and experience and especially the unpublished records of those who have worked on the lakes. The prerequisite for that goal is an effective library and records-holding system.

Similarly, a comprehensive record of historic specimens banked within agencies, universities and private institutions or held by individuals is sorely needed along with space to hold specimens and guidelines for specimen retention. The loss of crucial opportunities for retrospective analyses of trends can be profound. For example, the US federal Green Road laboratory in Ann Arbor, originally attached to the Bureau of Commercial Fisheries in NOAA then later to the US Department of

Interior, once had a collection of frozen alewife samples taken annually from 1964 through the mid-1990s. Lacking freezer space, these specimens were discarded in a house cleaning akin to triage of gravely wounded soldiers. With that action, the potential for retrospective research on the evolution of physical and physiological characters in the alewife population as it adapted to permanent presence in fresh water, and a means to measure how contaminant flows, uptake and congener sorting changed over time after POPs were banned in North America, were discarded as well many other research opportunities.

Scientists take and store specimens partly because they cannot know when specimens are collected all the questions they would like to ask about species or the media sampled. In a very real sense, historic specimens are one 'coin of the realm' of science; it must not be wasted or misspent and never discarded just to save a pittance. The time is long past when we should be discarding samples that can give us opportunities to understand more fully what has happened and why. That sort of analysis allows scientists to identify their errors and successes, thereby to learn how to manage better.

At present, besides the SAB, the IJC has two other advisory boards, the WQB and CGLRA. A similar pair of boards should be developed under a Compact agreement, but with expanded duties and requirements. First, I suggest the Water Quality Board be expanded to have much more prominent air and sediment components. Substantially, there are two media—water and air—by which species and materials, especially pollutants and alien species—recycle, enter and leave the lakes. Aerial inputs and losses are profound influences on water quality. Similarly, incorporation of materials into geochemically-stable sediments and recycling are important pathways influencing biological cycles. We cannot possibly understand water quality and impacts on the biota unless we address all media simultaneously; in this, the ecosystem-focused managers are entirely correct. To a limited extent, the present WQB has done this. But, if effective management is the goal, then we must understand all inputs, exports and storage phenomena including the rates of accumulation and loss by these systems. Furthermore, some body of qualified scientists should be reviewing these data and reporting trends routinely. I believe this board should have that function. This means centralizing water quality and air quality monitoring data from

JAMES P. LUDWIG, Ph.D

twelve jurisdictions, the International Air Deposition Network, other air monitoring programs and whatever sediment monitoring work is going forward in a Media Quality Board (MQB).

At present, much of these data are obscured and lost to easy access within agencies. For example, while sediment quality data are collected in many university studies and most of that eventually is published in peer-reviewed journals, much of data collected in planning for dredging operations, CDF construction and similar on-going project work under the requirements of environmental impact assessments ends up buried in agency reports and is lost effectively. Similarly, there are huge volumes of data collected by air and water discharge permit holders that lies in their reports to regulatory agencies. But, these data are virtually hidden from researchers, a sort of '*data obscura*'. In essence, these kinds of data sets cost nothing to collect in a central repository because private companies or their consultants have done that work. This loss of useful information is one contributor to ineffective management. A centralized information directorate can assemble these data sets at relatively low cost and make that information available widely across the entire Great Lakes watershed.

Assuming these changes are part of this directorate, the second fundamental role of a MQB shall be evaluation of data and trends and providing advice and reports to three audiences—the Compact Commission who will set priorities and select projects for implementation, those who that actually administer and build projects and those who operate programs of Great Lakes management. If we are ever to achieve true basin-wide transparent coordination of management, then all the parties and agencies within parties that do management programs must have equal access to all relevant information. This directorate should make sure that happens and initiate appropriate monitoring of the effectiveness of programs. Presently, the monitoring of progress and failures is haphazard at best, with failures the least likely to be considered, exposed and used to learn what not to do.

We desperately need a formal means to embrace our errors and to remove the stigma associated with making errors during honest effort. Making errors is part of living; it is long overdue that we recognize that error is one of the essential steps to true learning. That most difficult function will require a formal means of evaluation done routinely, operating much the same way the Government Accounting and Congressional Budget Offices do in the United States and the Inspector General does in Canada. The fact that transparent evaluation has been done infrequently in many agencies goes a long way toward explaining why ineffective programs are rarely deleted, glacially slow to adjust, often blundering on for years without any tangible changes, but always consuming scarce human and financial resources.

All to often, these failures to embrace errors are a manifestation of the 'fox-henhouse' syndrome. Consider the enduring problem of accurate fish consumption advisories over the human health hazards represented by bioaccumulated toxic substances. Quite literally, advisories of adjacent Great Lakes jurisdictions often do not match. Sometimes classes of compounds in foods that independent health authorities have documented to be dangerous are simply ignored. For example, at present virtually nothing is being done to inform the public about the dangers of endocrine disruptors now present in the fish taken from the lakes.

Perhaps the most egregious recent Great Lakes example of these deficiencies was the deletion of toxaphene from fish advisories between 1995 and 1999 even as concentrations were escalating rapidly by aerial transport from new Asian sources that reestablished high concentrations in Lake Superior fish and other high latitude North American lakes (Visser 2007). Presently, each state and province is free to set whatever advisories it wishes. If, for political reasons, lack of monitoring budgets, or to protect a home-grown industry, a state or province chooses to ignore a given contaminant class in their published advisories, they are perfectly free to do so. In some jurisdictions, there are no public review processes for proposed advisories.

I submit, if toxaphene is dangerous in Ontario-caught fish at 2 or 5 ppm, then it is in Michigan fish or Illinois fish too. It is absurd that some jurisdictions have ignored public health guidance in the past, yet this has been a recurrent pattern among fish advisories all over the basin (See Visser, 2007 for a complete discussion of this matter.). This is the kind of information that should be standardized, for the hazards to human health from contaminants are as ignorant of political boundaries as birds seeking the best nesting habitats, or fish on migrations. Hazards and risks have no relationship whatsoever to artificial political boundaries. If a single fish meal per month with a concentration of 0.2 ppm mercury is the maximum tolerable exposure for pregnant women (or those of child-bearing age) in Michigan, it is utterly fatuous to accept that 0.5 or 1 ppm is acceptable elsewhere in the basin, politics, economics or the presence of coal-fired power plants in those jurisdictions notwithstanding.

This is a problem by no means unique to the Great Lakes. In some places POPs-contaminated foods are actually recommended for consumption as 'native foods' on the justification that these are culturally appropriate. This occurs to the Inuit cultures of northern Canada at present (Visser *op cit.*). In my more pessimistic moments I cannot help but wonder if this Canadian disgrace is owing to incompetence, agency compartmentalization, or if it is a cynical means to destroy a people and a culture by recommending consumption of foods laden with toxic POPs. Any student of the history of North American colonization knows this kind of none-to-subtle approach has been a recurrent pattern since natives were given blankets from dead smallpox victims by the United States Army, spreading that often-fatal disease rapidly to native North Americans with no inherited immunity. While the Inuit native foods example of today may be a stark modern example of this mindset, a case can be made that the intentional omission of important data on contaminants and endocrine disruptors from Great Lakes state or provincial fish advisories are cousins of the same cynical strategy. Further, it is very convenient to omit warnings if the potential negative impacts on fishing license sales and associated businesses activities are the true concern.

If we are serious about prevention of these sorts of inequities, then a standard set of advisories with basin-wide application and full transparency about how the advisory concentrations were determined by the scientific community is required. In this case, either we evict the fishing interest foxes from the public henhouse or accept that as a society that we will pay a subtle set of very widely dispersed externalized costs owing to poor human reproductive outcomes, higher disease frequencies and lower mental performance (Stewart *et al.* 2005, 2008). The choice is that simple and stark when dealing with hidden contaminants in Great Lakes fish. The only means to find something hidden is to look for it. If you do not look you will not find it. That is why you monitor. And, you must be vigilant because things can change fast in an unregulated capitalistic business world dominated by the WTO and NAFTA, *de facto* protected by neoliberal policies that avoid effective control of externalized pollutants, especially when our world is connected by atmospheric transport.

Thus, I see the MQB structure as including a group of scientists that design, evaluate and oversee the development of long-term comprehensive monitoring datasets for the Great Lakes, including at least the following: The herring gull program of Canadian Wildlife Service; the International Air Deposition Network and any related work such as the UMBS Atmospheric and Climate Change Research Program; Fish advisories and fish monitoring programs; All biotic inventory programs for different taxa; All traditional basin-wide water quality parameter projects; All reported monitoring for parameters under water or air discharge permits; and, All other science related monitoring programs of a similar repetitive long-term nature. Accurate, complete and recent data are the bones of sound management; presently, that skeleton is incomplete and disarticulated because no one agency can afford to do all, or even most of what is required. The result? Great Lakes management is crippled.

The **Intergovernmental Management Directorate (IMD)** should be the body that disseminates information produced by KSPRD and the Compact Commission to all governmental bodies and assures that it is understood and incorporated into policies of the recipient parties through regular audits. I see this directorate as developing means of information sharing, public relations and auditing for the Compact. The information exchange function is relatively straight-forward, although it is reasonable to expect some difficulties as comprehensive information systems are established and integrated. It is likely to be particularly difficult to obtain information on routine monitoring done under permits as many agencies do not compile these data for third party use. Moreover, permit holders that have routine violations will very likely attempt to prevent the release and widespread dissemination of those data. That was the pattern of corporate polluters when the US established the 'Toxic Release Inventory': we should expect it to be repeated.

The audit function is also very likely to encounter resistance from established program managers for obvious reasons. Basically, the function of audits is to locate and correct errors, whether owing to omission, commission or lack of vision. Very few agencies, especially those unused to audits of their programs for performance, tolerate third-party audits gracefully. However, that is precisely what is required of the many Great Lakes programs that have only had their budgets audited. The science and performance-based audits most needed are those that match criteria and goals with progress of programs and projects that were designed to address those criteria and goals.

In all to many cases, existing programs developed a bit like 'Topsy'. Often, funds were directed toward a particular acute need without a clear mission statement or protocol of how to proceed, and very frequently with a lack of basic data on the nature of the problem. A perfect example of this was the way the US Food and Drug Administration (FDA) and other agencies reacted to the discovery of high levels of PCBs in Great Lakes fish between 1968 and 1970. FDA Action levels were established in 1972 without knowledge of the environmental behavior of these chemicals, inaccurate and incomplete toxicological analysis and a fundamental lack of information on how toxic mechanisms were induced inside of contaminated animals. In spite of many advances in knowledge in the next two decades, the FDA advice of 1972 remained substantially in place without critical review or change for the next 24 years. Most states deferred to the long-standing FDA advice in order to protect their fisheries and for economic reasons.

The fact that deferring to the FDA guidance protected fishing interests made this a convenient and palatable policy to the governments that sold fishing licenses. The advice to parties was not adjusted even partially until ten to fifteen years *after* verified information emerged on phenomena like selective sediment sorting, selective congener retention in food chains, congener-specific research showed that total PCB data did not reflect toxic potency of weathered mixtures and a fundamental understanding of the hazards was complete (Birnbaum 1993; Giesy *et al.* 1994d; Schecter 1994).

When we consider the high probability that new blue-green algal toxins with unknown toxic mechanisms, dosages and even routes into wildlife and people are likely to appear in the Great Lakes, we should learn from the PCB experience and assure that the pattern of institutionalized indifference in order to protect a *status quo* is never repeated. The IMD can provide both the audit function to measure success or failure and training for agencies' staffs seeking to develop clear mission statements under the Compact. In essence the IMD will be the staff translator of the directives of the Compact Commission and the technical advice of the KSPRD to and from the parties and their agencies.

The **Programs and Projects Directorate** (PPD) will develop and implement all specific projects approved and undertaken by the Compact Commission. The PPD shall administer all projects or programs contracted to agencies or third parties for Great Lakes research, monitoring, infrastructure development or maintenance and other matters under Commission authority and direction. An enormous effort will be required to integrate the program elements of the panoply of agency programs now distributed among the huge number of agencies presently active in the basin. This will not be done easily or quickly, partly because each agency and sub-agency will be highly territorial as they protect what they perceive to be their territory, interests and budgets. And, this is precisely where the executive leadership of the President, Prime Minister and cabinet level officers in the two federal and ten state or provincial governments will be the most critical. It cannot be accomplished without their leadership to force the bureaucracies under their control to comply with a new GLWQA requirement of a single integrated approach to Great Lakes management through a Compact. This will not be accomplished easily: but, it must be done very soon if we are ever to see the Great Lakes return to a self-sustaining, healthy ecological balance.

VII.

A final word.

THERE IS NO doubt we have done a horrid job managing the Sweetwater Seas for a century. The 100 years after the Boundary Waters Treaty was signed will be regarded by historians as the century when Canada and the United States finally recognized the need to control pollution to protect these precious public resources, but failed egregiously. To be sure, there has been progress, especially since the 1960s when obvious threats and severe damage became obvious to most observers. Yet, in spite of Herculean efforts by thousands of well-intentioned people, we have failed miserably. All of us must bear a part of the blame. On the occasion of the 100th anniversary of these official efforts to protect these precious waters, their condition was simply awful even as our management of these resources was chaotic. Worst, there is no clear multiparty vision of how to proceed to resurrect these lakes to health and productivity for themselves or the commonweal. It seems as though we have allowed ourselves to accept defeat. But, I refuse to accept that as the fate of our Sweetwater Seas. We are obligated to do better for our children.

Mao Tse-Tung one once said that a popular revolution was necessary every so often to achieve progress. Ghandi expressed it somewhat differently *'Civil disobedience becomes a sacred duty when the state becomes lawless or corrupt.'* Certainly, I do not subscribe to the violence and force recommended by revolutionaries to achieve change. Yet, I believe strongly that the moral force springing from the damage to our Sweetwater Seas is sufficient to justify a peaceful revolution in the way these resources are managed.

I have intended this book to be a call to debate the possible paths to effective change and to reignite the fires of public involvement, because our many efforts to eliminate threats and correct problems have failed miserably for more than a century. That is a sufficient length of time to be certain the structures of governance and existing management programs are egregious failures. And, I remind you of the truth that continuing to do what led to failure and expecting a better result is one hallmark of stupidity. We cannot expect better results by continuing to do what got us into this mess. Failed strategies, plans and institutions are sufficient justification for a radical changes to the way we manage these treasures for they the economic and ecological heart of North America, and a boundless source of beauty.

When I was courting my second wife I confronted all the issues of an older man (51) proposing marriage to a younger woman (37) from a different culture. One of the items we discussed was our differing means to approach change born of frustration. I told Alison that I was from a different era and would bring to our relationship a certain level of 'baggage' owing to that: but, mostly I was significantly older than her with a lot less patience than when I was younger. I have often explained to those who ask my age not that I am 72 now, but that I have survived to the 'age of no more bullshit' and refuse to tolerate more of it. I no longer simply 'go along to get along'; instead, I confront issues and problems directly without concern for the fallout from those I disturb.

On Great Lakes issues, regardless of our chronological ages, we need to mature our attitudes toward management of these precious resources by a refusal to accept any more bullshit over why we cannot deliver the commitments in a century old treaty and the four decades old GLWQA in order to prevent further injury to health. That is, we must bring forward the politicians and agencies forward into an age of no more bullshit, whether they like it or not, even if it means politicians we like as human beings lose their jobs.

Substantially, we have two choices. We can continue to stumble and bumble along with the same agencies of government, the prevailing fiefdom mindset of agencies and the fuzzy goals of the ecosystem approach. If we do, I suggest the probability that management will improve on a reasonable timetable is minute, approaching the probability of survival of a proverbial 'snowball in hell'. Our alternative is to determine what went wrong and why, without blaming any one, or any group, for the actions that promoted or fed failure to this point. In the words of Don Michael (1967), we must 'embrace our errors' to learn from them. Acknowledging failure is the single most difficult task we face. If we can do so, then genuine progress becomes at least a real possibility. If each of us remains defensive, promoting insular views or the conventional wisdom of our peer groups and the *status quo*, then continuous failure is inevitable. For many scientists and agency administrators, it is time to question the very paradigms we have used to frame our decisions on management and research for decades. In this book I have been especially critical to the point of harshness toward proponents of the nebulous ecosystem approach and much of the fisheries community because I believe these groups operate from failed paradigms. The same criticism is true of my own field.

Consider this example from environmental toxicology. Two decades ago Thomas and Colborn (1993) theorized that endocrine and immune systems were more sensitive to lower or moderate dose exposures than high doses of many endocrine disrupting synthetic chemicals. They were attacked roundly by many toxicologists who adhered to the fundamental toxicological paradigm that *'The dose makes the poison. Greater effects are caused by greater doses, and there is always a threshold of exposure concentration that leads to effects.'* However, numerous recent studies show that Thomas and Colborn were onto something substantial. For example, Steinberg *et al.* (2008) reported that pregnant rats exposed to a PCB blend of Aroclor™ mixtures did not have substantial effects at either high (10 mg/kg) or low dose (0.1 mg/kg) exposures, but that the intermediate dose of 1 mg/kg produced permanent effects on both the daughter (F_1) and granddaughter (F_2) generations female reproductive cycling and outcomes.

Not only does this and many other recent studies challenge the 'dose makes the poison' dictum of the classical toxicological paradigm, the fact that deleterious changes were evoked in two *successive* generations from a single exposure extends the idea of intergenerational damage far beyond the studies of the next generation (e.g. Stewart *et al.* 2008). Recently, Heindel and others in the human health field have summarized much new data that show epigenetic effects across generations when synthetic chemicals switch on or switch off genes that are later recombined to produce new offspring. Much of this damage occurs with low to moderate doses that do not cause overt damage to the exposed animal. Many endocrine disruptor chemicals present in Great Lakes fish humans eat may switch on unusual combinations of genes that contribute to or initiate many disease conditions including diabetes, thyroid anomalies, obesity and cancer in successive generations (Heindel 2010).

These new data suggest that the present strategy of benign neglect that depends on slow natural attenuation of contaminants in the Great Lakes as the remediation strategy may be very dangerous to humans and wildlife as doses are downshifted to intermediate, but still substantial, concentrations of many chemicals. A terrifying possibility is that by doing so, we throw open the door to poor health and many endocrine-mediated diseases with lifelong deleterious effects on subsequent human generations in the Great Lakes region.

Clearly, the 'tectonic plates' of toxicology are shifting; our toxicological paradigms must shift to accommodate and use the new knowledge properly. The larger community of Great Lakes scientists must commit to a thorough examination of our traditional paradigms and assumptions to be able to progress. We must choose this difficult path to change if we really do care about these once magnificent ecological systems. Or, we can be like the legendary desert bedouin and just fold up our tent, steal off silently into the night and try to forget the mess to which we all have contributed. Personally, I tried that by moving to Nova Scotia first, then Saskatchewan, now Alberta. It did not work.

I sense we are on the cusp of a huge cultural crisis in the way we see ourselves as citizens in western democracies. An element of this crisis spills into the Great Lakes related to the culture of "I-ness". Ever since President Reagan and British Prime Minister Margaret Thatcher articulated the concepts of neoliberalism for the masses legitimizing the ideas that greed and personal exploitation through market opportunities was not just a good value, but our most important value, we have slipped ever more into the mindset that our personal gain is the only accurate measure of societal success. But, whenever personal greed was the dominant social goal, community always suffered, just as occurred in Dicken's time of early industrial England and during the Great Depression.

JAMES P. LUDWIG, Ph.D

Look around and what do we see and hear about every day? It is I-phones, I-pods, I-reports, Facebook, Twitter and instant gratification that are the 'hip culture'. These are unmistakable signs of a North American culture oriented to the immediate desires of the individual, not the lifetime and multigenerational needs of the commonweal. It is quite remarkable, even humorous, how well the essence of this culture has been captured from time to time in music television (MTV). Perhaps the best example came from *Dire Straits* whose wonderful song about a neer-do-well appliance salesman watching a ridiculously rich rock star perform on television went like this:

> *"Man, that's the way you do it. Get your money for* [doing] *nothin and your chicks for free."*

Presently, we seem to be captured in a culture that celebrates only the individual, the individual's capacity to gather up wealth and resources for personal use and gratification, and the hedonism of accomplishing personal goals alone. One root of that philosophy is the myth of rugged American individualism that has celebrated the individual's achievements since the US was formed. But a huge price is isolation of people from their communities (one such community is the Great Lakes, a key piece of our commonweal) and the capacity to act together to solve problems.

And, when we have a pernicious neoliberal political philosophy at work legitimizing these values in both the US and Canada and perpetually reducing budgets for programs like Great Lakes restoration, our isolation can only increase even as our effectiveness withers. Then, our social contract of a people working together to preserve and enhance the lakes decays into ruin. Effective restoration of the Great Lakes will be expensive. That means those of us who pay taxes must accept increased burdens, regardless of our antipathy to larger, more expensive governments. It is time to pay the piper.

Daily we are bombarded through the broadcast media with actions of our neoliberal governments that incite us to nausea. For Americans these may include issues like Abu Grahib and Guantanamo Bay prisons and the controversial practices of human torture, glibly justified by the late Bush Administration as necessary to preserve the 'American Way'. Many Americans were utterly revolted that the rights we enjoy as citizens were trampled upon for our captives repeatedly, often sadistically. Sadly, it was continued under the Obama Administration.

In Canada, the recent prorogation of Parliament initiated by Stephen Harper is a similar challenge to our sense of who we are. During the run-up to prorogation we heard Prime Minister Harper claim shrilly that the threat of the opposition parties to topple the government in the first confidence vote of his newly elected minority government was a *coup d'etat*. Somehow, he brow-beat the Canadian Governor General to allow the prorogation of Parliament. In the long history of western parliamentary democracies a prorogation decision taken *only* to avoid a vote of no confidence had happened four times—by Adolf Hitler in 1933, Generalissimo Francisco Franco in 1936, Benito Mussolini in 1939 and Augusto Pinochet in 1973. As a new Canadian, I am utterly ashamed to find my Prime Minister in the same bed once occupied by these non-to-stellar examples of parliamentary democracy as each prepared for their own real *coup d'etat*. But then, perhaps I should not be so surprised since Mr. Harper describes his neoliberal administration as the 'Harper Government' rather than the Canadian Government.

In the long history of parliamentary democracies, decisions to prorogue parliaments often were the prelude to a true *coup d'etat*, but votes of 'no-confidence' never were the cause of a *coup*. A vote of no confidence for a minority party government only means either a coalition government or a new election in Canada. I see Prime Minister Harper's behavior as fully consistent with the neoliberal approach to most issues. Lie through a complicit media to establish doubt in an electorate that does not understand the way its government actually works (or does not work). Then, tell the lie often enough, find shills to promote the lie, and a confused public will fall into line. Indeed, Niccolo Machiavelli has been reincarnated and lives well north of the border, just as George W. Bush taught Americans to the south during the run up to his Second Gulf War!

We should be reflecting on what these kinds of radical departures from our shared democratic values and constitutional governments mean, exactly how these threats to true democracy were perpetrated and how the natural resources our societies depend upon are affected. These are the cultural taproots of our inability to protect the Sweetwater Seas. Worldwide we live in a time when the medium is the message, as so aptly put by McLuhan. Whoever controls the media with their message is apt to prevail. Modern neoliberal politicians and corporations have conspired relentlessly to get their mendacious messages out (Beder 2008), just as the recent history of the Iraq conflict and the prorogation decision in Canada show us vividly.

What has happened in the Great Lakes is a reflection of the broader ways we have implemented our values and created our cultures. Today, we ought never be surprised if we discern lies about the resources that are present in the Great Lakes and how these resources should be managed. Rather, we ought to ask who is lying, for what purpose, and how does that lie fit into a broader attempt to control the lakes for a neoliberal political agenda. Henry Giroux writing for the Truthout blog put it this way when confronting the effects of neoliberal politics and policies (Truthout, April 7, 2010):

'For over 30 years, the American public has been reared on a neoliberal dystopian vision that legitimates itself through the largely unchallenged claim that there are no alternatives to a market-driven society, that economic growth should not be constrained by considerations of social costs or moral responsibility and that democracy and capitalism were virtually synonymous. At the heart of this market rationality is an egocentric philosophy and culture of cruelty that sold off public goods and services to the highest bidders in the corporate and private sectors, while simultaneously dismantling those public spheres, social protections and institutions serving the public good. As economic power freed itself from traditional government regulations, a new global financial class reasserted the prerogatives of capital and systemically destroyed those public spheres advocating social equality and an educated citizenry as a condition for a viable democracy. At the same time, economic deregulation merged powerfully with the ideology of individual responsibility, effectively evading any notion of corporate responsibility, while effectively undercutting any sense of corporate accountability to a broader public.'

For at least the last thirty years, our societies have drifted ever closer to enshrining most of the economic and social concepts espoused by libertarians, neoliberals and their economists, particularly the school of economic thought driven forward by Milton Friedman and his colleagues four decades ago at the University of Chicago. But, markets driven by supply and demand, have no common social values or any means besides accumulating wealth and power to generate priorities for the society. The tendency for all of us in a neoliberal world is to maximize our own monetary gains and to forget about externalities that soon cripple our common resources.

In large measure, this became the sum of 'The American and Canadian Dreams'—accumulate as much wealth as possible, pay as few taxes as possible, and keep to yourself. An inexorable result is the concentration of wealth in the hands of the very few, a pattern of stealthy attacks on social programs like health care and natural resource management, and the privatization of public programs and resources solely for profits. Tax cuts, ostensibly to increase economic activity, nearly always rob resources from social programs and the commonweal and will lead eventually to the failure of our long-held social contract to succeed or fail as a whole society. As I write these opinions I see the credit, housing and economic debacles of the fall of 2008 through to today as inevitable results of these philosophies. Another cost has been the sacrifice of the Great Lakes and their immense natural resource value on the altar of those same mendacious philosophies of greed and exploitation for private gains.

In this time of severe economic and natural resource crises in the Great Lakes region it is interesting to revisit the writings of Charles Dickens who chronicled a time of great similarity in the England of the first half of the nineteenth century. Industries were running amok with no regulation, wealth was concentrated in the hands of a very few, public health and education were ignored, disease outbreaks were common and many thousands were out of work. The British social contract was in utter disarray following the rampant unregulated development of industries and the urbanization of that era.

In a real sense, the present pattern of globalization of unregulated or poorly regulated international trade that has permitted and even encouraged lead paints on our imported toys and PBDEs in the plastics of our cellphones and foams in our couches, contaminating our children, waters and wildlife are simply inevitable results of many neoliberal political initiatives. One wonders whether we have made much progress in the seventeen decades since Dickens described the horrid conditions

JAMES P. LUDWIG, Ph.D

of a rapidly industrializing England. The threats and mechanisms are different today, but the damage to the lakes and the true cause—greed—are remarkably similar.

Just as the market collapses, housing crisis, and banking catastrophes and scandals of the fall of 2008 have stimulated calls for reregulation of markets, I submit we must do the same re-examination of our social contract around the Great Lakes and many other social issues of the commonweal. And, we must do it now. Time is of the essence. So, educated your self on how we have come to this deplorable state for the Great Lakes, and choose a new path. Become a part of the solution, or just get out of the way while committing to pay enough in taxes to support the changes required. Either way, I suggest we all reflect on the sacred words in the Book of Common Prayer, to wit:

"We have done those things we ought not to have done, left undone those things we ought to have done, and there is no health in us."

If we are honest we will rephrase this confession to be:

We have done to the Great Lakes those things we ought not to have done, left undone those things we ought to have done, and there in no health in the Great Lakes.

Gaia cannot, and will not, help us make the necessary changes. In fact, as climate change is showing us vividly through increased storm frequencies and intensities all over the world, Gaia will exact a large price for our foolishness over unregulated atmospheric emissions. We will pay that price no matter what we do. This is not like the challenge of a bloated national debt our children alone will face, for we are facing these challenges every day in the Great Lakes region, even those aspects and costs largely concealed in a failing social contract for public services like health care, natural resource management and schools.

This is up to us. We have the power through full disclosure and the ballot box to force genuine change to happen. But change will elude us if we fail to accept the challenge to confront how the Great Lakes were despoiled for neoliberal goals and profits for the few. Now, what will you do to change this for the better? Will you participate or fold up your tent to steal silently away in the night for your narrow self-interest? Will you learn about and debate the pernicious effects of decades of decay of our Great Lakes resources promoted by our neoliberal governments? Will you ask whether this is the philosophical construct for the world you want for Canada and the United States, but especially for your children and grandchildren? Will you ask if an obscure young black man from south Chicago who understood Lake Michigan only as a place to retreat to for a moment of comfort and solace is relevant to you and the rest of us?

These are profound questions that will determine whether you are a competent member of our societies. The Sweetwater Seas and the Andres of the commonweal await your decisions.

Choose wisely.

Choose well.

But above all, choose quickly.

JAMES P. LUDWIG, Ph.D

EPILOGUE.

J UNE 20, 2013. **Cormorants and Herring Gulls**. This book has been a litany of our collective failures to protect the lakes. I would not be at all surprised if the text has left many readers deeply depressed and furious at agencies and me: I share those emotions. Yet today, I found a new glimmer of hope banding water birds in the company of brother Ted. Hundreds of nesting cormorants, a new colony of black-crowned night herons and an old colony of herring gulls all at Round Island, Lake Superior, a few miles above the Sault locks were visited and over two hundred banded. The gull chicks were normal and seemed to be healthy, as did the chicks of the other birds. Chicken and pork bones littered the gull spaces, indicating their dependence on nearby landfills. The herons were eating frogs, small perch and other fish typical of inland lakes. But those rascally cormorants were up to their usual tricks of exploitation of whatever fish in the lake were near their colony. We saw a few chubs, many alewives, sticklebacks and even four of those ecological horrors we call lamprey eels. In the decade from 1986-1995, our teams found one lamprey in their regurgitations of over 14,000 fish. Today, we found four adult lampreys here, each close to 18 inches long, among 216 regurgitated fish, mostly sticklebacks and alewives.

One of four lamprey eels found regurgitated in cormorant nests at Round Island, upper St. Marys River, Lake Superior on June 20, 2013. Photograph credit to Dr. Fred (Ted) Ludwig II.

Two gobies, an alewife and several sticklebacks found regurgitated in a cormorant nest at Naubinway Island, northern Lake Michigan on June 21, 2013.

The next day we elected to visit Naubinway Island, Cosmos birthplace, in northern Lake Michigan to see if there were substantial numbers of herring gulls and maybe a few unmolested cormorants nesting. We found both species nesting successfully. Of particular interest was the diet of the cormorants. We found it vastly different than reported in my previous studies (Ludwig *et al.* 1989, Diana *et al.* 1997) and closer to the diet cormorants' diet reported by Seefelt and Gillingham (2008) in the nearby Beaver Islands in 2003. I was able to identify 962 regurgitated fish: nearly half (436) were sticklebacks, a fourth were alewives (273), 217 (23%) were gobies and there was a smattering of logperch (19), troutperch (16) and a single small yellow perch. Previous work by dozens of researchers has found that cormorants eat whatever is living close to their nesting sites and abundant. These observations suggest that the control program for cormorants should credit their benefits to the fisheries at least as much as the supposed evidence of damage to yellow perch and other sport fish, which is poorly documented at best, and was misused cynically to justify the infamous 'cormorant holocaust' (Diana 2010).

We also looked at close to 800 young cormorants without finding one crossed bill bird or any others showing the dioxin-like related defects that once were so rampant among young cormorants, particularly in northern Lake Michigan and Green Bay. These few data point out the capability of the lakes to foster and sustain natural recoveries. The Great Lakes are resilient—if we just give them the chance to recover balance and ecological stability by controlling future biological and chemical pollution and cleaning up the legacy problems already here. But, in order to succeed, we must first clean up the political mess borne of neoliberalism that has allowed this to fester for so very long.

Now, let us be about finding the best ways to do that!

JAMES P. LUDWIG, Ph.D

Looking due south from the southeastern side of the Keweenaw Peninsula on the calm and beautiful evening of June 22, 2013, a view that justifies every effort to preserve and restore the Great Lakes.

LITERATURE CITED.

Adams, M. 2003. **Fire and Ice: The US and Canada and the myth of converging values.** Penguin Books. 224 pp.

Allen, T.F. H, B, L. Bandurski and A. W. King. 1993. The Ecosystem approach: Theory and ecosystem integrity. A report to the Science Advisory Board. *International Joint Commission.* ISBN 1-895085-78-0.

Ankley, G. T., D. E. Tillitt, J. W. Gooch and J. P. Giesy. 1989. Hepatic enzyme systems as biochemical indicators of the effects of contaminants on reproduction of Chinook salmon (*Oncorhynchus tschawytscha*). *Comparative Biochemistry and Physiology* **94**: 235-242.

Becker, R., M. Sultan, G. Boyer and E. Konopoko. 2006. Mapping variations of algal blooms in the lower Great Lakes. *Great Lakes Research Review* **7**: 14-17.

Beder, S. 2008. The corporate assault on democracy. *International Journal of Inclusive Democracy* **4**: 3-17.

Belyea, G.Y., S. L. Maruca, J. S. Diana, P. S. Schneeberger, S. J, Scott, R. D. Clark, Jr., J. P. Ludwig and C. L. Summer. 1999. Impact of Double-crested Cormorant predation on the Yellow Perch population in the Les Cheneaux Islands of Michigan. *Proceedings of the 1997 Wildlife Society Cormorant Symposium.*

Birnbaum, L. 1993. Re-evaluation of dioxin. July 15, 1993 presentation to the IJC Water Quality Board, *USEPA Research Triangle Park, Environmental Toxicology Division.* 19 pp.

Birrenkott, A. H., S.B. Wilde, J. J. Hains, J. R. Fischer, T. W. Murphy, C. P. Hope, P. G. Parnell and W. W. Bowerman. 2004. Establishing a food-chain link between aquatic plant material and Avian Vacuolar Myelinopathy in mallards (*Anas platyrhynchos*). *Journal of Wildlife Diseases* **40**: 485-492.

Bishop, C. A., R. J. Brooks, J. H. Carey, P. Ng, R. J. Norstrom, and D. S., Lean. 1991. The case for a cause-effect linkage between environmental contamination and development in the eggs of the common snapping turtle (*Chelydra s. serpentina*) from Ontario, Canada. *Journal of Toxicology and Environmental Health* **33**: 521-548.

Blaxland J. D. 1951. Newcastle disease in shags and cormorants and its significance as a factor in the spread of the disease among domestic poultry. *Veterinary Records* **63**: 731-733.

Borgmann, U. and D. M. Whittle. 1991. Contaminant concentration trends in Lake Ontario lake trout (*Salvelinus namaycush*): 1977 to 1988. *Journal of Great lakes Research* **17**: 368-381.

W. W. Bowerman. 1993. Regulation of Bald Eagle (*Haliaeetus leucocephlus*) productivity in the Great Lakes basin. Ph.D dissertation, *Michigan State University*, East Lansing. 189 pp.

Bowerman, W. W., T.J. Kubiak, J. B. Holt, D. L. Evans, R. G. Eckstein, C. R. Sindelar, D. A. Best and K. D. Kozie. 1994. Observed abnormalities in mandibles of nestling bald eagles (*Haliaeetus leucocephalus*). *Bulletin of Environmental Contamination and Toxicology* **53**: 450-457.

Bowerman, W. W., J. P. Giesy, D. A. Best and V. J. Kramer. 1995. A review of factors affecting productivity of bald eagles in the Great Lakes region: implications for recovery. *Environmental Health Perspectives* **103**: 51-59.

Boyer, G. L. 2006. Toxic cyanobacteria in the Great Lakes: More than just the western basin of Lake Erie. *Great Lakes Research Review* **7**: 2-7.

Braden, J. B., L. O. Taylor, D. Won, N. Mays, A. Cangelosi and A. A. Patunru. 2008a. Economic benefits of remediating the Buffalo River, New York Area of Concern. *Journal of Great Lakes Research* **34**: 631-648.

Braden, J. B., D. Won, L. O. Taylor, N. Mays, A. Cangelosi and A. A. Patunru. 2008b. Economic benefits of remediating the Sheboygan River, Wisconsin Area of Concern. *Journal of Great Lakes Research* **34**: 649-660.

Braune, B. M. and R. J. Norstrom. 1989. Dynamics of organochlorine compounds in herring gulls: III. Tissue distribution and bioaccumulation in Lake Ontario gulls. *Environmental Toxicology and Chemistry* **8**: 957-968.

Brouwer, A. 1989. Inhibition of thyroid hormone transport in plasma of rats by polychlorinated biphenyls. *Archives of Toxicology* **153**: 625-632.

Burkhard, L., D. Armstrong and A. Andren. 1985. Partitioning behavior of polychlorinated biphenyls. *Chemosphere* **14**: 1703-1716.

Chopra, S. 2009. **Corrupt to the Core.** KOS publishing, Caledon, ON. ISBN 978-0-9731945-7-9. 340pp.

Clark, T. P., R. J. Norstrom, G. A. Fox, and H. T. Won. 1987. Dynamics of organochlorine compounds in herring gulls (*Larus argentatus*): II. A two-compartment model and data for ten compounds. *Environmental Toxicology and Chemistry* **6**: 547-559.

Colborn, T., A. Davidson, S. N. Green, R. A. Hodge, C. I. Jackson and R. A. Liroff. 1991. **Great Lakes, Great Legacy?** *The Conservation Foundation*, Washington, DC, and *The Institute for Research on Public Policy*, Ottawa, Ontario. 301 pp.

Commoner, B. 1966. **Science and Survival.** Viking Press, New York. 150 pp.

Cook, P.M., J.A. Robbins, D.D. Endicott, K. B. Lodge, P.D. Guiney, M.K. Walker, E. W. Zabel and R. E. Peterson. 2003. Effects of aryl hydrocarbon hydroxylase receptor-mediated early life stage toxicity in lake trout populations in Lake Ontario during the 20th century. *Environmental Science and Technology* **37**: 3864-3877.

Cooper, W.C. 1995. Risks of organochlorine contaminants to Great Lakes ecosystems are overstated. *Ecological Applications* **5**: 293-298.

Crawford, R.J.M., .M. Allbright and C.W. Heyl. 1992. High mortality of cape cormorants (*Phalacrocorax capensis*) off western South Africa caused by *Pasturella multocida. Colonial Waterbirds* **15**: 236-238.

DeGuise, S., S.D. Shaw, J. S. Barclay, J. Brock, A. Brouwer, E. Dewailly, P. A. Fair, M. Fouriner, P. Grandjean, L. J. Guillette, Jr., M. E. Hahn, C. Koopman-Esseboom, R. J. Latcher, A. Matz, R. J. Norstrom, C. R. Perkins, L. Schwacke, J. U. Skaare, J. Sowles, DJ. St.Aubin, J. Stegeman and J. E. Whaley. 2001. Consensus Statement: Atlantic Coast Contaminants Workshop 2000. *Environmental Health Perspectives* **109**: 1301-1302.

Diana, J. S., C.A. Jones D.O Lucchesi and J.C. Schneider. 1987. Evaluation of the yellow perch fishery and its importance to the local economy of the Les Cheneaux Islands area. Final Report LRP-8C-7. Coastal Management Program, *Michigan Department of Natural Resources*. 59 pp.+ appendices.

Diana, J.S., G.Y. Belyea, and R. D. Clark, Jr., Eds. 1997. History, status and trends in populations of yellow perch and double-crested cormorants in Les Cheneaux Islands, Michigan. Eds. Special Report 17, *Michigan Department of Natural Resources, Fish Division.*

Diana, J. S. 2010. Should cormorants be controlled to enhance yellow perch in Les Cheneaux Islands? A commentary on Felder (2008). *Journal of Great Lakes Research* **36**: 190-194.

Delzell, E. J., J. Doull, J. P. Giesy, D. Mackay, I. C. Monro and G. M. Williams. 1994. Interpretative review of the potential adverse effects of chlorinated organic chemicals on human health and the environment: polychlorinated PCBs. *Regulatory Toxicology and Pharmacology* **20** (Special Supplement 1, part 2). Academic Press, NY.

Durnil, G. 1995. **The making of an environmental conservative.** Indiana University Press, Bloomington. ISBN 0-253-32873-X.

JAMES P. LUDWIG, Ph.D

Elbrecht, A. and R. G. Smith. 1992. Aromatase enzyme activity and sex determination in chickens. *Science* **255**: 467-470.

Environment Canada. 1991. Toxic Chemicals in the Great Lakes and associated effects. Synopsis. 51 pp.

Fair, P. A., J.S. Reid, T. Hulsey, G. Mitchum, E. Worth, J. Adams, E. Zolman and G. D. Borsard . 2007. Association of polybrominated diphenyl ethers (PBDEs) blubber concentrations with health status of bottlenose dolphins (*Tursiops truncatus*) along the southeast United States. Poster presented at *Society of Environmental Toxicology and Chemistry annual meeting*, Milwaukee, WI, November, 2007.

Finkelstein, M., B. S. Keitt, D. D. Croll, B. Tershy, W. M. Jarman, S. Rodriguez-Pastor, D. J. Anderson, P. R. Sievert and D. R. Smith. 2006. Albatross species demonstrate regional differences in North Pacific marine contamination. *Ecological Applications* **16**: 678-686.

Fox, G. A., A. P. Gilman, D. B. Peakall and F. W. Anderka. 1978. Behavioral abnormalities of nesting Lake Ontario herring gulls. *Journal of Wildlife Management* **42**: 477-483.

Fox, G. A., D.V. Weseloh, T.J. Kubiak, and T.C. Erdman. 1991a. Reproductive outcomes in colonial fish-eating birds: A biomarker for developmental toxicants in Great Lakes food chains. I. Historical and ecotoxicological perspectives. *Journal of Great Lakes Research* **17**: 153-157.

Fox, G. A., B. Collins, E. Hayakawa, D.V. Weseloh, J.P. Ludwig, T.J. Kubiak, and T.C. Erdman. 1991b. Reproductive outcomes in colonial fish-eating birds: A biomarker for developmental toxicants in Great Lakes food chains. II. Spatial variation if ther occurrence and prevalence of bill defects in young double-crested cormorants in the Great Lakes 1979-1987. *Journal of Great Lakes Research* **17**: 158-167.

Fox, G. A. 1991. Practical causal inference for ecoepidemiologists. *Journal of Toxicology and Environmental Health* **33**: 359-373.

Freeman R. 2003. Opening rivers to trojan fish: The ecological dilemma of dam removal in the Great Lakes. *Conservation in Practice* **3**: 35-40.

Fry, D. M., C.K. Toone, S.M. Speich and R.J. Peard. 1987. Sex ratio skew and breeding patterns of gulls: demographic and toxicological considerations. *Studies in Avian Biology* **10**: 26-43.

Giesy, J. P. and R. L. Graney. 1989. Recent developments in and intercomparisons of acute and chronic bioassays and bioindicators. *Hydrobiologica* **188/189**: 21-60.

Giesy, J. P., D. A. Verbrugge, R. A. Othout, W. W. Bowerman, M. A. Mora, P. D. Jones, J. L. Newstead, C. Vandervoort, S. N. Heaton, R. J. Aulerich, S. J. Bursian, J. P. Ludwig, M. Ludwig, G. A. Dawson, T. J. Kubiak, D. A. Best, and D. E. Tillitt. 1994a. Contaminants in fishes from Great Lakes-influenced sections and above dams of three Michigan rivers I: Concentrations of organochlorine insecticides, polychlorinated biphenyls, dioxin equivalents, and mercury. *Archives of Contamination and Toxicology* **27**: 202-212.

Giesy, J. P., D. A. Verbrugge, R. A. Othout, W. W. Bowerman, M. A. Mora, P. D. Jones, J. L. Newstead, C. Vandervoort, S. N. Heaton, R. J. Aulerich, S. J. Bursian, J. P. Ludwig, G. A. Dawson, T. J. Kubiak, D. A. Best, and D. E. Tillitt. 1994b. Contaminants in fishes from Great Lakes-influenced sections and above dams of three Michigan rivers II: Implications for the health of mink. *Archives of Environmental Contamination* **27**:213-223.

Giesy, J. P., D. A. Verbrugge, R. A. Othout, W. W. Bowerman, M. A. Mora, P. D. Jones, J. L. Newstead, C. Vandervoort, S. N. Heaton, R. J. Aulerich, S. J. Bursian, J. P. Ludwig, M. Ludwig, G. A. Dawson, T. J. Kubiak, D. A. Best, and D. E. Tillitt. Contaminants in fishes from Great Lakes-influenced sections and above dams of three Michigan rivers III: Concentrations of organochlorine insecticides, polychlorinated biphenyls, dioxin equivalents, and mercury: Implications for the health of eagles. *Archives of Contamination and Toxicology* **27**: 224-252.

Giesy, J. P., J. P. Ludwig, and D. E. Tillitt. 1994d. Deformities in birds of the Great Lakes region: Assigning causality. *Environmental Science and Technology* **28**: 128-135.

Gilbertson, M.O. 2007. Injury to Health: A forensic audit of the Great Lakes Water Quality Agreement (1972-2005), with special reference to congenital Minamata Disease. Ph.D. Thesis, University of Stirling, Stirling, Scotland, United Kingdom.

Gilbertson, M. O. 2009. Index of congenital Minimata Disease (CMD) in Canadian areas of concern in the Great Lakes. Submitted to *Environmental Toxicology and Chemistry*.

Gilbertson, M.O., G.A. Fox, H. Henry, J.P. Ludwig. 1990. New strategies for Great Lakes toxicology. Editorial commentary. *Journal of Great Lakes Research* **16**: 625-627.

Gilbertson, M.O, G.A. Fox, J.P. Ludwig, and T.J. Kubiak. 1991. The Great Lakes embryo mortality, edema and deformity syndrome (GLEMEDS). *Toxicology and Environmental Health* **33**: 455-520.

Gilbertson, M. O. and A. E. Watterson. 2007. Diversionary reframing of the Great Lakes Water Quality Agreement. *Journal of Public Health Policy* **28**: 201-215.

Gilbertson, M. O., and J. Brophy. 2001. Community health profile of Windsor, Ontario: Anatomy of a Great Lakes Area of Concern. *Environmental Health Perspectives* **109** Supplement 6: 827-843.

Giroux, H. 2010. Commentary on Truthout Blog, April 7, 2010, WWW.

Glaser, L. C., I. K. Barker, D. V. Weseloh, J. Ludwig, R. M. Windingstad, D. W. Key, and T. K. Bollinger. 1999. The 1992 epizootic of Newcastles Disease in double-crested cormorants of North America. *Journal of Wildlife Diseases* **35**: 319-330.

Gore, A. 2007. **The Assault on Reason.** Penguin Press. ISBN 978-1-59420-122-6. 308 pp.

Grasman, K. A. 1995. Immunological and hematological biomarkers for contaminants in fish-eating birds of the Great Lakes. Ph.D thesis. Virginia Technological University, Blacksburg. 176 pp.

Grasman, K. A., G. A. Fox, P. F. Scanlon, and J. P. Ludwig. 1996. Organochlorine-associated immunosuppression in prefledgling Caspian terns and herring gulls from the Great Lakes: An ecoepidemiological study. *Environmental Health Perspectives* **104** (Supplement 4): 829-842.

Grasman, K. A., S. Fuhrman, M. Langeland, M. McRae, and L. Williams. 2013. Health and reproductive impairments in colonial waterbirds in the Saginaw Bay and River Raisin Areas of Concern. Poster at 2013 SETAC conference.

Harvey, C. J., M. P. Ebner and C. K. White. 2008. Spatial and ontogenetic variability of sea lamprey diets in Lake Superior. *Journal of Great Lakes Research* **34**: 434-449.

Hilscherova K., K. Kannan, H. Nakata, N. Hanari, N. Yamashita, P. W. Bradley, J. M. McCabe, A. B. Taylor and J. P. Giesy. 2003. Polychlorinated dibenzo-*p*-dioxin and dibenzofuran concentration profiles in sediments and flood-plain soils of the Tittabawassee River, Michigan. *Environmental Science and Technology* **37**: 468-474.

Heindel, J. 2010, The developmental origins of disease: Environmental pharmaceuticals and epigenetic mechanisms. Powerpoint presentation to Guelph Conference on Pharmaceuticals and epigenetic mechanisms of diseases. February 27, 2010, Guelph, Ontario.

Hoffman, D. J., B. A. Rattner, L. Sileo, D. Docherty, and T. J. Kubiak. 1987. Embryotoxicity, teratogenicity and aryl hydrocarbon hydroxylase activity in Forster's terns on Green Bay, Lake Michigan. *Environmental Research* **42**: 176-184.

Hornshaw, T. C. and R. J. Aulerich. 1983. Feeding Great Lakes fish to mink: Effects on mink and accumulation and elimination of PCBs by mink. *Journal of Toxicology and Environmental Health* **24**: 933-946.

JAMES P. LUDWIG, Ph.D

Hubbs, C. L. and K. F. Lagler. 1958. **Fishes of the Great Lakes Region.** *The University of Michigan Press.* Ann Arbor. 213 pp.

International Joint Commission. 1989a. Revised Great Lakes Water Quality Agreement of 1978. Agreement with annexes and terms of reference, November 22, 1978, phosphorus load reduction supplement and protocol of November, 1987.

International Joint Commission. 1989b. Proceedings of the workshop on cause-effects linkages, March 28-30, 1989, Chicago, IL. Ed. M. Gilbertson. *Council of Research Managers.* 45pp.

International Joint Commission. 1990a. The International Joint Commission and the Boundary Waters Treaty. 24 pp.

International Joint Commission 1990b. Proceedings of the roundtable on contaminant-caused reproductive problems in salmonids. Eds. M. Mac and M. Gilbertson. Report to the International Joint Commission by *the Biological Effects Subcommittee of the Ecological Committeee, Science Advisory Board.* September 24, 25, 1990.

International Joint Commission. 1991. Persistent toxic substances: Virtually eliminating inputs to the Great Lakes. The interim report of the Virtual Elimination Task Force. ISBN 1-895085-27-6.

International Joint Commission. 1996. Eighth biennial report on Great Lakes water quality. 48 pp.

International Joint Commission, USEPA & National Sea Grant. 2006. Synthesis of public comment on the forthcoming review by the federal governments of Canada and the United States of the Great Lakes Water Quality Agreement. 74 pp.

Jacobson, J.L., S. W. Jacobson and H.E.B. Humphrey. 1990a. Effects of *in utero* exposure to polychlorinated biphenyls and related contaminants on cognitive functioning in young children. *Journal of Pediatrics* **116**: 38-45.

Jacobson, J. L., S. W. Jacobson and H.E.B. Humphrey. 1990b. Effects of exposure to PCBs and related compounds on growth and activity in children. *Neurotoxicology and Teratology* **12**: 319-326.

Jacobson, J. L. and S. W. Jacobson. 1996. Intellectual impairments in children exposed to polychlorinated biphenyls *in utero. New England Journal of Medicine* **335**: 783-789.

Jones, P. D., G. T. Ankley, D. A. Best, R. Crawford, N. DeGalan, J. P. Giesy, T. J. Kubiak, J. P. Ludwig, J. L. Newsted, D. E. Tillitt, and D. A. Verbrugge. 1993a. Biomagnification of bioassay-derived 2,3,7,8 tetrachlorodibenzo-*p*-dioxin equivalents. *Chemosphere* **26**: 1203-1212.

Jones, P. D., J. P. Giesy, J. L. Newstead, D. A. Verbrugge, D. L. Beaver, G. T. Ankley, D. E. Tillitt, K. B. Lodge, and G. J. Niemi. 1993b. 2,3,7,8-tetrachlorodibenzo-*p*-dioxin equivalents in tissues of birds at Green Bay, Wisconsin, USA. *Archives of Environmental Contamination and Toxicology* **24**: 345-354.

Jones, P. D., D. J. Hannah, S. J. Buckland, P. J. Day, S. V. Laetham, L. J. Porter, J. P. Giesy, H. J. Auman, J. P. Ludwig and C. L. Summer. 1994a. PCBs and 2,3,7,8-substituted polychlorinated dibenzo-*p*-dioxins and dibenzofurans in albatross tissues from the central Pacific Ocean. *Organohalogen Compounds* **20**: 137-140.

Jones, P. D., J. P. Giesy, J. L. Newstead, D. A. Verbrugge, J. P. Ludwig, M. E. Ludwig, H. J. Auman, R. Crawford, D. E. Tillitt, T. J. Kubiak and D. A. Best. 1994b. Accumulation of 2,3,7,8-tetrachlorodibenzo-*p*-dioxin equilavents by double-crested cormorant (*Phalacrocorax auritus*, Pelicaniformes) chicks in the North American Great Lakes. *Ecotoxicology and Environmental Safety* **27**: 192-209.

Kannan, N., S. Tanabe, T. Wakimoto and R. Tatsukawa. 1987. Coplanar polychlorinated biphenyls in Aroclor and Kanechlor mixtures. *Journal of the Association of Official Analytical Chemists* **70**: 451-454.

Kannan, N., S Tanabe and R. Tatsukawa. 1988. Toxic potential of non-*ortho* and mono-*ortho* coplanar PCBs in commercial PCB

JAMES P. LUDWIG, Ph.D

preparations: 2,3,7,8-T$_4$CDD toxic equivalence factors approach. *Bulletin of Environmental Contamination and Toxicology* **41**: 267-276.

Karcher, S. I., D. G. Franks, S. W. Kennedy and M. E. Hahn. 2006. The molecular basis for differential dioxin sensitivity in birds: Role of the aryl hydrocarbon receptor. *Proceedings of the National Academy of Science, USA* **103**: 6252-6257.

J. A. Keith. 1966. Reproduction in a DDT-contaminated population of herring gulls. *Journal of Applied Ecology* **3** (Supplement): 57-70.

Kerkvleit, N. I., L. B. Steppan, J, A. Brauner, J. A, Deyo, M. C. Henderson, R. S. Tomar and D. R. Behler. 1990. Influence of the Ah locus on the humoral immunotoxicology of 2,3,7,8-tetrachlorodibenzo-*p*-dioxin: Evidence for Ah-receptor-dependent and Ah-receptor-independent mechanisms for immunosuppression. *Toxicology and Applied Pharmacology* **105**: 26-36.

Klasson-Wehler, E., A. Bergman, M. Athanasiadou, J. P. Ludwig, H. J. Auman, K. Kannan, M. Van Den Berg, A. J. Murk, L. A. Feyk, and J. P. Giesy. 1998. Hydroxylated and methylsulfonyl polychlorinated biphenyl metabolites in albatrosses from Midway Atoll, North Pacific Ocean. *Environmental Toxicology and Chemistry* **17**: 1620-1625.

Koopman-Esseboom, C., N. Nynke-Kuperus, M. A. J. de Riddert, C. G. van der PaauwL, M. T. Tunistra and P. J. J Sauer. 1996. Effects of polychlorinated biphenyl/dioxin exposure and feeding type on infants' mental and psychomotor development. *Journal of Pediatrics* **97**: 700-706.

Kreibel. D., J. Tickner, P. Epstein, J. Lemmons, R. Levins, E. L. Loechler, M.Quinn, R. Rudel, T. Schettler and M. Stoto. 2001. The precautionary principle in environmental science. *Environmental Health Perspectives* **109**: 871-876.

Kubiak, T. J., H. J. Harris, L. M. Smith, D. E. Docherty, and T. C. Erdman. 1989. Microcontaminants and reproductive impairment of the Forster's tern on Green Bay, Lake Michigan, 1983. *Archives of Environmental Contamination and Toxicology* **18**: 706-727.

Kuhns, L. A. and M. B. Berg. 1999. Benthic invertebrate community responses to round goby (*Neogobius melanostomas*) and zebra mussel (*Dreissena polymorpha*) invasion in southern Lake Michigan. *Journal of Great Lakes Research* **25:** 910-917.

Kurita, H. 1987. Mercury Contamination in Deer Lake Ecosystem. MS thesis, Michigan State University, Department of Fisheries and Wildlife. 97 pp.

Kvach, Y. and C. A. Stepian. 2008. Metazoan parasites of introduced round and tube-nosed gobies in the Great Lakes: Support for the "enemy release hypothesis". *Journal of Great Lakes Research* **34**: 23-35.

Lack, D. 1954. **The Natural Regulation of Animal Numbers.** Oxford, Clarendon Press. 343 pp.

Lindeman, R. L. 1940. The trophic-dynamic aspect of ecology. *Ecology* **23**: 399-418.

Ludwig, F. E. 1943. Ring-billed gulls of the Great Lakes. *Wilson Bulletin* **55**: 234-244.

J. P. Ludwig. 2013. Evidence of contamination-driven population source-sink regions in the Great Lakes: Survivorship and recruitment in the Caspian tern population 1922-2007. MS in preparation for submission to *Journal of Great Lakes Research.*

Ludwig, J. P., C. L. Summer, H. J. Auman, T. L. Colborn, R. M. Rolland, and J. P. Giesy. 1997a. Contaminants and by-catch effects on Laysan and Black-footed Albatross populations of the North Pacific Ocean. Chapter 19 in **Albatross Biology and Conservation.** Eds. R. Gales and G. Robertson, Australia. ISBN 0 949324 82 5.

Ludwig, J. P., S. I. Apfelbaum and J. P. Giesy. 1997b. Ecotoxicological effects of watershed contamination. *Proceedings of the 1996 USEPA symposium assessing the cumulative impacts of watershed development*

JAMES P. LUDWIG, Ph.D

on aquatic ecosystems and water quality. pp. 241-250. March, 1996, Chicago, Il.

Ludwig, J. P. 1996a. Contaminants effected widespread changes of Great Lakes populations and communities. [Letter to editor response to Great Lakes Forum]. *Ecological Applications* **6**: 962-965.

Ludwig, J. P., H. Kurita-Matsuba, H. J. Auman, M. E. Ludwig, C. L. Summer, J. P. Giesy, D. E. Tillitt, and P. D. Jones. 1996b. Deformities, PCBs and TCDD-equivalents in double-crested cormorants (*Phalacrocorax auritus*) and Caspian terns (*Hydroprogne caspia*) of the upper Great Lakes 1986-1991: Testing a cause-effect hypothesis. *Journal of Great Lakes Research* **22**: 172-197.

Ludwig, J. P. 1995a. Science, research, and public policy in the Great Lakes: Making science subservient to politics on IJC boards. [Invited editorial] *Journal of Great Lakes Research* **21**: 159-160.

Ludwig, J. P., H. J. Auman, D. V. Weseloh, G. A. Fox, J. P. Giesy, and M. E. Ludwig. 1995b. Evaluation of the effects of toxic chemicals in Great Lakes cormorants: Has causality been established? *Colonial Waterbirds* **18** (Special Publication): 60-69.

Ludwig, J.P., J.P. Giesy, C. L. Summer, W.W. Bowerman, S. Heaton, R Aulerich, S. Bursian, H.J. Auman, P.D. Jones, L.L. Williams, D.E. Tillitt, and M.O. Gilbertson. 1993a. A comparison of water quality criteria in the Great Lakes basin based on human or wildlife health. *Journal of Great Lakes Research* **19**: 789-807.

J. P. Ludwig, H.J. Auman, H. Kurita-Matsuba, M. E. Ludwig, L. M. Campbell, J. P. Giesy, D. E. Tillitt, P. D. Jones, N. Yamashita, S. Tanabe, and R. Tatsukawa. 1993b. Caspian tern reproduction in the Saginaw Bay ecosystem following a 100-year flood event. *Journal of Great Lakes Research* **19**: 96-108.

Ludwig, J.P., C.A. Hall, H. Auman, and M.E. Ludwig. 1989. Feeding ecology of double-crested cormorants in the upper Great Lakes 1986-1989. *Jack-Pine Warbler* **67**: 117-129.

Ludwig, J.P. and D.D. Bromley. 1988. Observations on the 1965 and 1966 mortalities of alewives and ring-billed gulls in the Saginaw Bay, Lake Huron ecosystem. *Jack-Pine Warbler* **66**: 2-19.

Ludwig, J.P. 1984. Decline, resurgence and population dynamics of Michigan and Great Lakes double-crested cormorants. *Jack-Pine Warbler* **62**: 91-102.

Ludwig, J.P. 1982. Governance of scientific research projects through error embracing in the 1980's. *Michigan Academician* **14**: 181-189.

Ludwig, J.P. 1979. Present status of the Caspian tern population of the Great Lakes. *Michigan Academician* **11**: 69-77.

Ludwig, J.P. 1974. Recent changes in the ring-billed gull population and biology in the Laurentian Great Lakes. *Auk* **91**: 575-594.

Ludwig, J.P. and C.E. Ludwig. 1969. The effect of starvation on insecticide contaminated herring gulls removed from a Lake Michigan colony. *Proceedings of the 12th Conference of the International Association for Great Lakes Research* **18**: 53-60.

Ludwig, J.P. 1968. Dynamics of ring-billed gull and Caspian tern populations of the Great Lakes. *Ph.D. Dissertation*, University of Michigan, Ann Arbor. 73 pp.

Ludwig, J.P., and C.S. Tomoff. 1966. Reproductive success and insecticide residues in Lake Michigan herring gulls. *Jack-Pine Warbler* **44**: 77-86.

Ludwig, J. P. 1963. Return of herring gulls to natal colony. *Bird Banding* **34**: 68-72.

Ludwig, J.P. 1962. A survey of the gull and tern populations of Lakes Huron, Michigan, and Superior. *Jack-Pine Warbler* **40**: 104-120.

Mac, M.J. and C.C. Edsall. 1991. Environmental contaminants and reproductive success of lake trout in the Great Lakes: an epidemiological approach. *Journal of Toxicology and Environmental Health* **33**: 375-394.

MacKay, D. and M. Gilbertson. 1991. Signs of intelligent life in the Great Lakes ecosystem? Editorial *Environmental Toxicology and Chemistry* **10**: 559-561.

MacPherson, L.W. 1956. Some observations on the epizootiology of Newcastle Disease. *Canadian Journal of Comparative Medicine* **20**: 155-168.

McFarland, V.A. and J.U. Clarke. 1989. Environmental occurrence, abundance and potential toxicity of polychlorinated biphenyl congeners: Considerations for a congener-specific analysis. *Environmental Health Perspectives* **81**: 225-239.

McKinney, J.D., J. Fawkes, S. Jordan, K. Chae, S. Oatley, R.E. Coleman and W. Briner. 1985. 2,3,7,8-tetrachlorodibenzo-*p*-dioxin (TCDD) as a potent and persistent thyroxine agonist: A mechanistic model for toxicity based on molecular reactivity. *Environmental Health Perspectives* **61**: 41-53.

Michael, D. M. 1967. **The Unprepared Society.**

Michigan Audubon Society. 1991. Cause-Effect Linkages II Symposium Abstracts. Eds. S. Schneider and R. Campbell. September 27-28, 1991. Traverse City, MI. 46pp.

Mora, M.A., H.J. Auman, J.P. Ludwig, J.P. Giesy, D.A. Verbrugge and M.E. Ludwig. 1993. Polychlorinated biphenyls and chlorinated insecticides in plasma of Caspian terns: Relationships with age, productivity and colony site tenacity in the Great Lakes. *Archives of Environmental Contamination* **24**: 320-331.

Muir, D. C.G., P. D. Jones, H. Karlsson, K. Koczansky, G.A. Stern, K. Kannan, J. P. Ludwig, H. Reid, C. J. R. Robertson and J.P. Giesy. 2002. Toxaphene and other persistent organochlorines in three species of albatrosses from the north and south Pacific Ocean. *Environmental Toxicology and Chemistry* **21**: 413-423.

Muir, T. and M. Zegarac. 2001. Societal costs of exposure to toxic substances: Economic and health costs of four case studies that are candidates for environmental causation. *Environmental Health Perspectives* **109**: Supplement 6: 885-903.

Murk, A.J., J.H. J. van den Berg, J.H. Koeman, and A. Brouwer. 1991. The toxicity of tetrachlorobenzyltoluenes (Ugilec 141) and polychlorobiphenyls (Aroclor 1254 and PCB-77) compared in Ah-responsive and Ah-nonresponsive mice. *Environmental Pollution* 72: 57-67.

Murphy, T.A Lawson, C. Nalewajko, H. Murkin, K. Oguma and T. McIntyre. 2000. Algal toxins—Initiators of avian botulism? *Environmental Toxicology* **15**: 558-567.

Oliver, B.G., M.N. Charlton and R.W. Durham. 1989. Distribution, redistribution and geochemistry of polychlorinated biphenyl congeners and other chlorinated hydrocarbons in Lake Ontario sediments. *Environmental Science and Technology* **23**: 200-208.

Peterson, R.E., M.D. Seefeld, B.J. Christian, C.L. Potter, C.K. Kelling and R.E. Keesey. 1990. The wasting syndrome in 2,3,7,8-tetrachlorodibenzo-*p*-dioxin toxicity: Basic features and their interpretation. In *The Banbury Report—Biological mechanisms of dioxin action.* Cold Spring Harbor Laboratory. 291-308.

Reid, S.M. and N.E. Mandrak. 2008. Historical changes in the distribution of threatened channel darter (*Percina copelandi*) in Lake Erie with general observations on the beach fish assemblage. *Journal of Great Lakes Research* **34**: 324-333.

Rogan, W.J., B.C. Gladen, K-LHung, S.L. Koong, L.Y. Shih, J.S. Taylor, Y.C. Wu, D. Yang, N.B. Ragan and C.C. Hsu. 1979. Congenital poisoning by polychlorinated biphenyls and their contaminants in Taiwan. *Science* **241**: 334-336.

Safe, S. 1990. Polychlorinated biphenyls (PCBs), dibenzo-p-dioxins (PCDDs), dibenzofurans (PCDFs) and related compounds: Environmental and mechanistic considerations which support the development of toxic equivalency factors. *Toxicology* **21**: 51-88.

Schug, T.T., R. Abugyan, B. Blumberg, T. J. Collins, D. Crews, P. L. Defur, S. M. Dickerson, T. M. Edwards, A. C. Gore, L. J. Guillette, T. Hayes, J. J. Heindel, A. Moores, H. B. Patisaul, T. L. Tal, K. A. Thayer, L. N. Vandenberg, J. C. Warner, C. S. Watson, F. S. vom Saal, R. T. Zoeller, K. P. O'Brien and J. P. Myers. 2012. Designing endocrine disruption out of the next generation of chemicals. *Green Chemistry* DOI: 10.1039/c2cg35055f.

Schwartz, P.M., S.W. Jacobson, G. Fein. J.L. Jacobson and H. A.Price. 1983. Lake Michigan fish consumption as a source of polychlorinated biphenyls in human cord serum, maternal serum, and milk. *American Journal of Public Health* **83**: 113-117.

Schaeffer, J.S., D.M. Warner and T.P. O'Brien. 2008. Resurgence of emerald shiners (*Notropis antherinoides*) in Lake Huron's main basin. *Journal of Great Lakes Research* **34**: 395-403.

Seamans, M.L., J.P. Ludwig, K. Stromborg, F.E. Ludwig II, and F.E. Ludwig. 2012. Annual survival of double-crested cormorants from the Great Lakes 1979-2006. *Waterbirds* **35**: 23-30.

Schantz, S.L., D.M Gasior, E. Polverejan, R.J. McCaffery, A.M. Sweeney, H.E.B. Humphrey, and J.C. Gardiner. 2001. Impairments of memory and learning in older adults exposed to polychlorinated biphenyls via consumption of Great Lakes fish. *Environmental Health Perspectives* **109**: 605-611.

Schecter, A. Ed. 1994. **Dioxins and Health**. Plenem Press, NY. 792 pp.

Seefelt, N. and J.C. Gillingham. 2008. Bioenergetics and prey consumption of breeding double-crested cormorants in the Beaver archipelago, northern Lake Michigan. *Journal of Great Lakes Research* **34**: 122-133.

Seegal, R.F. and S.L. Chance. 1994. Neurochemical and behavioral sequelae of exposure to dioxins and PCBs. Pp. 409-447 in *Dioxins and Health* Ed. A. Schecter, Plenum Press, NY, 792 pp.

Silkworth, J.B., D.S. Cutler, P.W. O'Keefe and T. Lipinkas. 1993. Potentiation and antagonism of 2,3,7,8 tetrachlorodibenzo-*p*-dioxin effects in a complex environmental mixture. *Toxicology and Applied Pharmacology* **119**: 236-247.

Simmers, J.W., S.I. Apfelbaum, and L.F. Bryniarski. 1990. Assessment of avian botulism control pilot project at the Dike 14 confined dredged material disposal facility, Cleveland, Ohio. Miscellaneous paper EL 90-23, *U. S. Army Engineers, Waterways Experiment Station, Vicksburg, MS.*

Sitar, S.P., H.M. Morales, M.T. Mata, B.B. Bastar, D.M. Dupras, G.D. Kleaver, and K.D. Rathbun 2008. Survey of siscowet lake trout at their maximum depth in Lake Superior. *Journal of Great Lakes Research* **34**: 276-286.

Smith, L.M., T.R. Schwartz and K. Feltz. 1990. Determination and occurrence of AHH-active polychlorinated biphenyls, 2,3,7,8-tetrachloro-*p*-dioxin and 2,3,7,8-tetrachlorodibenzofuran in Lake Michigan sediment and biota: The question of their relative toxicological significance. *Chemosphere* **21**: 1063-1085.

Steinberg, R.M., D.M. Walker, T.E. Juenger, M.J. Woller, and A.C. Gore. 2008. Effects of perinatal polychlorinated biphenyls on adult female rat reproduction: Development, reproductive physiology and second generational effects. *Journal of Biology of Reproduction* **78**: 1091-1101.

Stewart P., S. Fitzgerald, J. Reihman, G. Brooks, E. Lonky, T. Darvill, J. Pagano, and P. Hauser. 2003. Prenatal PCB exposure, the corpus callosum, and response inhibition. *Environmental Health Perspectives* **111**: 1670-1677.

Stewart P. W.E. Lonky, J. Reihman, J. Pagano, B.B. Gump, and T. Darvill. 2008. The relationship between prenatal PCB exposure and intelligence (IQ) in 9-Year-Old Children. *Environmental Health Perspectives* **116:** 1416-1422.

Struger, J. and D.V. Weseloh. 1985. Great Lakes Caspian terns: Egg contaminants and biological implications. *Colonial Waterbirds* **8**: 142-149.

Summer, C.L. 1992. An avian ecosystem indicator: The reproductive effects induced by feeding Great Lakes fish to white leghorn laying hens. MS thesis, Department of Animal Science, Michigan State University, East Lansing. 116 pp.

Summer, C.L., J.P. Giesy, S. Bursian, J.A. Render, T.J. Kubiak, P.D. Jones, D.A. Verbrugge and R.J. Aulerich. 1996. Effects induced by feeding organochlorine-contaminated carp from Saginaw Bay, Lake Huron to laying white leghorn hens II. Embryotoxic and teratogenic effects. *Journal of Toxicology and Environmental Health* **49**: 409-438.

Swackhamer, D.L., B.D. McVeely and R.A. Hites. 1988. Deposition and evaporation of polychlorobiphenyl congeners to and from Siskiwit Lake, Isle Royale, Lake Superior. *Environmental Science and Technology* **22**: 664-672.

Swain, W.R. 1991. Effects of organochlorine chemicals on the reproductive outcome of humans who consumed contaminated Great Lakes fish: An epidemiologic consideration. *Journal of Toxicology and Environmental Health* **33**: 587-639.

Tansley, A.G. 1935. The use and abuse of vegetational concepts and terms. *Ecology* **16**:284-307.

Tillitt, D.E. and J.P. Giesy. 1991. Characterization of the H4IIE rat hepatoma cell bioassay as a tool for assessing toxic potency of planar halogenated hydrocarbons in environmental samples. *Environmental Science and Technology* **25**: 87-92.

D.E. Tillitt, G.T. Ankley, D.A. Verbrugge, J.P. Giesy, J.P. Ludwig, and T.J. Kubiak. 1991. H4IIE rat hepatoma cell bioassay-derived 2,3,7,8-tetrachlorodibenzo-p-dioxin equivalents in colonial fish-eating waterbird eggs from the Great Lakes. *Archives of Environmental Contamination and Toxicology* **21**: 91-101.

D.E. Tillitt, G.T. Ankley, J.P. Giesy, J.P. Ludwig, H. Kurita, D.V. Weseloh, P.S. Ross, C.A. Bishop, L. Sileo, K.L. Stromborg, J. Larson and T.S. Kubiak. 1992. Polychlorinated biphenyl residues and egg mortality in double-crested cormorants from the Great Lakes. *Environmental Toxicology and Chemistry* **11**:1281-1288.

Tillitt, D. E. and J. P. Giesy. 2013. Ecotoxicology of organochlorine chemicals in birds of the Great Lakes. *Environmental Toxicology and Chemistry* **32**: 490-492.

Thomas, K. B and T. Colborn. 1993. Organochlorine endocrine disruptors in human tissue. In **Chemically-induced alterations in sexual and functional development: The wildlife-human connection.** 1993. Eds. T. Colborn and C. Clement. Princeton Scientific Publishing, Princeton, NJ.

Trasande, L. P.L. Landrigan and C. Schecter. 2005. Public health and the environmental consequences of methylmercury toxicity to the developing brain. *Environmental Health Perspectives* **113**:590-596.

USEPA. 2008. Great Lakes basinwide botulism coordination workshop proceedings. June 24, 25, 2008. Detroit, MI. *Great Lakes National Program Office and Sea Grant National Program.* 950-R-08-005. 25 pp.

Visser, M. 2007. **Cold Clear and Deadly**. Michigan State University Press, East Lansing. 192 pp.

Watzin, M.C., E.B. Miller, A.D. Shambaugh, and M.A. Kreider. 2006. A partnership approach to monitoring cyanobacteria in Lake Champlain. *Great Lakes Research Review* **7**: 8-13.

Weseloh, D.V., S.M. Teeple, and M. Gilbertson. 1983. Double-crested cormorants of the Great Lakes: egg-laying parameters, reproductive failure and contaminant residues in eggs, Lake Huron 1972-1973. *Canadian Journal of Zoology* **61**: 427-436.

Weseloh, D.V., P.J. Ewins, J. Struger, P. Mineau, C.A, Bishop, S. Postupalsky and J.P. Ludwig. 1995. Double-crested cormorants of the Great Lakes: Changes in population size, breeding distribution and reproductive output between 1913 and 1991. *Colonial Waterbirds* **18** (Special Publication I): 48-59.

Williams, L.L., J.P. Giesy, N. DeGalan, D.A. Verbrugge and G.T. Ankley. 1992. Prediction of concentrations of 2,3,7,8 tetrachlorodibenzo-*p*-dioxin equivalents (TCDD-EQ) in trimmed chinook salmon fillets from Lake Michigan from total concentrations of PCBs and fish size. *Environmental Science and Technology* **26**: 1151-1159.

Wobeser, G., F.A. Leighton, R. Norman, D. J. Myers, D. Onderka, M.J. Pybus, J.L. Neufeld, G. A. Fox and D.J. Alexander. 1993. Newcastle disease in wild water birds in western Canada, 1990. *Canadian Veterinary Journal* **34**: 353-359.

Wren, C.D. 1991. Cause-effect linkages between chemicals and populations of mink (*Mustela vison*) and otter (*Lutra Canadensis*) in the Great Lakes basin. *Journal of Toxicology and Environmental Health* **33**: 549-586.

Yamashita, N., S. Tanabe, J.P. Ludwig, H. Kurita, M.E. Ludwig, and R. Tatsukawa. 1993. Embryonic abnormalities and organochlorine contamination in double-crested cormorants (*Phalacrocorax auritus*) and Caspian terns (*Hydroprogne caspia*) from the upper Great Lakes in 1988. *Environmental Pollution* **79**: 163-173.

Science, Research and Public Policy in the Great Lakes: Making Science Subservient to Politics on IJC Boards.

THIS EDITORIAL SUPPOSES readers have read and understand the GLWQA [Great Lakes Water Quality Agreement]. The Science Advisory Board (SAB) and Water Quality Board (WQA) do not conform to the GLWQA, nor to the annexes and terms of reference—especially with reference to memberships and purposes of the SAB. These boards are now politicized and act as barriers to effective policy. It is time the IJC Commissioners (re)acquainted themselves with the content of the GLWQA wherein the roles of the SAB and WQB are distinguished clearly. New members having expertise consistent with the distinct scientific and political advisory roles of these boards are sorely needed. The Council of Great Lakes Research Managers (CGLRM) was narrowly established of government research administrators.

The SAB is chartered to be the IJC's and WQB's research advisor. The SAB's central roles are to evaluate the quality of published science, advise what topics should be investigated, evaluate emerging trends and address technical issues. Published science is to be reviewed for accuracy, adequacy of experimental design, and relevance to the important issues that the commission has identified (e.g. toxic chemicals, invasive species, etc.). However, *bona fide* active research scientists with credible training and Great Lakes experience are decreasing in numbers on the SAB. Recent appointments of nonscientist policy specialists and advocates of special interests are evidence of IJC preoccupation with attaining political balance in lieu of attention to science. One eminent scientist was recruited to serve on the SAB last year only to be told recently he was no longer acceptable because commissioners believed they knew what was wrong with the lakes and policy persons were what the SAB needed. Just imagine what that conclusion would have meant to our knowledge of the Great Lakes were it promoted 20 years ago, and how it will limit our understanding of the Great Lakes 20 years from now! The current preoccupation of IJC commissioners to force the two boards to speak with one voice and prepare a single biennial report is the final irrefutable evidence of the descent of the SAB into a political role. The commissioners themselves fail to understand the differing roles and purposes of IJC advisory bodies as set forth in the GLWQA. Who led the commission to make non-scientist, policy and special interest appointments to the SAB and for what reasons?

Scientists are trained to understand research designs, interpret data relevance to hypotheses, determine statistical adequacy of analyses and related matters of science and scientific peer review. Lawyers, policy specialists and interest group representatives are advocates of particular interests. Agency administrators are frequently not knowledgeable about science, or have failed to keep up, and some lack the basic skills for this task. While scientists are also prone to judge controversies according to their biases (and sometime by who employs them), the rigor of the scientific method and formal peer review are proven means to generate scientific consensus. Unfortunately, scientific consensus on the SAB has been replaced with political consensus. The present SAB members are well-intentioned, dedicated and sincere appointees. However, it is also true they are more a mélange of interest group representatives than scientists. The current US Chairman, a politically adept administrator of high skill, great likeability, but modest science credentials illustrates the problem. Some SAB members have no science credentials: others are out of date or untrained for today's science issues—persistent toxic chemicals, invasive species, global warming, etc.—that must be addressed by research. Promoting and evaluating that knowledge is the reason the SAB exists. It is as absurd that these people advise the IJC officially on the

JAMES P. LUDWIG, Ph.D

quality, meaning and practice of Great Lakes research and science as for me to offer religious advice to a theologian.

If the IJC wants an effective *Science* Advisory Board, then much of the current SAB membership must not be reappointed. To be effective, The SAB must focus on the issues of quality of published science and needed research as the GLWQA and terms of reference demand. An SAB with its own agenda cannot review science and research findings without political taint. The SAB has degenerated into a means to achieve politically-acceptable consensus.

The WQB must have a broader representation on it than the SAB, simply because the questions of water quality criteria, standards and enforcement are policy decisions arrived at by political consensus processes. The WQB is supposed to put forth improved public policies that integrate peer reviewed science endorsed by the SAB, the views of interest groups and the realities of what is possible through agencies that effect policies. The WQB sets forth policy recommendations to the IJC commissioners in its biennial reports and—in the past—through multiple task forces working on specific issues. This operational structure makes the WQB the right place for all stakeholders to bring diverse interests forward into debates on policies to devise strategies for improved Great Lakes Programs and the logical place for political consensus.

The WQB is dominated by agency representatives who have the dual agendas of review of water quality issues and justification of their agencies as protectors of resources. **There is a clear vested interest of many WQB members to highlight their successful programs and hide their failing ones.** Admitting that present strategies and policies to clean-up toxicants, prevent alien species invasions, promote endangered species, etc. are ineffective is to admit agency failure. That is a negative career decision since administrators report to politicians who do not want to hear bad news, regardless of importance. Self-evaluation of agency goals and policies is often a self-serving gesture that tends to happen just after a new political administration is elected. The WQB has been a body facilitating *program changes* to improve Great Lakes water quality while the issues were simple and easily addressed such as nutrients in sewage. It is very unlikely to continue desirable change when the issues are more complex, less well understood, or require risk-taking behaviors so long as it is a fiefdom of agency administrators.

Finally, the CGLRM, now composed chiefly of those who manage government funding programs, should be broadened to include additional managers of non-government funding sources—businesses, industries, and foundations. Governments are strapped for research funds, a situation likely to get worse. Most private funders lack access to (or chose not to use) networks of qualified peer-reviewers who could assist their organizations in funding decisions. Excluding non-traditional sources of funding leads to their alienation.

Environmentalists claim that money from industries is "dirty". Industrialists often denigrate *any* projects funded through environmental groups as "bad science". Neither view is reasoned, nor can be supported with hard data. Reviews of published results almost always shows that who funded research is far less important than the peer-reviewed product. Good science stands up to the test of time as other scientists independently verify the conclusions. A glaring deficiency of the CGLRM is its preoccupation not to review, and thereby, to endorse continuation funding of many ongoing agency programs *de facto*. Yet, it is exactly sort of review that the IJC is mandated to do by treaty and annexes. To believe that the present CGLRM coordination of research has much to do with the needs of Great Lakes resources is naïve: it has far more to do with preserving flows of research and management dollars into accepted pathways.

The current structure, memberships and functions of these advisory boards are manifestations of the old government pattern to guarantee staff security and minimize critical reviews. It is long past the time when the IJC should embrace its treaty role of reviewer of government actions (or inactions) with vigor and determination to effect beneficial change. The first step toward this treaty requirement is changing the memberships and charges give to IJC advisory boards. Some years ago, Don Michael, a social scientist interested in how scientific data were used (The Unprepared Society) stated the only effective way to perform any complex scientific or engineering task filled with uncertainties was to study and embrace the errors made, in order to avoid repeating them. If the IJC is to restore itself as an effective leader working to improve Great

Lakes management, then the errors in advisory board memberships and the charges given those boards must be acknowledged, embraced and corrected. The IJC's advisory boards are broken. They must be fixed. It is wrong to foster the present structure, roles and memberships just because the governments are comfortable with ineffective benign advice. Ultimately, the CGLRM could coordinate research priorities and increase funds from all sources—if the SAB and WQB roles are properly refocused to the intent of the GLWQA and the SAB is insulated from politics by a focus restricted to science instead of advocacy,

Make no mistake, we scientists who feed our research programs at the public trough are doing the public's business. The research community would be well advised to address this matter. We all are part of this mess. We watched it happen and did very little to rectify it. We had better help make changes, or be prepared for the public wrath that always follows publically-funded failures. Whether the cause was benign neglect, stupidity, ignorance or corruption is not relevant. The resources we profess to protect and an institution we have revered and depended upon for improving the lakes—the IJC—are both in dire straits.

Journal of Great Lakes Research. 1995. **21**(2) 159-160.

To the editor: 4 September, 1995

Ecological Applications performed a valuable service by elevating the debate over organochlorines in the Great Lakes above the news media into a forum. However, it is most unfortunate that the lead articles neither back up their statements with adequate literature reviews, nor keep a focus on the effects of organochlorines. These papers confuse the science of effects with policy debates over a proposed chlorine ban and regulatory matters. These are very different issues with distinct economic and ecological significance.

In the lead article (Cooper, 1995), *only one* of the five citations cited to support the case comes from the peer-reviewed literature. I take issue with at least the following unsupported statements:

1.) **"that the 'Great Lakes are dying' and must be protected at all costs."** I know of no such claims by Great Lakes scientists and object to its use unless it can be documented.

2.) that **"laboratory data on toxic effects of these substances on mink (Mustela vison), eagles (Haliaeetus leucocephalia [sic]), salmon (Onorhyncus sp. [sic]), and other predators are presented as scientific proof that these potential impacts are real. Once again, science is being used to give credibility to and advocate (sic) group."** This claim is simply wrong; it confuses observations and data with policies and political decisions. It was *field observations* by ecotoxicologists that recorded and measured the same suite of effects produced in laboratory studies by organochlorines in surrogate test species. These studies documented the presence of these compounds at the same or greater doses than those that elicit identical effects in test species. The best work showed dose:response relationships with a robust degree of statistical significance (e.g. Tillett et al. 1992, Mora et al. 1993). Effects were reasonably linked to particular organochlorines, including pesticides (Ludwig and Ludwig 1969; Weseloh et al. 1973) polychlorinated dibenzo-*p*-dioxins (PCDDs), polychlorinated dibenzo-furans (PCDFs), and polychlorinated biphenyls (PCBs) (Gilbertson et al. 1991, Yamashita et al. 1993, Giesy et al. 1994c, Schecter

JAMES P. LUDWIG, Ph.D

1994; also, see the cause-effects linkage papers in *Journal of Toxicology and Environmental Health* **33**[4] and the *Journal of Great Lakes Research* **19**[4]) and other chemicals. Peer-reviewed research implicates all of these chemical groups, other Ah-receptor active compounds (naphthalenes, PBBs, etc.), and neurologically-active organochlorines that have a different mode of action than the ah-receptor-mediated mechanism (Devito and Birnbaum 1994, Kerkvleit 1994, Giesy et al. 1994b, Seegal and Schantz 1994). These plieotropic effects are evidence of a system-wide, non-genetic, non-habitat related cause. The commonality of effects across so many species and taxa is potent evidence of a common, albeit very complex, chlorinated organic chemical cause. Fox (1991) codified the criteria for making cause-effects linkages between toxic chemicals and effects in populations.

3.) That **"natural selection maintains quality control by eliminating maladapted individuals irrespective of the selection pressure."** While this statement is probably true more often than not, in this context Cooper is really stating that organochlorines are just another kind of natural selection. He believes that chemicals are not important to Great Lakes populations or community structure. While it is true that there are small, largely insignificant, natural sources of toxic chemicals, I know of no case where the concentrations of these chlorinated substances are great enough to kill or impair the reproductive potential of individuals, let alone exert a significant consistent selection pressure on natural populations. The highly toxic, endocrine-disruptive (Colborn and Clement 1993, Theobald and Peterson 1994) and developmental (Yamashita et al. 1993, Devito and Birnbaum 1994) effects of synthetic organochlorine chemicals are present at concentrations in the Great Lakes that kill or impair reproduction in many populations according to their species' sensitivities. Organochlorines are proven selection agents in Great Lakes populations of at least lake trout (*Oncorhynchus kisutch*; Mac and Edsall 1991), bald eagles (*Haliaeetus leucocephalus*; Gilbertson 1991. Bowerman 1993, Giesy et al. 1994b c, Bowerman et al. 1995) Forsters tern (*Sterna fostori*; Kubiak et al. 1989), Caspian tern (*Hydroprogne* *caspia*; Ludwig et al. 1993a, Mora et al. 1993), herring gull (*Larus argentatus*; Keith 1966, Ludwig and Tomoff 1966, Ludwig and Ludwig 1969, Fry et al. 1987) double-crested cormorant (*Phalcrocorax auritus*; Weseloh et al. 1983, Tillett et al.1991, 1992, Jones et al. 1993) and mink (*Mustela vison*; Wren 1991, Giesy et al. 1994 b,c).

There is good reason to suspect organochlorine damage to Great Lakes common tern (*Sterna hirundo*), black tern (*Chlidonias nigra*), osprey (*Pandion haliaetus*), snapping turtle (*Chelydra serpentina*; Bishop et al. 1991, Struger et al. 1993) and river otter (*Lutra Canadensis*; Wren 1991) from abrupt declines of their Great Lakes populations after 1960. Probably the only reason why declines of these species were not linked to organochlorines is that few scientists were monitoring their shy, small or economically insignificant populations when exposures became important. By the time anyone suspected a contaminants cause for their declines, their populations were too small and dispersed to study effectively. The standard explanation offered by Cooper that exotic species introductions and habitat changes are sufficient to explain the decimation of all these species flies in the face of the number of species damaged plus the common effects in taxa of all predatory residents on the Great Lakes. The coincidence of effects over the entire system when effects of habitat loss and exotic species invasions were very different in different parts of the basin is powerful evidence of a basin wide chemically mediated cause (Fox et al. 1991).

It is much closer to the truth to state that there are no well-studied upper trophic level predators in the Great Lakes whose populations have not been affected by chlorinated hydrocarbon exposures than to accept **Cooper's opinion the "the ambient concentrations, exposures and observable ecological effects might have been present at sufficient concentrations in the 1960s and 1970s to warrant consideration, but they are definitely not there today."** The peer-reviewed literature says otherwise. The chemicals were there then. They are there now, and in mixtures of much higher toxicity than was present in the original discharged mixtures (Tillitt et al. 1992, Williams et al. 1992, Ludwig et al. 1993a, Giesy et al. 1994c) owing to physical environmental sorting processes (Burkhard et al. 1985, Oliver et al. 1989). Organochlorines have damaged, are damaging and will continue to damage both individuals and populations in the Great Lakes. The 30-year old population models invoked by Cooper do not explain these effects. Whole assemblages of organisms have been altered grossly, possibly forever. The peer-reviewed literature favors an unambiguous statement that both the Great Lakes community structure and populations have been damaged by organochlorines. And, lest anyone forget, injury and damage are the core of laws, treaties and water quality agreements that give legal structure to management of these resources. Documented damage calls out for remediation under these vehicles. Remediation of organochlorines is very expensive, especially as we do not know how to do it safely.

Evidence of ecological damage must be kept separate from policy questions, something that none of the papers in the forum accomplished. Proposed actions like the chlorine ban and Great Lakes Water Quality Initiative only begin with solid evidence of ecological damage. The real problem is that identifying and measuring damage does not provide either the knowledge, or a means, to perform remediation. However, the debate has been prosecuted on both sides as though this was the case, and under the assumption that point-source discharges were the problem. It is clear that the active sources to the water column for most organochlorines are contaminated sediments, atmospheric deposition and internal recycling, three virtually intractable sources to aquatic biota. These sources cannot be regulated: therewith, there is no political incentive to deal with them. It will be virtually impossible to address one source (atmospheric); remediation of another (sediments) may be technically infeasible at reasonable costs. Sediment disturbance or removal may cause unacceptable effects locally during remediation projects. Nothwithstanding these failures to effect clean-ups, and thereby control damage to Great Lakes species, attempts to discredit the peer-reviewed linking exposures to effects are misguided. As a society we need remediation research and development, not polemics over good and bad science on the validity of effects research. Peer-review and repetitions of critical work have already shown what is good ecotoxicological science.

Two of ecology's "laws", Liebigs law of the minimum and Shelford's law of tolerance provide insight into the role of contaminants in the Great Lakes. The best example may lie with the double-crested cormorant, a native species resident on the Great Lakes that prospered until the widespread use of dichlorodiphenyltrichloroethane (DDT) rendered it impossible to reproduce (Weseloh et al. 1983, Ludwig et al. 1995). This species is exquisitely sensitive to dichlorodiphenyldichloroethene (DDE)-mediated eggshell thinning. After 1950-1955, this population declined steadily from thousands of pairs nesting on islands in all of the Great Lakes until 125 breeding pairs remained at eight sites in Lakes Huron and Erie in 1972-1973. Although the species has a very high intrinsic rate of natural increase, at least 2-3 fold greater than its Great Lakes competitors, it has an extreme sensitivity to DDE effects on its eggshells (Low Adverse Effect Concentration = 3 mg/kg on a mass basis). DDE causes total reproductive failure at levels above about 15 mg/kg. Eggs from Great Lakes colonies averaged 22 mg/kg in 1972. Only five years after the ban on DDT use, the species resumed a normal reproductive pattern (Ludwig 1984, Ludwig et al. 1995). An immense population explosion has followed in the last 20 years. It is also reasonable to suspect that the negative impacts of organochlorines on formerly competitive Great Lakes species, especially the herring gull, and on the tertiary predators great horned owls, bald eagles, mink and herring gulls are much less frequent now than before 1960. A recent analysis of the published data suggested that the cormorant population has, in the long term, actually benefited from the presence of organochlorines owing to depression of the tertiary predator community that one helped exert natural controls on this, now very abundant, "pest" (Ludwig et al. 1995).

The very slow recovery of the herring gull population and the recent explosion of the ring-billed gull population on the Great Lakes are other examples where complex predator-prey and competitive interactions strongly limit or increase the intrinsic rate of natural increase for each species in the organochlorine-enriched Great Lakes (Ludwig 1974). *Specific types of organochlorine contamination have acted as limiting factors.* These exposures have different effects on different species (Giesy et al. 1994b). The toxicologically sensitive species which respond at the low end of the dose:response curve for PCBs, like mink (Wren 1991, Giesy 1994d), or for DDT/DDE, like cormorants, or those at the end of food webs, *especially the tertiary predators*, are most at risk (Ludwig et al. 1993b). This is potent evidence of wholesale alterations to the entire community structure of the Great Lakes. Some species' populations were devastated, others benefited from organochlorine exposures, and some were devastated only to recover to pest status when environmental

JAMES P. LUDWIG, Ph.D

mixtures of organochlorines changed. This is exactly what one should expect to see from a widespread common chemical perturbation to an ecosystem over time.

Reprinted from Ecological Applications **6**(3): 962-965.

CPSIA information can be obtained
at www.ICGtesting.com
Printed in the USA
LVHW022312211122
733714LV00001B/43